THE SERMON ON THE MOUNT

Explorations in Christian Practice

Ed Gallagher

The Sermon on the Mount: Explorations in Christian Practice
Cypress Bible Study Series
Published by Heritage Christian University Press

Copyright © 2021 by Ed Gallagher

Manufactured in the United States of America

Cataloging-in-Publication Data
Gallagher, Ed (Edmon Louis), 1979–
The Sermon on the Mount: Explorations in Christian Practice / by Ed Gallagher
p. cm. — (Cypress Bible Study Series)
Includes bibliographic references (p.) and indexes.
ISBN 978-1-7347665-4-7 (pbk.)
1. Bible. Sermon on the Mount—Criticism, interpretation, etc. 2. Theology, Doctrinal. I. Author. II. Title. III. Series
BT380. 2. G35 2021 226.906—DC20
Library of Congress Control Number: 2020919908

Cover design by Brad McKinnon and Brittany Vander Maas
Interior design by Brad McKinnon
Cover image "Sermon on the Mount" by Fra Angelico, Fresco im Markuskloster in Florenz (1437–45) https://commons.wikimedia.org/wiki/File:Frescoangelico100216.jpg

All rights reserved. No part of this publication may be reproduced, distributed, stored in a retrieval system, or transmitted in any form or by any means without the prior written permission of the publisher, except in the case of brief quotations embodied in critical reviews and certain other noncommercial uses permitted by copyright law.

For information:
Heritage Christian University Press
3625 Helton Drive
PO Box HCU
Florence, AL 35630
www.hcu.edu

To Sam and Joy Bell,
for giving me Jodi
and loving my kids

Contents

Preface		ix
List of Abbreviations		xix
1.	Life in the Kingdom of Heaven	3
2.	The Good Life, According to Jesus	25
3.	Salt and Light	39
4.	Fulfilling the Law and the Prophets	51
5.	Personal Relationships	65
6.	Marriage and Divorce	93
7.	How to Be Religious	129
8.	The Lord's Prayer	145
9.	Handling Possessions	171
10.	Judge Not	189
11.	The Way of Life	207
12.	A Solid Foundation	221
Appendix: Questions for Reflection		239
Glossary		249
Bibliography		255
Subject Index		265
Index of Ancient Literature		269
Scripture Index		271

Preface

> *I think I am right in saying that I would only achieve true inner clarity and honesty by really starting to take the Sermon on the Mount seriously.*
>
> —Dietrich Bonhoeffer[1]

Repent! For you are about to enter the Sermon on the Mount, and you're going to realize how bad you are at Christianity. Sometimes you need to realize that. Actually, you probably need that fact firmly implanted in your mind at all times. Like the horse Bree in *The Horse and His Boy*, we often think we're a lot better at life than we really are, and we need an encounter with Aslan to get our thinking straight. As the elderly hermit told the humiliated Bree, "My good Horse, you've lost nothing but your self-conceit."[2]

---

1. Letter from Dietrich Bonhoeffer to his brother, Karl-Friedrich, Jan. 14, 1935; in *London, 1933–1935*, ed. Keith Clements, trans. Isabel Best, Dietrich Bonhoeffer Works 13 (Minneapolis: Fortress, 2007), 284–85.

2. C. S. Lewis, *The Horse and His Boy*, The Chronicles of Narnia (New York: HarperCollins, 1954), 161, in Chapter Ten, "The Hermit of the Southern March."

Reading the Sermon on the Mount is a good way to lose your self-conceit about what a great Christian you are.

When we encounter Jesus in this Sermon, what we're going to realize is that Christianity is both harder and easier than we often think. We will find in Matthew 5–7 that Jesus does not settle for half-hearted obedience or lackluster faith. He doesn't settle even for outstanding obedience and faith.

> Christ says "Give me All. I don't want so much of your time and so much of your money and so much of your work: I want You. I have not come to torment your natural self, but to kill it. No half-measures are any good. I don't want to cut off a branch here and a branch there, I want to have the whole tree down. I don't want to drill the tooth, or crown it, or stop it, but to have it out. Hand over the whole natural self, all the desires which you think innocent as well as the ones you think wicked—the whole outfit. I will give you a new self instead. In fact, I will give you Myself: my own will shall become yours."[3]

You read the Sermon with its call to perfection (Matt 5:48), and you realize how hard Christianity is. Impossible, really. Jesus knows this, too. He has told us that our perfect obedience is unnecessary because his obedience counts for us. Now that's easy! All we have to do is accept that offer, and it's gravy. But then Jesus does expect us to do what he says, so we're back to it's being hard. Look, I can't resolve

---

3. C. S. Lewis, *Mere Christianity* (New York: Macmillan, 1952), 153, in the chapter called "Is Christianity Hard or Easy?"

the perpetual tension within Christianity of the relationship between faith and works, but what I can try to do here is sum it up in a catchy little motto: "Christianity is both harder and easier than you thought."[4]

The whole Sermon on the Mount relates to the call to repentance in Matthew 4:17: "Repent, for the kingdom of heaven has come near." The Sermon unpacks what repenting looks like. Remember that John the Baptist has already called for repentance based on the same reasoning: "the kingdom of heaven has come near" (3:2). And John has also told his listeners that they should produce "fruit worthy of repentance" (3:8). Again, the Sermon shows us fruit worthy of repentance.

Housekeeping Items

This book arose from a series of studies at the Sherrod Ave. Church of Christ in Florence, Alabama. I wrote these lessons during the Winter of 2018/19, and three men from our congregation taught the material to different groups. Thank you David Webb, Jimmy Highland, and Brad Hall for teaching during that quarter and for using this material in a trial run. I have updated some of the material since then, and various other people have consented to read portions of it and offer their comments. None of them agreed with everything I said; I'm thankful for their candid and helpful responses.

---

4. Alright, even that line I stole from C. S. Lewis. But, look, there are worse sins than ripping off C. S. Lewis. Would that more preachers did the same!

Somehow, I ended up with only twelve chapters, which might be annoying to some readers who are looking for Bible class material and want thirteen lessons. Sorry. It shouldn't be too hard to divide one of the chapters into two lessons. Might I suggest you consider doing this with Chapter Five?

Once again, Jamie Cox, Brad McKinnon, and Brittany Vander Maas have done amazing work to get this book off of my computer and into the form you now see. Aside from work on this book specifically, let me highlight Jamie's work as librarian at Overton Memorial Library. Her continued insistence on having books in the library (not all libraries are interested in such things) has made this book possible. I couldn't have written it without a well-stocked library; I wouldn't have had anything to say.

My wonderful wife, Jodi, gives me the strength and support to do this kind of work, and she continually challenges me not only to understand the words of Scripture but to live them out. My kids fill our home with excitement and joy, providing endless preaching illustrations. Thank you Miriam, Evelyn, Josiah, Jasmine, Marvin, and Ellie. Some of you might actually want to read this book. My parents, Tim and Judy Gallagher, have never been anything but supportive. Though Jesus didn't say it, the past twenty years have demonstrated the truth of the beatitude, "Blessed is he who has happy and helpful in-laws." Thank you, Sam and Joy.

Entering the Sermon: First Steps

Before you do anything else, before you read another word in this book, you should read the Gospel of Matthew, the whole thing, in order to get a sense of who Jesus is, what his ministry was all about, and how this Sermon fits into that ministry. Then you can finish this Preface.

The Sermon on the Mount is found only in Matthew's Gospel, but Luke records some sayings of Jesus very similar to what we find in the Sermon on the Mount. The chart below shows you where the parallels are. The few that I've noted in Mark are not really parallel, but sorta. I didn't include John in the chart because…well, if you don't know, I'm not going to tell you.

	Matthew	Mark	Luke
Beatitudes	5:1–12	—	(6:20–23)
Salt of the earth	5:13	(9:50)	(14:34–35)
Light of the world	5:14–15	(4:21)	(8:16)
Good deeds	5:16	—	—
Fulfilling the Law	5:17–20	—	(16:17, heaven & earth)
Anger = murder	5:21–22	—	—
Leave your gift, make peace	5:23–24	—	—

Make peace w/accuser	5:25–26	—	12:58–59
Lust = adultery	5:27–28	—	—
Eye/hand causes sin	5:29–30 (cf. 18:8–9)	9:43–47	—
Divorce	5:31–32 (cf. 19:9)	10:11	16:18
Swearing	5:33–37	—	—
Lax talionis	5:38–42	—	(6:29–30)
Love your enemy	5:43–48	—	(6:27–28, 32–36)
Almsgiving in secret	6:1–4	—	—
Praying in secret	6:5–6	—	—
Praying without babbling	6:7–8	—	—
Lord's prayer	6:9–13	—	11:1–4
Forgiveness necessary	6:14–15		11:1–4
Fasting in secret	6:16–18	—	—
Treasure in heaven	6:19–20	—	—
Where your treasure is	6:21	—	12:34

Eye important	6:22–23	—	11:34–36
Can't serve two masters	6:24	—	16:13
Don't worry	6:25–34	—	12:22–31
Don't judge	7:1–2	—	(6:37)
Log and splinter	7:3–5	—	6:41–42
Pearls before swine	7:6	—	—
Ask & receive	7:7–8	—	11:9–10
Heavenly Father responds to requests	7:9–11	—	11:11–13
Golden Rule	7:12	—	6:31
Narrow gate	7:13	—	(13:24)
False prophets	7:15	—	—
Trees & fruit	7:16–20	—	6:43–45
Lord, lord...	7:21–23	—	(13:25–27)
Two builders	7:24–27	—	6:46–49
Teaching w/ authority	7:28–29	(1:27)	(4:32)

Now for some helpful resources. First, the Bible Project.[5] Surely you know about it by now. These wonderful, brief

---

5. See www.bibleproject.com.

videos available on their website or YouTube cover many topics in the Bible and every book of the Bible, some more than once. You can find two videos on the Gospel of Matthew. After you read through the entire Gospel and compare the relevant portions of Luke's Gospel, watch these videos from the Bible Project, and then read through the Gospel again. That's Step 1 (or, maybe, Steps 1–4). Then you can read my book, since you're already holding it. That's Step 5.

Next, you can do a couple of different things. Maybe you'll want to take a look at some movie versions of the Sermon. Filmmakers have often dramatized the life of Jesus, and they almost always include the Sermon on the Mount, often an abbreviated version, maybe just with the Beatitudes and the Lord's Prayer. Looking at some of these portrayals might help you think about how it really went, how far Jesus' voice carried, whether anyone really might have thought they heard Jesus say, "Blessed are the cheesemakers," what the crowds looked like gathered on the mountain, how he delivered the lines, the intonation of his voice and such. At YouTube, you can find the Sermon on the Mount scene from the films *King of Kings* (1961, with Jeffrey Hunter as Jesus), *The Greatest Story Ever Told* (1965, with Max Von Sydow as Jesus), and *Jesus of Nazareth* (1977, with Robert Powell as Jesus). And then there are those word-by-word dramatizations of the Gospel of Matthew you could look for.

Or maybe you'll want some more books on the Sermon. Here are two books that I found helpful.

When I started writing on the Sermon on the Mount, I picked up Scot McKnight's commentary and constantly interacted with it.[6] You'll notice, especially in the first several chapters (well, not so much Chapter One) how frequently I cite McKnight. I'd recommend you go ahead and get McKnight's commentary. It's well done and easy to read. Actually, in my book's original form as Bible class material for teachers at church, I gave each of my teachers a copy of McKnight's book and then provided these lessons so that they would have two perspectives on the Sermon, sometimes united and sometimes divided.

The essential twentieth-century work on the Sermon on the Mount was published in German under the title *Nachfolge* in 1937 by a 31-year-old Lutheran pastor and professor named Dietrich Bonhoeffer. This work was translated by R. H. Fuller into English in 1948 and given the title *The Cost of Discipleship*, under which title it has become a classic. This first translation has been reprinted many times in various editions. Fuller's translation is beautifully done, and some of its phrasing has entered into the common parlance of American Christianity, such as the famous line from Chapter Four, "When Christ calls a man, he bids him come and die." Unfortunately, the translation also deviates from Bonhoeffer's German in various ways, not least in its many gaps. A newer, scholarly translation was published in 2001—now titled simply *Discipleship*, in closer correspondence to the German title—as part of a 17-volume series containing all of Bonhoffer's writings, called "Dietrich Bonhoeffer Works" and published by Fortress Press

---

6. Scot McKnight, *Sermon on the Mount*, The Story of God Bible Commentary (Grand Rapids: Zondervan, 2013).

(Minneapolis). It is this translation that I use in the following chapters.[7]

The reason Bonhoeffer's book has become a classic is probably twofold: the work itself is amazing, but also the life of its author is amazing. First, the work: Bonhoeffer's *Discipleship* refuses to explain away Jesus' Sermon and its implications for modern people, but unflinchingly deals with those dramatic implications, particularly where the words of Jesus convict modern Christians for laziness and the promotion of "cheap grace." During his lifetime, for basically all of his adult life (he was born in 1906), Bonhoeffer opposed the Third Reich. He was imprisoned in April 1943, was subsequently implicated in the 20 July Plot against Hitler, and was hanged by the Nazis on April 9, 1945, only a few weeks before Hitler took his own life. If you want to read up on Bonhoeffer, there are plenty of options. The full biography by Marsh,[8] or the brief biography by Matthews.[9] Or for an intense, scholarly evaluation of Bonhoeffer, there is now an Oxford Handbook.[10] And if you

---

7. Dietrich Bonhoeffer, *Discipleship*, DBWE 4 (Minneapolis: Fortress, 2001). The "E" at the end of the series abbreviation stands for "English" in order to distinguish this series from the corresponding German series, Dietrich Bonhoeffer Werke.

8. Charles Marsh, *Strange Glory: A Life of Dietrich Bonhoeffer* (New York: Knopf, 2014).

9. John W. Matthews, *Bonhoeffer: A Brief Overview of the Life and Writings of Dietrich Bonhoeffer* (Minneapolis: Lutheran University Press, 2011).

10. Philip G. Ziegler and Michael Mawson, eds., *The Oxford Handbook of Dietrich Bonhoeffer* (Oxford: Oxford University Press, 2019).

just want a helpful introduction to Bonhoeffer and his most well-known publications, there's a nice little book by Kelly.[11] Bonhoeffer's life and death has imparted an importance and an urgency to his works, and especially to his most famous and beloved work, *Discipleship*.

There's a ton of other stuff on the Sermon, and some of that stuff is really helpful. In this age of the proliferation of publication, one has to make choices about what to read, and I chose to read every word of McKnight's commentary and Bonhoeffer's *Discipleship*, but you'll also find in the notes that I did not limit myself to these sources. Nevertheless, there's a lot of good work on the Sermon that I didn't get to. You might want to turn to that literature. I hope this book provides some guidance on some of the literature on the Sermon that I have found valuable. More than that, I hope this book provides some guidance on the Sermon and the power, the life-defining power, it holds for modern disciples.

LIST OF ABBREVIATIONS

Old Testament

Gen	Genesis
Exod	Exodus
Lev	Leviticus
Num	Numbers
Deut	Deuteronomy

---

11. Geffrey B. Kelly, *Reading Bonhoeffer: A Guide to His Spiritual Classics and Selected Writings on Peace* (Eugene, OR: Cascade, 2008).

Josh	Joshua
Judg	Judges
Ruth	Ruth
1–2 Sam	1–2 Samuel
1–2 Kgs	1–2 Kings
1–2 Chr	1–2 Chronicles
Ezra	Ezra
Neh	Nehemiah
Esth	Esther
Job	Job
Ps	Psalms
Prov	Proverbs
Eccl	Ecclesiastes
Song	Song of Solomon
Isa	Isaiah
Jer	Jeremiah
Lam	Lamentations
Ezek	Ezekiel
Dan	Daniel
Hos	Hosea
Joel	Joel
Amos	Amos
Obad	Obadiah
Jonah	Jonah
Mic	Micah
Nah	Nahum
Hab	Habakkuk
Zeph	Zephaniah
Hag	Haggai
Zech	Zechariah
Mal	Malachi

New Testament

Matt	Matthew

Mark	Mark
Luke	Luke
John	John
Acts	Acts
Rom	Romans
1–2 Cor	1–2 Corinthians
Gal	Galatians
Eph	Ephesians
Phil	Philippians
Col	Colossians
1–2 Thess	1–2 Thessalonains
1–2 Tim	1–2 Timothy
Titus	Titus
Phlm	Philemon
Heb	Hebrews
Jas	James
1–2 Pet	1–2 Peter
1–2–3 John	1–2–3 John
Jude	Jude
Rev	Revelation

THE SERMON ON THE MOUNT

I

LIFE IN THE KINGDOM OF HEAVEN

From that time Jesus began to proclaim, "Repent, for the kingdom of heaven has come near." (Matt 4:17)

The Sermon on the Mount is challenging. If you think Jesus is all about making you feel good, you haven't read the Sermon on the Mount. I'm not saying the Sermon makes me feel bad, but it doesn't make me feel good. I don't know who could read that Sermon and think, "I'm kinda wonderful." If you're that person, you need to read more closely.

This Sermon is the first major block of Jesus' teaching in the Gospel of Matthew, and therefore the first major block of Jesus' teaching in the New Testament, according to our present (and long traditional) arrangement of the books. Here readers encounter for the first-time what Jesus is up to. Well, sort of. Matthew has already made it clear, in the very first statement of his Gospel, that Jesus is the son of David and the son of Abraham. Jesus has also called on people to repent because of the imminence of the kingdom of heaven (see the epigraph above). He has started bidding certain people to abandon their occupations to follow him around (4:18–22). What does he want from these people? And what is this kingdom of heaven that he's announcing? The Sermon on the Mount explains.

The Sermon is important. Even if we just take it by itself, just those three chapters without the context of the Gospel in which they appear, the Sermon would be powerful and important. But placing the Sermon in the context of the Gospel of Matthew and of the ministry of Jesus clarifies what Jesus is trying to accomplish with this discourse, why he is saying these things to the people assembled on that mountain. Let's think a little more about the Gospel of Matthew and Jesus' ministry, and we'll save the Sermon itself for the next chapter (and the next ten after that).

THE SERMON IN MATTHEW

The Sermon on the Mount appears only in the Gospel of Matthew. A lot of the same material in the Sermon appears also in the Gospel of Luke (with some slight parallels in Mark), but in different contexts, not one long speech like we have in Matthew. Many of the parallels in Luke appear in the so-called Sermon on the Plain starting at Luke 6:20 (with the title taken from Luke 6:17) and in the speech recorded in Luke 12.[1]

In the Gospel of Matthew, the Sermon on the Mount is the first of five lengthy discourses by Jesus. For about a century now, scholars have often thought that Matthew aimed at presenting specifically five discourses for a special reason.[2] There is some

---

1. See the preface above for a chart listing all of these parallels.
2. This analysis of Matthew's Gospel goes back to Benjamin W. Bacon, "The Five Books of Matthew Against the Jews," *The Expositor* 25 (1918): 56–66. At Wikipedia, look for "Five Discourses of Matthew."

credence to the notion that Matthew presents the five discourses as a special series, since each of the discourses ends with a comment such as, "When Jesus had finished all these words" (see 7:28; 11:1; 13:53; 19:1; 26:1). The five discourses are as follows:

> The Sermon on the Mount, chs. 5–7
> Missionary Discourse, ch. 10
> Parables, ch. 13
> Discourse on the Church, ch. 18
> Olivet Discourse, chs. 23–25

What would be the reason that Matthew would present Jesus as delivering specifically five discourses? Well, notice that to deliver his first discourse, Jesus first ascends a mountain (5:1).[3] If you think about someone in the Bible going up a mountain to deliver a message to God's people, you think of Moses, especially if it's a fivefold message. Think about some other parallels between Moses and Jesus, like their parents having to hide the newborn Savior from the baby-killing king, and fasting for forty days, and being tempted in the wilderness.[4] It's fairly common for scholars to argue that Matthew presents Jesus as a new Moses, transmitting a new Torah to a renewed Israel.

This fivefold structure demonstrates the importance of the Sermon within the Gospel of Matthew. It is not the only major discourse, but it is the first major discourse. Jesus will later be able

---

3. Other mountaintop experiences in Matthew: 15:2; 17:1–13; chs. 24–25, 28:16–20.

4. Jonathan T. Pennington, *The Sermon on the Mount and Human Flourishing: A Theological Commentary* (Grand Rapids: Baker, 2017), 139–40.

to give much more instruction on the kingdom of heaven, particularly in the parables of chapter 13, but here in the Sermon on the Mount, in a much more straightforward way than in the parables, Jesus reveals what type of kingdom he is proclaiming, and what type of person will be able to be a part of this kingdom—specifically, someone who surpasses in righteousness even the scribes and Pharisees (5:20), or, to put it a different way, someone "who does the will of my Father in heaven" (7:21).

THE KINGDOM OF THE HEAVENS

Jesus is not just the new Moses; he's also the new David—and this is emphasized in Matthew's Gospel more than in the other Gospels. The title "son of David" appears about ten times (see Exploration 1.2), more than elsewhere, presenting Jesus as the long-awaited king who has come to fulfill the promise to David of an eternal kingdom (2 Sam 7:12–16). Jesus has come to establish a kingdom.

In the Gospel of Matthew, Jesus talks about the kingdom of heaven, or, more precisely, the kingdom of the heavens. In the original Greek of the Gospel of Matthew, the phrase always uses the plural heavens (all thirty-two times). "The kingdom of the heavens" appears nowhere else in the New Testament. In Mark and Luke (and a few times in John), Jesus talks about the kingdom of God, never the kingdom of heaven/the heavens. Matthew also uses the phrase "kingdom of God" a few times (12:28; 19:24; 21:31, 43), but Matthew clearly prefers the phrase "kingdom of heaven" over "kingdom of God." In fact, sometimes when different Gospels tell the same story about Jesus, Matthew uses the phrase "kingdom of heaven" where Mark and/or Luke use the phrase "kingdom of

God."[5] So, the appearance of "kingdom of heaven" in Matthew is weird, and it demands some explanation.

I hope it's okay with you if I skip all the wrong explanations that have been proposed over the years and just get to the one that's right. (If you're into reviewing all the various scholarly proposals for such things, there are massive commentaries waiting for you.)[6] The phrase "kingdom of heaven" rather than "kingdom of God" emphasizes the heavenly nature of the kingdom and probably relies on the picture of the kingdom in the book of Daniel. Remember that in Daniel 7, the kingdoms of the earth are represented as nasty beasts, and then "one like a son of man coming with the clouds of heaven" receives a kingdom from the Ancient of Days (7:13–14). The fact that the earthly kingdoms are pictured as beasts, whereas the kingdom of the Ancient of Days is handed over not to a beast but to one like a son of man, establishes a strong contrast between God's kingdom (ruled by a son of man) and earthly kingdoms (ruled by beasts). Moreover, the book of Daniel refers to God as "the God of heaven" (2:19, 37, 44; cf. 2:28; 5:23; 6:27). Nebuchadnezzar needed to learn in Daniel 4 that "heaven rules" (4:26). One of the more important Old Testament verses about the kingdom of God is Daniel 2:44, which says that "the God of heaven will establish his kingdom."

---

5. E.g., Matt 4:17 // Mark 1:15; Matt 5:3 // Luke 6:20; Matt 13:11 // Mark 4:11 // Luke 8:10. For all of the appearances of the phrase "kingdom of heaven" in Matthew's Gospel along with their parallels in the other Gospels, see Exploration 1.1.

6. But skip the massive commentaries and just read Jonathan T. Pennington, *Heaven and Earth in the Gospel of Matthew* (Leiden: Brill, 2007). If that leaves you still wanting more, then you can go to the massive commentaries.

This theme in Daniel provides helpful background for understanding the phrase "kingdom of heaven" in Matthew's Gospel. Remember that, like Daniel, Matthew also refers to God's heavenly abode with the frequent phrase "Father in heaven" (actually, "in the heavens"), appearing around fifteen times—especially in the Sermon on the Mount (5:16, 45, 48; 6:1, 9; 7:11, 21)—though the other Gospels rarely use the phrase (only in Mark 11:25). Matthew's version of the Lord's Prayer famously addresses "Our Father in heaven (the heavens)" (6:9), while Luke's version starts with a simple address to "Father" (11:2). In fact, the word "heaven" (οὐρανός, *ouranos*) appears eighty-two times in Matthew's Gospel, far more than in any other New Testament writing, and more than in the other three Gospels combined.[7] Both Matthew and Daniel relate God particularly to heaven in order to contrast his rule with earthly powers. The phrase "kingdom of heaven" fits within this broader emphasis. The kingdom announced by Jesus will not be at all like the earthly, beastly kingdoms with which people are so familiar. Jesus' kingdom will be ruled by heaven.

EXPLORATION 1.1
Kingdom Language in Matthew's Gospel

"kingdom of the heavens" (32x; twice at 5:19)
 1. 3:2, Repent, for the kingdom of the heavens is at hand.

---

7. The majority of these appearances of the word "heaven" features the plural "heavens," including (as I've already mentioned) every reference to the "kingdom of the heavens." There are twenty-seven appearances of the word "heaven" in the singular: Matt 5:18, 34; 6:10, 20, 26; 8:20; 11:23, 25; 13:32; 14:19; 16:1–3 (4x); 18:18 (2x); 21:25 (2x); 22:30; 23:22; 24:29 (first appearance), 30 (2x), 35; 26:64; 28:2, 18.

2. 4:17, Repent, for the kingdom of the heavens is at hand.
   - (Mk 1:15, "kingdom of God")
3. 5:3, Blessed are the poor in spirit, for theirs is the kingdom of the heavens.
   - (Lk 6:20, "kingdom of God")
4. 5:10, Blessed are those who have been persecuted for the sake of righteousness, for theirs is the kingdom of the heavens.
5. 5:19, Whoever then annuls one of the least of these commandments, and teaches others *to do* the same, shall be called least in the kingdom of the heavens; but whoever keeps and teaches *them*, he shall be called great in the kingdom of the heavens.
6. 5:20, For I say to you that unless your righteousness surpasses *that* of the scribes and Pharisees, you will not enter the kingdom of the heavens.
7. 7:21, Not everyone who says to Me, 'Lord, Lord,' will enter the kingdom of the heavens, but he who does the will of My Father who is in heaven *will enter.*
8. 8:11, I say to you that many will come from east and west, and recline *at the table* with Abraham, Isaac and Jacob in the kingdom of the heavens.
   - (≈ Lk 13:28, "kingdom of God"; Lk 13:29, "kingdom of God")
9. 10:7, And as you go, preach, saying, 'The kingdom of the heavens is at hand.'
   - (≈ Lk 9:2, "kingdom of God")
10. 11:11, Truly I say to you, among those born of women there has not arisen *anyone* greater than John the

Baptist! Yet the one who is least in the kingdom of the heavens is greater than he.
- (Lk 7:28, "kingdom of God)

11. 11:12, From the days of John the Baptist until now the kingdom of the heavens suffers violence, and violent men take it by force.
- (≈ Lk 16:16, "kingdom of God")

12. 13:11, To you it has been granted to know the mysteries of the kingdom of the heavens, but to them it has not been granted.
- (Mk 4:11, "kingdom of God"; Lk 8:10, "kingdom of God")

13. 13:24, The kingdom of the heavens may be compared to a man who sowed good seed in his field.

14. 13:31, The kingdom of the heavens is like a mustard seed, which a man took and sowed in his field.

15. 13:33, The kingdom of the heavens is like leaven, which a woman took and hid in three pecks of flour until it was all leavened.

16. 13:44, The kingdom of the heavens is like a treasure hidden in the field, which a man found and hid *again*, and from joy over it he goes and sells all that he has and buys that field.

17. 13:45, Again, the kingdom of the heavens is like a merchant seeking fine pearls.

18. 13:47, Again, the kingdom of the heavens is like a dragnet cast into the sea, and gathering *fish* of every kind.

19. 13:52, Therefore every scribe who has become a disciple of the kingdom of the heavens is like a head of a household, who brings out of his treasure things new and old.
20. 16:19, I will give you the keys of the kingdom of the heavens.
21. 18:1, At that time the disciples came to Jesus and said, "Who then is greatest in the kingdom of the heavens?"
22. 18:3, Truly I say to you, unless you are converted and become like children, you will not enter the kingdom of the heavens.
    - (≈ Mk 10:15, "kingdom of God"; Lk 18:17, "kingdom of God")
23. 18:4, Whoever then humbles himself as this child, he is the greatest in the kingdom of the heavens.

24. 18:23, For this reason the kingdom of the heavens may be compared to a king who wished to settle accounts with his slaves.
25. 19:12, and there are *also* eunuchs who made themselves eunuchs for the sake of the kingdom of the heavens.
26. 19:14, Let the children alone, and do not hinder them from coming to Me; for the kingdom of the heavens belongs to such as these.
    - (Mk 10:14, "kingdom of God"; Lk 18:16, "kingdom of God")
27. 19:23, Truly I say to you, it is hard for a rich man to enter the kingdom of the heavens.
    - (Mk 10:23, "kingdom of God"; Lk 18:24, "kingdom of God")

28. 20:1, For the kingdom of the heavens is like a landowner who went out early in the morning to hire laborers for his vineyard.
29. 22:2, The kingdom of the heavens may be compared to a king who gave a wedding feast for his son.
30. 23:13, But woe to you, scribes and Pharisees, hypocrites, because you shut off the kingdom of the heavens from people; for you do not enter in yourselves, nor do you allow those who are entering to go in.
31. 25:1, Then the kingdom of the heavens will be comparable to ten virgins, who took their lamps and went out to meet the bridegroom.

"kingdom of God" (4x or 5x; some Greek manuscripts have the phrase "kingdom of God" at 6:33, but other Greek manuscripts have "his kingdom.")

1. 12:28, But if I cast out demons by the Spirit of God, then the kingdom of God has come upon you. (Lk 11:20, "kingdom of God")
2. 19:24, Again I say to you, it is easier for a camel to go through the eye of a needle, than for a rich man to enter the kingdom of God. (Mk 10:25, "kingdom of God"; Lk 18:25, "kingdom of God")
3. 21:31, Truly I say to you that the tax collectors and prostitutes will get into the kingdom of God before you.
4. 21:43, Therefore I say to you, the kingdom of God will be taken away from you and given to a people, producing the fruit of it.

"gospel of the kingdom" (the Greek phrase does not appear in other Gospels, but cf. Lk 16:16)
1. 4:23, Jesus was going throughout all Galilee, teaching in their synagogues and proclaiming the gospel of the kingdom, and healing every kind of disease and every kind of sickness among the people.
2. 9:35, Jesus was going through all the cities and villages, teaching in their synagogues and proclaiming the gospel of the kingdom, and healing every kind of disease and every kind of sickness.
3. 24:14, This gospel of the kingdom shall be preached in the whole world as a testimony to all the nations, and then the end will come.

other kingdom language
1. 6:10, Your kingdom come. Your will be done, on earth as it is in heaven. (Lk 11:2, "Your kingdom")
2. 6:33, But seek first His kingdom and His righteousness, and all these things will be added to you. (Lk 12:31, "His kingdom")
3. 8:12, but the sons of the kingdom will be cast out into the outer darkness; in that place there will be weeping and gnashing of teeth.
4. 13:19, When anyone hears the word of the kingdom and does not understand it, the evil *one* comes and snatches away what has been sown in his heart. This is the one on whom seed was sown beside the road.
5. 13:38, and *as for* the good seed, these are the sons of the kingdom; and the tares are the sons of the evil *one.*

> 6. 13:41, The Son of Man will send forth His angels, and they will gather out of His kingdom all stumbling blocks, and those who commit lawlessness.
> 7. 13:43, Then the righteous will shine forth as the sun in the kingdom of their Father.
> 8. 16:28, Truly I say to you, there are some of those who are standing here who will not taste death until they see the Son of Man coming in His kingdom. (Mk 9:1, "kingdom of God after it has come with power"; Lk 9:27, "kingdom of God)
> 9. 20:21, Command that in Your kingdom these two sons of mine may sit one on Your right and one on Your left.
> 10. 25:35, Then the King will say to those on His right, 'Come, you who are blessed of My Father, inherit the kingdom prepared for you from the foundation of the world.
> 11. 26:29, But I say to you, I will not drink of this fruit of the vine from now on until that day when I drink it new with you in My Father's kingdom. (Mk 14:25, "kingdom of God"; Lk 22:16, "until it is fulfilled in the kingdom of God"; Lk 22:18, "until the kingdom of God comes")

What Kind of Kingdom?[8]

The first words out of the mouth of Jesus in the Gospel of Mark consist of an announcement that the kingdom of God would soon

---

8. This section first appeared in the opening chapter of *The Ekklesia of Christ*, Berean Study Series (Florence, AL: HCU Press, 2015).

commence (Mark 1:15). (In Matthew, the same announcement appears [4:17], but it's not quite the first thing Jesus says in the Gospel.) Such an announcement would have been received by Jesus's contemporaries with, perhaps, a mix of anticipation (the oppressed crowds), trepidation (the political leaders), and disbelief (nearly everyone). For hundreds of years Judah had been dominated by foreign powers, from the Assyrians to the Babylonians to the Persians, Greeks, and now the Romans. While some first-century Jews no doubt longed for the time when God would establish his kingdom, others had probably long since ceased holding their breath.

The announcement by Jesus signaled the impending fulfillment of a variety of Old Testament promises. To be sure, God has always been king, and in that sense he has had a kingdom.[9] But the prophets had in varying ways envisioned a time when God would reign as king more fully and visibly than he currently did. The pivotal promise appears in 2 Samuel 7. God would establish David's dynasty, guaranteeing that one of his descendants would always reign over Israel (vv. 12–16). Through this "son of David" God would reign, for the son of David would also be the "son of God" (v. 14).

It quickly became apparent that the immediate descendants of David in no way lived up to the great promise of 2 Samuel 7. Though Solomon accomplished some great things (1 Kings 3–10)—and, by the way, David related God's promise directly to Solomon (1 Kings 2:4; 1 Chron 28:6), not some future descendant—this immediate son of David also oppressed the people (1 Kings 12:4), promoted idolatry (1 Kings 11:1–8), and indirectly caused

---

9. For OT passages mentioning the kingship of God, see Psalms 47:2; 93:1; 95:3; 97:1; 98:6; 99:1; cf. 1 Samuel 8:7.

the division of the kingdom into two separate nations (Judah and Israel) following his death (1 Kings 12:1–15).

Most of the other kings of Judah and Israel weren't even that righteous. Even while the Davidic dynasty was going strong, Isaiah longed for a time when "a shoot will spring from the stem of Jesse" (Isa 11:1). This new king from David's line—Jesse was David's father (1 Sam 16:1)—would bear the divine Spirit and would judge the people with righteousness, lifting up the poor and slaying the wicked (Isa 11:2–5). In his days there would be universal peace, even between animals and men, so much so that children need have no fear of poisonous snakes (Isa 11: 6–9). The reign of this king would usher in a time of paradise, and God would reign through him.

Other prophets presented their own visions of what it would look like when God reigned, when he would establish his kingdom. Ezekiel, a priest, imagined an enormous temple (chs. 40–48) from which flowed a great river watering life-giving trees (47:1–12) and, most importantly, God himself inhabited this temple (43:5). God would live among his people. Micah imagined God as a shepherd who would "assemble the lame and gather the outcasts" to be his kingdom (4:6–8). Sometimes in these visions of God's kingdom, the Gentile nations flocked to Zion to learn God's will and join in worshipping him (cf. Mic 4:1–3; Isa 2:2–4; cf. Isa 56:1–8; 60). Often it was imagined that twelve tribes of Israel would be regathered under one king, the new David (Jer 23:5–6; Ezek 37:15–28).

And so, though some people may have doubted the sanity of Jesus, no one could doubt his meaning when he declared that the time had finally arrived when God would begin to reign. Indeed, Jesus was the one through whom God would inaugurate his kingdom; he was the Messiah, as Peter and the apostles finally realized (Matt 16:16). When he cast out demons, the kingdom had come near (12:28). When he healed people of their diseases, he engaged in battle with the evil forces arrayed against God (19:28; cf. Luke 13:16). He fought with Satan in the wilderness, and he overcame (Matt 4:1–11). His twelve chosen disciples (10:1–4) represented the regathered tribes of Israel (cf. Luke 22:30), just as he also attracted followers from roughly the geography of David's kingdom (Matt 4:23–25). He was the one, as Isaiah prophesied, on whom the Spirit rested (Luke 4:16–21). He was the son of David whose throne would be established forever (Matt 1:1).

EXPLORATION 1.2
Christ Language in Matthew

Christ (= Messiah) in Matthew's Gospel

1:1, The record of the genealogy of Jesus the Messiah, the son of David, the son of Abraham.

1:16, Jacob was the father of Joseph the husband of Mary, by whom Jesus was born, who is called the Messiah.

1:17, So all the generations from Abraham to David are fourteen generations; from David to the deportation to Babylon, fourteen generations; and from the deportation to Babylon to the Messiah, fourteen generations.

1:18, Now the birth of Jesus Christ was as follows.

2:4, Gathering together all the chief priests and scribes of the people, he inquired of them where the Messiah was to be born.

11:2, Now when John, while imprisoned, heard of the works of Christ, he sent *word* by his disciples.

16:16, Simon Peter answered, "You are the Christ, the Son of the living God."

16:20, Then He warned the disciples that they should tell no one that He was the Christ.

22:42, "What do you think about the Christ, whose son is He?" They said to Him, "*The son* of David."

23:10, Do not be called leaders; for One is your Leader, *that is*, Christ.

24:5, For many will come in My name, saying, "I am the Christ," and will mislead many.

24:23, Then if anyone says to you, "Behold, here is the Christ," or "There *He is*," do not believe *him*.

26:63, But Jesus kept silent. And the high priest said to Him, "I adjure You by the living God, that You tell us whether You are the Christ, the Son of God."

26:68, and said, "Prophesy to us, You Christ; who is the one who hit You?"

27:17, So when the people gathered together, Pilate said to them, "Whom do you want me to release for you? Barabbas, or Jesus who is called Christ?"

27:22, Pilate said to them, "Then what shall I do with Jesus who is called Christ?" They all said, "Crucify Him!"

"Son of David" in Matthew's Gospel

1:1, The record of the genealogy of Jesus the Messiah, the son of David, the son of Abraham.

1:20, But when he had considered this, behold, an angel of the Lord appeared to him in a dream, saying, "Joseph, son of David, do not be afraid to take Mary as your wife; for the Child who has been conceived in her is of the Holy Spirit."

9:27, As Jesus went on from there, two blind men followed Him, crying out, "Have mercy on us, Son of David!"

12:23, All the crowds were amazed, and were saying, "This man cannot be the Son of David, can he?"

15:22 And a Canaanite woman from that region came out and *began* to cry out, saying, "Have mercy on me, Lord, Son of David; my daughter is cruelly demon-possessed."
(the title does not appear in Mark 7:24-30)

20:30-31 And two blind men sitting by the road, hearing that Jesus was passing by, cried out, "Lord, have mercy on us, Son of

David!" The crowd sternly told them to be quiet, but they cried out all the more, "Lord, Son of David, have mercy on us!"
// Mark 10:47-48 // Luke 18:38-39

21:9, 15 The crowds going ahead of Him, and those who followed, were shouting, "Hosanna to the Son of David; Blessed is He who comes in the name of the Lord; Hosanna in the highest!" ... But when the chief priests and the scribes saw the wonderful things that He had done, and the children who were shouting in the temple, "Hosanna to the Son of David," they became indignant.
// Mark 11:10 ("our father David") // Luke 19:38 ("king", no David)

22:42, 43, 45 "What do you think about the Christ, whose son is He?" They said to Him, "*The son* of David." He said to them, "Then how does David in the Spirit call Him 'Lord,' ... If David then calls Him 'Lord,' how is He his son?"
// Mark 12:35-37 // Luke 20:41-44

Notes:
- Mark has no additional references to "son of David" aside from those that are paralleled in Matthew.
- Luke's birth narrative has several references to "son of David" not paralleled in Matthew (1:27, 32, 69; 2:4, 11); otherwise, only in parallels with Matthew.
- "son of David" never appears in John but see John 7:42.
- The rest of the NT has the theme rather infrequently: Romans 1:3; 2 Timothy 2:8; Revelation 5:5; 22:16.

Jesus as a messiah was different from what had been anticipated, and he spoke of a different kind of kingdom from what was expected. Not only was he David's son, but he was David's lord (Matt 22:41–46). In the kingdom preached by Jesus, blessings were pronounced on the poor in spirit, the merciful, the peacemakers (5:3–12). Jesus' kingdom was one that welcomed sinners (9:9–13) and prostitutes (21:31–32) and—worse yet—Gentiles (cf. Isa 2:2–4) while the most religious individuals were threatened with exclusion (Matt 8:11–12). This king, this expected one, who healed the sick and opened the eyes of the blind and preached the gospel to the poor (Matt 11:2–6), strangely refused to proclaim himself king openly (Matt 16:20; cf. John 6:15) and did not take up arms against Israel's enemy, Rome (Matt 26:52). Indeed, just the opposite: he allowed himself to be mocked, tortured, and crucified by Rome. Certainly, an odd type of king.

Yet the crucifixion was central to Jesus's notion of the kingdom. It was, after all, at the moment of crucifixion when Jesus received his royal crown (Matt 27:29) and hung under a sign proclaiming him king (27:37). He had warned his disciples that this was going to happen (16:21; 17:22–23; 20:17–19) and that they themselves would have to do similarly (10:38; 16:24). In Jesus's kingdom the first would be last (19:30) and the leaders would be servants (20:25–28; cf. John 13:1–10).

The citizens of Jesus's kingdom would be characterized by self-sacrifice (Matt 25:31–46), love (22:34–40), and commitment to one another (18:15–18). They would live by an elevated ethic, beyond normal interpretations of Moses's law (5:17–48). Not just adultery, but even lust was prohibited. Not just murder, but even hate was forbidden. Loving neighbors was fine, but citizens of this new kingdom would love their enemies. They would go the extra mile and turn the other cheek. They would do their righteous deeds to be noticed not by men but by God (6:1–18). They would trust God to provide their daily needs as they sought, above all, his kingdom (6:25–34). They would refuse to judge others but would walk the strait and narrow path (7:1–14). By living out the teachings of Jesus they would prove themselves to be citizens of the kingdom of heaven (7:21).

When "all authority in heaven and on earth" has been given to Jesus following his suffering and resurrection (Matt 28:18)—that is, following his victory over death and the evil powers (Col 2:15; Heb 2:14–15)—what Jesus has been announcing throughout his ministry has now come to pass: he is king over heaven's kingdom. If the kingdom does not appear as we might have guessed from the prophetic visions, Jesus himself had cautioned us: only those who are born again can see the kingdom of God (John 3:3). Only renewed eyes of faith can discern the reign of God in the small group of Jews who stubbornly insist that the man crucified as a traitor had truly been and truly is the Messiah, the king in a newly established kingdom. When people accept this message and obey the teachings of Jesus the Messiah (Christ), God transfers them out of the kingdom of darkness and into the kingdom of his dear son (Col 1:13).

But the kingdom of God is not yet fully revealed. Jesus inaugurated it but has not yet brought it to completion. We still pray for God's kingdom to come (Matt 6:10)[10] because we long for the time when all creation will bow before Jesus and acclaim him lord (Phil 2:9–11; Rev 5:13). The church is an outpost of the kingdom of God now, a community already living under the rule of God in

---

10. For discussion of this prayer, see Chapter 8 below.

accordance with the ethic Jesus established, looking forward to inheriting the kingdom (Matt 25:34; Rom 8:17; cf. 1 Cor 6:9; 15:50) at the consummation of all things.

Does the Sermon on the Mount Apply to Us?

Have you heard this question before? Here's the logic behind it: if the New Covenant instituted by Jesus required his death to take effect (cf. Heb 9:16–17), and if the church—of which we are a part—didn't really begin until Acts 2, then it would seem that the actual ministry of Jesus took place under the Old Covenant, and all the words coming out of Jesus' mouth during his earthly life apply to Judaism more than to Christianity. I have heard this idea before. I have heard people say that Christians should not derive instructions for living from the Gospels. This is the opposite extreme of those red-letter Christians who emphasize exclusively the words of Jesus. Both positions are wrong.

Yes, the Sermon on the Mount does apply to modern Christians. Without touching on every element of the previous paragraph that makes me cringe, let me suggest the following line of thought, that I think would especially appeal to people in churches of Christ. We have long proclaimed (and rightly so) that the kingdom of heaven is manifested now in the church. We are not waiting for the kingdom to be established (even if we are waiting for it to be fully realized; see Chapter 8); the kingdom has been established (cf. Col 1:13), and we are a part of it. This entire chapter has sought to demonstrate that the point of the Sermon on the Mount is to unveil the nature of the kingdom and the nature of life in the kingdom. If all of that is true, how could we say that the kingdom life as set forth by our king is irrelevant to life in the kingdom.

Sure, there are aspects of the Sermon on the Mount that apply more directly to a first-century Jew than to a Christian. We are not going to go to the temple in Jerusalem (which hasn't existed for nearly two millennia) to offer a gift at the altar (Matt 5:23), but we do figuratively offer our gifts to God at his altar (cf. Heb 13:10), so it's not too hard to see how even this verse could apply to us.

Jesus our King is sitting on the mountain ready to instruct us on how to be citizens of heaven's kingdom. Are you sure you're ready to find out?

2

THE GOOD LIFE ACCORDING TO JESUS
MATTHEW 5:3-12

These people who have been turning the world
upside down have come here also. (Acts 17:6)

How would you describe "the good life"? If you picture "the good life" in your mind, what do you imagine? What about the phrase "the blessed life"? Both of these terms (oftentimes) are closely related to the American Dream, which involves independence—financial independence and political independence and religious independence. We don't want anyone telling us what to do; we don't want to be obligated to anyone. The American Dream entails owning a home outright and having enough wealth to be free from any financial anxiety. When we picture "the good life," perhaps images of a beach house come to mind, or maybe a Victorian Christmas, with children quietly playing by the fire in a living room with a Christmas tree and a piano. Or maybe you start humming a tune by Joe Walsh.

When you picture the good life, you probably don't picture "the poor in spirit" or "hungering and thirsting after righteousness" or being persecuted. But Jesus wants to assure you that the good life, the blessed life, is not about financial and political independence but is about these characteristics that we would more readily associate with a miserable life. Jesus begins his most famous sermon by describing the good life in a way that no one expected, and we still largely ignore.

Terminology

We call this section of the Sermon "the Beatitudes." The word "beatitude"—completely unrelated to the word "attitude"—comes from the Latin *beatus*, which means "blessed." So, a beatitude is a blessing.

But the New Testament was written in Greek, not in Latin, and the Greek word at the start of each beatitude is *makarios* (μακάριος).[1] That's why sometimes instead of "beatitudes" these sayings are called "macarisms." According to the standard dictionary of New Testament Greek,[2] *makarios* means "fortunate" or "happy." I don't like the translation "happy" because it just describes a feeling that can come and go, and Jesus isn't talking about the way these people feel. He is talking about the "fortunate" situation that they are in, so I like the translation "fortunate" best. Another option is to translate "flourishing"; this also is a word that's not about feelings but about situation. "Fortunate are the

---

1. Actually, it's plural *makarioi*. The word appears 50x in the NT, including 13x in Matthew. Aside from the 9x in the beatitude section of Matthew, it also appears in 11:6; 13:16; 16:17; 24:46.

2. BDAG = Frederick W. Danker, Walter Bauer, William F. Arndt, and F. Wilbur Gingrich, *A Greek-English Lexicon of the New Testament and Other Early Christian Literature*, 3d ed. (Chicago: University of Chicago Press, 2000).

poor in spirit..." or "flourishing are the poor in spirit...." I think either of those options captures what Jesus is trying to say. Or, I think we could even translate it, "the poor in spirit are living the good life... those who are persecuted are living the good life...."[3]

In the Septuagint (the Greek translation of the Old Testament), *makarios* is the word used in Psalm 1, "*Makarios* is the man who walks not in the counsel of the wicked...." Here again, the word "fortunate" (or "flourishing" or "living the good life") is probably the best translation. This man may or may not be happy, but he is in a fortunate situation because the life that he is leading makes him like a strong tree, whereas the life that he is avoiding would make him like chaff. How fortunate to be a person who meditates on God's law!

Here in Psalm 1, the original Hebrew word for "fortunate" or "blessed" is *ashrē* (אשרי). There is another Hebrew term often rendered "blessed" (*barak*, ברך), but these two words are not the same. *Barak* means to bless someone, as in, to pronounce a blessing on someone, like what Isaac did for Jacob when Jacob stole Esau's blessing (Gen 27:27). When the Septuagint translated this text, it did not use the term *makarios* but rather the term *eulogeō* (εὐλογέω).

It can get a little confusing, but the important difference is this:

Hebrew *ashrē* = Greek *makarios* = a state of being = fortunate, flourishing
Hebrew *barak* = Greek *eulogeō* = an action performed on someone else = to bless someone

---

3. You could even say, "Congratulations to the one who is poor in spirit...."

All that to say that in the Beatitudes, Jesus is not using the word *eulogeō*, he is not "blessing" people, or saying that they will be blessed by God. He uses the word *makarios*, meaning that these people are in a fortunate situation. Admittedly, not everyone follows this logic. Scot McKnight, for instance, thinks that Jesus is pronouncing blessings on people, or, more specifically, that these are the people who are blessed by the God of Israel.[4] No doubt, that idea is true, but that idea is not what Jesus is getting at with the beatitudes. He is not drawing a connection to the blessings and curses in Leviticus 26 and Deuteronomy 28, as McKnight thinks. Jesus is describing the kind of people that are living the good life.

Jonathan Pennington gives a good explanation:

> It is problematic if we treat macarisms and woes as promises and prohibitions, as blessings and curses, because this is not how they function in the divine economy. Macarisms and woes are invitations to living based on sapiential reflections, not divine speech of reward and cursing.[5]

A little later Pennington describes the beatitudes as "sapiential invitations to the kind of life that will experience flourishing."[6]

---

4. See discussion in Scot McKnight, *The Sermon on the Mount*, Story of God Bible Commentary (Grand Rapids: Zondervan, 2013), 31–36.

5. Pennington, *The Sermon on the Mount and Human Flourishing*, 53 (but see all of his ch. 2). Pennington also suggests (50n35) a possible distinction between the two different ways of pronouncing the English word blessed, as to whether the accent is on the first syllable (bléssed/blest = active) or the second syllable (blesséd = state of being).

6. Pennington, *The Sermon on the Mount and Human Flourishing*, 54.

THE BIZARRO WORLD OF THE BEATITUDES

Commentators have different ways of trying to capture the strangeness of the beatitudes. The beatitudes paint a picture of life that is upside down or inside out, that is the opposite of the way we normally think about life, or, at least, the good life. In comic books, this is the bizarro world.[7] In this bizarro world depicted by Jesus, you're considered fortunate if you are poor in spirit, or mourning, or humble. In the world that we usually inhabit, the opposite of these characteristics are valued: we usually consider those fortunate who are happy, who are not mourning, who are powerful and confident, who know how to get their way, who live a peaceful and secure life. This picture of the good life largely determines what we want out of life (peace, security, happiness, etc.), just as it has defined the American Dream.

Jesus challenges us to enter into a bizarro world with him. He wants to reorient what we want out of life. He wants to challenge our assumptions about what a fortunate life looks like. He wants to redefine for us the good life.

THE BEATITUDES IN MATTHEW

People can look at Matt 5:3–12 and arrive at different lists of beatitudes. It depends on how many beatitudes you think there are. Wikipedia thinks there are eight, which is a common enumeration.[8] But many people also count nine, which I think

---

7. There is a Wikipedia entry on "Bizzaro World." But for a nice introduction to the concept, go to YouTube and look for the brief (35-second) Seinfeld video "Bizzaro Explained."

8. See "Beatitudes" at Wikipedia.

makes more sense. If you count eight, you understand verses 11–12 as an appendix; if you count nine, you understand these verses to contain the ninth beatitude. The form of v. 11 is a little different from the other beatitudes.

Luke has a set of beatitudes—only four instead of Matthew's nine—at Luke 6:20–23, and he balances these macarisms with a set of woes (6:24–26). Matthew also has a set of woes, but they come much later in the story (Matt 23). The beatitudes in Luke also read a little differently. Instead of "poor in spirit," as in Matthew, Luke has just "poor." Instead of hungering after righteousness, as in Matthew, in Luke these fortunate people are just hungry. While the emphasis might be different depending on which version we are reading (Matthew or Luke), the main point is the same either way—Jesus redefines the good life.

Why the difference in wording between the two sets of beatitudes? Jesus might have said similar but different things on different occasions, sometimes saying "blessed are the poor" (Luke) and sometimes "blessed are the poor in spirit" (Matthew). The alternative view, that Jesus actually said "blessed are the poor," and Matthew clarified the meaning by adding the words "in spirit," is advocated by McKnight.[9] Luke's Beatitudes—just like Matthew's—present an unexpected view of the good life. In Luke 6:20, Jesus says that it is the poor who are fortunate, whereas we would normally think that they are unfortunate. The hungry are fortunate (Luke 6:21), contrary to our usual judgments. In both lists (Matthew's and Luke's), those people usually considered unfortunate are actually highly valued in the kingdom of heaven.

---

9. McKnight, *The Sermon on the Mount*, 37.

In Matthew, the beatitudes are as follows:

Condition	Outcome
poor in spirit (spiritually destitute)	kingdom of heaven
mourn	comforted
humble/meek	inherit the earth[10]
hunger and thirst for righteousness	filled
merciful	shown mercy
pure in heart	see God
peacemakers	called the sons of God
persecuted for the sake of righteousness	kingdom of heaven
those insulted for me	reward is great in heaven

I like how McKnight divides up the Beatitudes into three sets of three, with one group focusing on the humble poor, the middle group focusing on those who pursue justice, and the last group

---

10. Bonhoeffer: "when the realm of heaven will descend, then the form of the earth will be renewed, and it will be the earth of the community of Jesus"; Dietrich Bonhoeffer, *Discipleship*, DBWE 4 (Minneapolis: Fortress, 2001), 105. McKnight would probably not see this comment from Bonhoeffer to be in opposition to McKnight's own insistence that the word "earth" here should actually be translated "land" and refers specifically to the "land promise" made to Abraham (Gen 12:7), and thus Jesus means the land of Israel in particular (*The Sermon on the Mount*, 42–43).

focusing on those who create peace.[11]

As it turns out, the perfect model for each of these beatitudes is Jesus himself. Matthew's Gospel will go on to show us that Jesus is "gentle and lowly in heart" (11:29), he mourns for Jerusalem (23:37–39),[12] he hungers and thirsts for righteousness (4:4), he is merciful (9:27; 15:22; 17:15; 20:30–31), pure in heart, attempts to make peace, and he is persecuted for righteousness' sake.

Notes on a Few of the Beatitudes

Not everything about the Beatitudes is obvious. Some of the difficulty is that it's hard to know exactly how to live out what seems at first to be rather straightforward encouragement (such as "blessed are the peacemakers"). Another element of difficulty is that some of the statements do not seem very straightforward, at least not to twenty-first-century Americans (such as "blessed are the poor in spirit"). Here we'll discuss a few difficult spots.

Poor in Spirit

Luke's version (6:20) just says "poor," which is—perhaps—a little easier to understand, even if we would want to immediately qualify Jesus' statement by pointing out that poverty is not unequivocally a fortunate postion, and wealth is not always a por-

---

11. McKnight, *The Sermon on the Mount*, 37–38. See also McKnight's helpful discussion of each beatitude on pp. 38–49.

12. As McKnight (*The Sermon on the Mount*, 41) points out, the people in the beatitude are mourning probably not for a recently deceased spouse but rather for the degradation of the people of Israel due to their own sin. Jesus' mourning over Jerusalem fits the model precisely.

tent of doom (or, so the book of Proverbs teaches). But at least we know what "poor" means: what does "poor in spirit" mean? We might first think of humility, but Jesus is about to declare the humble blessed (#3), and it would be nice to find some different meaning for "poor in spirit." But the two are probably very closely related. The opposite of spiritual poverty is probably in some ways arrogance, but also boldness, self-assertion. Those who are spiritually poor—which does not mean anything close to "poor with respect to God," as this macarism makes clear—consider spiritual matters ahead of physical matters, and they mourn (see the next beatitude) over their sinfulness, and the sinfulness of God's people. There's hardly any greater need for Christians this year than to emphasize again this first beatitude, to abandon self-assertiveness, to hold up as models those who are poor in spirit. And there's hardly anything this year less likely to occur.

The Kingdom of Heaven

Jesus attaches the promise of the kingdom of heaven to two Beatitudes: #1 "blessed are the poor in spirit"; and #8 "blessed are those who are persecuted for righteousness' sake"; "for theirs is the kingdom of heaven." Jesus doesn't use the word "inherit" here like he does in Beatitude #3 ("blessed are the meek"), but the thought seems similar—the poor in spirit or the persecuted ones are going to inherit the kingdom of heaven. It's not uncommon for the New Testament to talk about certain people inheriting (or not inheriting) the kingdom of heaven.[13] Jesus also frequently talks

---

13. See also Matthew 25:34; Romans 4:13; 8:17; 1 Corinthians 6:9–10; 15:50; Galatians 3:29; 5:21; Titus 3:7; Hebews 6:17; James 2:5; 1 Peter 1:4.

about the type of people who are "kingdom of heaven" people.[14] You might say that's what his entire ministry is about. We talked more about this in the previous chapter, but here I'll just remind you that Jesus has come to establish the kingdom of heaven (or, of the heavens; cf. 4:17), and the actual phrase "kingdom of heaven" is unique to Matthew's Gospel—"kingdom of God" appears elsewhere—indicating the heavenly nature of the kingdom (a theme also in John 18:36). What I want to emphasize here is that, in the Beatitudes, the people who might have been thought cursed by God are precisely the ones who are "kingdom of heaven" people, and if we press the point that the kingdom is said to be "theirs," belonging to them, we could say what is definitely affirmed elsewhere, that the children of God are not just subjects in God's kingdom but co-heirs with Jesus (Rom 8:17) destined to reign alongside him (Rev 22:5).

Inherit the Earth (or Land?)

The third Beatitude says that the meek will inherit the earth. It's pretty common for commentators to link this promise to the land-promise to Abraham in Genesis 12:7, a promise reaffirmed several times in Scripture (e.g., Gen 28:13; Psa 37:11), a promise that specifically relates to the "land" (not "earth") of Israel. The word translated "earth" in Matthew 5:5 could just as easily be translated "land." The main Greek dictionary for New Testament study (BDAG) gives six main definitions for this word, the first being "earth" and the last four all more-or-less being different nuances of "land."[15] Let's assume for a moment that Jesus is tapping into

---

14. E.g., Matt 7:21; 8:11–12; 18:3; 19:12, 14, 23–24; 21:43.
15. BDAG 196 (for the full reference, see note 2 above).

this ancient promise of the land, a promise apparently unfulfilled in Jesus's day since many contemporary Jews probably did not feel like the land on which they resided belonged to them, since the Romans were their overlords. This land promise in Scripture is related to security, something like the ancient Israelite version of the American Dream: owning your own land meant you didn't have to serve a foreign power, you didn't have to be afraid. In this way it was also closely connected with the kingdom of God—or, rather, the kingdom of the heavens—for when God established his kingdom (so the theory went) then he would bring back together the scattered Israelites to have them dwell securely in the land once more, each under his own vine and fig tree (Mic 4:4). So I don't think Jesus meant the meek would literally inherit the earth, or even literally inherit the land of Israel, but I think his promise of inheriting the land taps into the Old Testament theme of the land and corresponds to inheriting the kingdom of heaven.

THEY WILL SEE GOD

The Bible has some interesting (and complex) things to say about seeing God. Of course, you know, "you cannot see my face, for no one shall see me and live" (Exod 33:20). This verse appears in the same chapter of the Bible in which we read, "the Lord used to speak to Moses face to face, as one speaks to a friend" (Exod 33:11). Whatever it means that Moses spoke to God "face-to-face"—whatever it means for God to have a face—this privilege marks Moses as the Lord's most intimate confidant (Num 12:6–8). Seeing God, being in his presence, is held out as a hope: "I will dwell among the Israelites, and I will be their God" (Exod 29:45), rarely and only fleetingly experienced (e.g., Ezek 1). The sixth Beatitude promises that those who are pure in heart will see God, no doubt meaning that their position as honored saints within the kingdom of heaven will finally put them in close proximity to the God whom they have longed to see. As the loud voice from the throne says in the hearing of John, "See, the home of God is among people, and he will dwell with them, and they will be his people, and God himself will be with them" (Rev 21:3).

Peacemakers

What are we to make of the peacemakers in Beatitude #7? We are supposed to be peacemakers, but what exactly does that mean? How far do we take the idea? Can we defend ourselves from harm? (Jesus has something to say about that later in the Sermon, so we'll talk about it when we get to Matt 5:39.) McKnight defines peacemaking as "an active entrance into the middle of warring parties for the purpose of creating reconciliation and peace," and he says that peacemaking is not being "nice" or "tolerant" or soft-pedaling around differences.[16] I like the way he puts all of this, though this definition doesn't really solve the much bigger problem of how to put this into practice. McKnight goes on to discuss briefly pacifism (a position toward which he leans) and whether the ethic of Jesus applies to nations or only individuals.[17] His conclusion: "Privatizing one's kingdom ethics is not the way of Jesus."[18] I myself am not so sure about that. I don't see anywhere in the New Testament where Jesus or an inspired writer talked

---

16. McKnight, *The Sermon on the Mount*, 47.
17. See also his lengthier discussion at pp. 130–38, and my own response to it in chapter 5 below.
18. McKnight, *The Sermon on the Mount*, 48.

about how nations ought to behave. McKnight apparently thinks that what applies to individuals also applies to nations, but that's only one way to think about these issues, and I don't see that the New Testament expresses any opinion one way or the other. I know that what Jesus says in this Sermon applies to individuals, but I'm not sure in what way it would apply to nations, and really, I think this kind of discussion is a distraction from the radical nature of Jesus's teaching.

We have plenty of trouble being "peacemakers" in our personal relationships, in our homes with our spouses, with our children, with our co-workers, with people at church—I mean, good grief, have you seen Twitter?—we have so much trouble here that we really need to focus on these daily struggles without getting lost in a philosophical discussion (with definite practical implications, to be sure) about whether it's okay for a nation to go to war with another nation, or whether a Christian could serve in the military. Of course, we should have those discussions, too, and when we do we should return to the Sermon on the Mount as one key passage informing such discussions, but for now we can simply note that Jesus did not have those particular issues in mind (even if his statements here have implications for those particular issues).

The complexities of this issue should keep us in the middle between two ditches. I say that even as I recognize that the radical nature of Jesus's teaching cannot easily be described as "staying in the middle."

Conclusion

Sometimes we use the phrase "the in-crowd" to refer to a group of people that we want to be like. We want to be in "the in-crowd" because those are the people who enjoy life, that everybody wants to be around, who appear successful, like life is easy for them. Jesus begins his sermon by destroying our notions of the in-crowd. The people that Jesus wants to lift up before our eyes as worthy of our congratulations are not those we think of as constituting the in-crowd—quite the opposite. These beatitudes call on us to reconsider what our life's aspirations are. Do we want to be rich and powerful? Do we hunger after fortune and glory? Do we want a nice, easy life? None of those ideas can be found in Jesus's list of people who are fortunate. The bizarro world depicted by Jesus, otherwise known as the kingdom of heaven, commends a different set of values, a different vision of the good life.

3

SALT AND LIGHT
MATTHEW 5:13-16

> Salt is good, but if the salt has lost its saltiness, how will you make it salty again? Have salt in yourselves, and be at peace with one another. (Mark 9:50)

How much should disciples of Jesus resemble the world around them? This perennial question has no easy answers. Due in part to their Christian beliefs, the Amish live very distinctive lives, much more distinctive than many conservative Christians would tolerate. Most of us think there's no problem with driving a car or having electricity, but we still struggle with which movies it's okay for a Christian to see, or what kind of music we can listen to, or what clothing we can wear, or whether we can eat in a restaurant that has an open bar, or whether we can participate in "mixed bathing," or school dances, or...all kinds of things.

One of the reasons we struggle with these questions is because the Bible doesn't necessarily provide straightforward answers, and the guidance it does contain could support contrary approaches. Paul's famous "When in Rome..." statement that he becomes all things to all men (1 Cor 9:22) tends to support the idea that Christians need to look like "normal people" if we are to win an audience in this world. But the same apostle counsels Christians to abstain from every form of evil (1 Thess 5:22), and he denied that a believer had anything in common with an unbeliever (2 Cor 6:14–16).

Modern Christians who emphasize 1 Corinthians 9:22 also usually mention that Jesus seemed to enjoy the company of sinners more than that of religious people. On the other hand, the statements in the Sermon on the Mount definitely exhort separation from the behaviors of the world. The idea that followers of Jesus can be compared to salt and light supports this way of thinking—Christians ought to be distinct, their influence obvious, just as the influence of salt and light is obvious.

You Are Salt

The word "salt" appears in only three passages in the Gospels, one in each of the Synoptic Gospels.

> You are the salt of the earth. But if the salt should lose its taste, how can it be made salty? It's no longer good for anything but to be thrown out and trampled under people's feet. (Matt 5:13)

> For everyone will be salted with fire. Salt is good, but if the salt should lose its flavor, how can you season it? Have salt among yourselves and be at peace with one another. (Mark 9:49–50)

> Now, salt is good, but if salt should lose its taste, how will it be made salty? It isn't fit for the soil or for the manure pile; they throw it out. Let anyone who has ears to hear listen. (Luke 14:34–35)

Jesus uses the same sort of language in each of these passages, but the context is quite different. Only our passage in the Sermon on the Mount explicitly says that Jesus' disciples are salt.

EXPLORATION 3.1
Salt in the Bible[1]

In the ESV, the word "salt" appears 46x in the Bible, only 10x in the NT (mostly in the mouth of Jesus, as we surveyed above). Here are the appearances in the Old Testament:

Geography
- Salt Sea (Gen 14:3; Num 34:3, 12; Deut 3:17; Josh 3:16; 12:3; 15:2, 5; 18:19)
- city of salt (Josh 15:62)
- valley of salt (2 Sam 8:13 // 1 Chr 18:12; 2 Kgs 14:7 // 2 Chr 25:11 // Ps 60 superscription)
- salt pits (Zeph 2:9)
- salt land (Job 39:6; Jer 17:6)

Religious Uses
- seasoning for incense (Exod 30:35)
- seasoning for offerings (Lev 2:13; Ezek 43:24)

---

1. Of course, Wikipedia has an entry on "Salt in the Bible."

- salt of the covenant (Lev 2:13)
- covenant of salt (Num 18:19; 2 Chr 13:5)

Other Occurrences
- Lot's wife as a pillar of salt (Gen 19:26)
- destroying agricultural abilities (Deut 29:23; Judg 9:45)
- purifying water (miraculously; 2 Kgs 2:20–21)
- food (Ezra 4:14; Job 6:6)
- list (Ezra 6:9; 7:22)
- rubbing newborns (Ezek 16:4)
- salt water (Ezek 47:11)

In the New Testament, aside from the Synoptic Gospels, the word "salt" appears in only two passages:

> Let your speech always be gracious, seasoned with salt, so that you may know how you should answer each person. (Col 4:6)

> Does a spring pour forth from the same opening both fresh and salt water? Can a fig tree, my brothers, bear olives, or a grapevine produce figs? Neither can a salt pond yield fresh water. (Jas 3:11–12)

It might have been nice if Jesus had defined exactly what he meant by calling his disciples salt. Exactly which properties of salt did you have in mind, Jesus? On the other hand, this failure to specify leaves the relationship between disciples and salt open to our imagination. And—as you know—people have come up with all sorts of connections. The most prominent ones I've heard have to do with salt giving flavor to foods, or salt as a preservative, or salt making people thirsty.

In antiquity, salt was extremely valuable, sometimes used as currency.[2] The word "salary" derives from the Latin word for salt. It is this quality of salt that Dietrich Bonhoeffer emphasizes:

> Now they are described using the image of the most indispensable commodity on earth. They are the salt of the earth. They are the noblest asset, the highest value the world possesses. Without them the earth can no longer survive. The earth is preserved by salt; the world lives because of these poor, ignoble, and weak people, whom the world rejects. It destroys its own life by driving out the disciples, and—O wonder! —the earth may continue to live because of these outcasts.[3]

My own experience with salt suggests to me that the salty flavor is the primary characteristic that we should consider. (Jesus himself seems to emphasize the flavor of salt in his statement.) I think about how powerful just a little bit of salt is in a recipe. Put some pot roast on somebody's plate without any salt and they'll choke it down; add just a few sprinkles of salt and they'll gobble it up and ask for seconds.

I make pizza every Friday night, starting with the dough, and I've messed up the dough every which way. I've forgotten to include just about every ingredient except for the flour. I make

---

2. In the Wikipedia article on "Salt," see the section called "History." Or see Mark Kurlansky, *Salt: A World History* (New York: Penguin, 2002).

3. Dietrich Bonhoeffer, *Discipleship*, DBWE 4 (Minneapolis: Fortress, 2001), 110–11.

three pizzas, and only a single teaspoon of salt goes into the dough for all three pizzas combined. You would think that such a little amount of salt would hardly be noticeable, especially in something like pizza, since the dough is going to be covered in sauce and cheese and various toppings (pepperoni, onion, and olives, in our case). But I'll tell you what—I'll never forget the salt again. I might forget something else, but I'm going to make sure the salt goes into the dough, because the one time I forgot to include that little bit of salt, the pizza was awful. Bland. We ate it, but only after sprinkling a little salt on top of the finished pizza.

A little salt has a big influence.

I think what Jesus is getting at is that his disciples, though few in number, can—or rather, will—have a big influence on others around them. His disciples, those who hear his words and enact them, will be obvious in their effect on society.[4]

Part of the reason this interpretation of the salt statement makes sense is because of the parallel statement regarding light.

You Are Light

Light is a much more common theme in Scripture than salt. From the first chapter of the Bible —"Let there be light" (Gen 1:3)—to the last —"the Lord God will give them light" (Rev 22:5)—the theme of light is ubiquitous and important.

Light and dark have obvious connections to knowledge. We talk about the Dark Ages as a period of poor education, whereas the

---

4. For an interesting economic-impact analysis of the effect of churches within their communities, see Ram A. Cnaan, *The Other Philadelphia Story: How Local Congregations Support Quality of Life in Urban America* (Philadelphia: University of Pennsylvania Press, 2006).

Enlightenment is a time of increased learning. When someone gets an idea, we say that a lightbulb turned on. The Bible also talks about light in connection to knowledge. "Your word is a lamp to my feet and a light to my path" (Ps 119:105).

Another way of thinking about the contrast between light and dark is a moral one: darkness is evil, and light represents goodness. Paul tells the Ephesians, "you were once darkness, but now you are light in the Lord. Live as children of light" (Eph 5:8). He warns them away from "the unfruitful works of darkness" (5:11).

These two ways of thinking about light—knowledge and morality—are closely intertwined and both are probably at play in the Sermon on the Mount. The disciples are the light of the world in the sense that they live according to the enlightened ethic of Jesus.

But light is a helpful image also because light shares the property of salt that we explored earlier: a little bit goes a long way. It is this idea that Jesus' illustrations highlight: the disciples as light are a city on a hill, or a lamp on a lampstand. The influence of disciples is obvious.

We used to live in Cincinnati, and we used to love approaching the city from the south, heading north on I-75. Cincinnati is bordered on the south by the Ohio River, so the entire city butts up against the water. You don't come to Cincinnati little by little, like you do Nashville; you arrive in Cincinnati all at once. So, coming up I-75 at night, we'd head around a little bend in the interstate and the entire lit-up city would appear all at once. It wasn't even on a hill, but down in a valley, but still the effect was dazzling. It could not be hidden.

Losing Flavor, Hiding Light

Jesus warns that salt that has lost its flavor is worthless. I haven't really been able to get an answer as to whether this scenario imagined by Jesus is possible—can salt actually lose its flavor? The closest I've come to an answer is that if enough impurities are mixed with the salt, it can lose its saltiness. But whether or not it is actually possible for salt to become unsalty, the point Jesus is making is clear. If I had some salt that didn't work, that didn't salt my food, I certainly wouldn't keep using it. I'd get rid of it quickly. It wouldn't be worth anything.[5]

As the salt of the world, Jesus's disciples must maintain their flavor. Whether or not salt can lose its flavor, it is by all means possible for disciples to lose their flavor. At which point, Jesus says, they have forfeited their value.

So also, disciples can obscure the light shining through them. Jesus goes on to define that light as "good deeds":

> Let your light shine before others, so that they may see your good works and give glory to your Father in heaven. (5:16)

The extent to which we allow our light to shine is the extent to which we carry out the instructions of Jesus, living according to his teachings and thereby influencing the world.

---

5. See the comment on this verse in the online NET Bible (note 14), which points to a passage in the Babylonian Talmud, tractate Bekhorot 8b, as indicating that the idea of salt losing its flavor was considered impossible, like a camel going through the eye of a needle (Matt 19:24).

The idea that people are light for the world is not original with this Sermon. Already, Israel had been described in these terms, for example in Isa 49:1–6.[6] Jesus is adopting this ancient description and applying it to his followers.

THE CHRISTIAN INFLUENCE

Bonhoeffer points out, "When Jesus calls his disciples 'the salt,' instead of himself, this transfers his efficacy on the earth to them. He brings them into his work."[7] Similarly, we recall that Jesus said about himself, "I am the light of the world" (John 8:12), but in the Sermon he gives that description to his followers. As Bonhoeffer said, Jesus entrusts his work to his disciples.

I appreciate Scot McKnight's view that the two metaphors, salt and light, refer to different missions.[8] The "salt of the earth," which McKnight persuasively translated "salt of the land (of Israel)," refers to the mission to the Jews. A reader of Matthew's Gospel cannot help but notice the verses where Jesus restricts his ministry to the "lost sheep of the house of Israel," even instructing his disciples to avoid ministering to Samaritans and Gentiles (cf. Matt 10:5–6; 15:24). But this restriction was for a limited time only; at the end of the Gospel, the risen Jesus tells his disciples that they should in turn make disciples of all nations (Matt 28:19). They are

---

6. I really like the way Scot McKnight (*The Sermon on the Mount*, Story of God Bible Commentary [Grand Rapids: Zondervan, 2013], 58–59) connects the light theme of Matt 5:14 with the Bible's depiction of Israel as light, particularly in view of Matt 4:14–16, immediately before the Sermon.

7. Bonhoeffer, *Discipleship*, 111.

8. McKnight, *The Sermon on the Mount*, 57.

to be "the light of the world."

The impact of the Christian is not always as we might wish. We recall that even in the case of Jesus, "the light shone in the darkness, and the darkness did not comprehend it" (John 1:5). Nevertheless, light always makes some sort of impact on the darkness; a city set on a hill cannot be hidden. So also, in the case of the disciples: they "are to see the inevitability of their impact on the Gentile world."[9] The Lord was with Joseph, and that fact was obvious to everyone around him (Gen 39:3).

The challenge of these descriptions (salt and light) is that in order to have the impact on our communities and this world that Jesus envisions for us, we must live out the words of this Sermon. The Sermon is the blueprint for how to be salt and light in the world, and it would be no exaggeration to respond, "easier said than done."[10]

Conclusion

How much should disciples of Jesus resemble the world around them? In the Sermon on the Mount, Jesus stresses how unlike the world his disciples ought to be. They ought to be like salt and light. The world ought to notice their presence or their absence. If they maintain their saltiness by living out Jesus's instructions—if they let their light shine by doing the good deeds that Jesus enjoins—

---

9. McKnight, *The Sermon on the Mount*, 59.

10. McKnight's illustration of a church in Illinois that he believes is fulfilling this "salt and light" mandate in the modern world (*The Sermon on the Mount*, 60–61) might spur an interesting discussion in a class setting.

then they will make an impact on the world, and people will give glory to God.

4

FULFILLING THE LAW AND THE PROPHETS
MATTHEW 5:17-20

> Don't think that I came to abolish the Law or the
> Prophets. I did not come to abolish but to fulfill.
> (Matt 5:17)

What role does the Old Testament play in the Christian religion? This issue has exercised Christian theologians from the very earliest days. The apostle Paul stressed that Christians are not under law (Rom 6:14; Gal 5:18) and are therefore not bound by the specific requirements of the Torah, such as circumcision. On the other hand, Paul quoted the Old Testament, including the Torah, frequently, not only to prove that Jesus is the Messiah, but even to instruct Christians on proper behavior (e.g., 1 Cor 10). When Paul said that all Scripture is inspired and useful for teaching and rebuking and correcting and training (2 Tim 3:16–17), he surely had the Old Testament in mind, and his own use of the Old Testament bears out the point.

In the second century, a teacher in Rome named Marcion made a sharp distinction between Christianity and the Old Testament, even to the point of denying that the Old Testament is Christian

Scripture. The Old Testament is for Jews, Marcion said, and the New Testament is for Christians. While Marcion's views won some followers, the majority of Christians have rejected Marcionism as basically heretical.[1] A person cannot read the New Testament and fail to see how important the Old Testament is. Jesus quotes the Old Testament frequently in order to explain who he is and what he is doing (cf. Luke 4:1–13, 17–21).

The issue is a difficult one for many Christian groups, and certainly this has been the case for my own religious group, the churches of Christ. Modern churches of Christ in America are associated with the American Restoration Movement (a.k.a., the Stone-Campbell Movement), which have had a conflicted view of the Old Testament. Sometimes people in churches of Christ are accused of not believing in the Old Testament, and sometimes we say things that feed into that perception, things like, "The Old Testament is not authoritative for the Christian."[2] This idea is connected to our traditional emphasis on the proper distinction between the Old Testament and the New Testament, an emphasis that goes back to the 1816 "Sermon on the Law" by Alexander Campbell.[3] Campbell was concerned mostly with the use of the

---

1. For more, see ch. 2 in Ronald E. Heine, *Reading the Old Testament with the Ancient Church: Exploring the Formation of Early Christian Thought* (Grand Rapids: Baker, 2007).

2. I have heard a professor at a university affiliated with churches of Christ make this statement publicly, but in a rather off-hand way (i.e., it wasn't the main point of what he was talking about). I have also heard a professor from another Christian group say that people in churches of Christ do not believe in the Old Testament.

3. The sermon was printed in Campbell's journal *The Millennial Harbinger* in September 1846 and has been reprinted many times, e.g. in

Old Testament to establish doctrines like infant baptism (based on an analogy with circumcision in the Old Testament) and the so-called Christian Sabbath. To understand why you can't use circumcision or the Sabbath command to establish Christian practice, you have to understand how the Old Testament relates to the Christian. But Campbell was no Marcionite; he believed that the Old Testament was authoritative for Christians[4]—its presentation of God is authoritative for us, its view of the Messiah is authoritative for us, and even the Law has some continuing authority, at least as it reveals to us the character of our God. Even in respect of Christian practice, note how Paul in 1 Corinthians 9:9 quotes the law of Deuteronomy 25:4.

In the Gospel of Matthew, we have already encountered the Old Testament on a number of occasions. We have seen that Jesus (1:22-23; 2:5-6, 15, 17-18, 23; 4:14) and John the Baptist (3:3) fulfill Scripture, and Jesus overcomes the devil by quoting Deuteronomy (4:1-11). It's not until after the Sermon on the Mount that we read stories about Jesus in conflict with Jewish leaders in regard to the Law (Matt 9:9-17; 12:1-14; etc.), but hints of conflict come already in John the Baptist's condemnation of the Pharisees and Sadducees (3:7-10). Jesus wants to make clear now, at the beginning of his public ministry, that his teaching—though distinct from that of other religious leaders—should not be considered an overturning of Jewish Scripture. He has not come to throw out the Jewish Bible but to fulfill it.

Campbell's book *Familiar Lectures on the Pentateuch* (1867) available on Google Books.

4. As mentioned in the previous note, Campbell delivered a series of lectures on the Pentateuch in which he expounded on the Torah because of its continuing authority for Christians.

The Law and the Prophets

In Matthew 5:17, Jesus mentions "the Law and the Prophets." This common phrase is an ancient way of referring to the Old Testament.[5] The "law" means the law of Moses, the Torah or Pentateuch, the first five books of the Old Testament. The "prophets" refers to the rest of the Old Testament. In truth, the entire Old Testament was considered prophetic, even the Pentateuch, since Moses was the greatest of the prophets (Deut 34:10–12).

In these verses, Jesus teaches us about the meaning of the Old Testament, which in his day constituted all of Scripture. According to Scot McKnight, "Our passage is the most significant passage in the entire Bible on how to read the Bible ... because Jesus tells us here how to read the Bible."[6] What does Jesus tell us the Bible is about? He shows here that if you want to read it correctly, you have to read below the surface.

Fulfilling Scripture

The concept of "fulfillment" is important in Matthew.[7] The use of the word "fulfill" (πληρόω, *pleróō*) in 5:17 is already the seventh

---

5. The phrase "the law and the prophets" appears also in Matt 7:12; 22:40; Luke 16:16; Acts 13:15; Rom 3:21.

6. McKnight, *The Sermon on the Mount*, Story of God Bible Commentary (Grand Rapids: Baker, 2014), 66. The other passages McKnight cites as important for learning how to read the Bible are Luke 24:13–49; Gal 3:19–25; Rom 9–11; and the Epistle to the Hebrews.

7. For a treatment of this theme similar to mine, see Iain Provan, *The Reformation and the Right Reading of Scripture* (Waco, TX: Baylor University Press, 2017), 115–18.

time in the Gospel that this word has appeared. Mostly up to now, various Scriptures have been fulfilled in the life of Jesus: Isa 7:14 was fulfilled in the conception of the child who is Immanuel ("God with us"; Matt 1:22–23); Hosea 11:1 is fulfilled in the family of Jesus escaping Egypt (Matt 2:15); Jeremiah 31:15 is fulfilled in the outcry surrounding Herod's murder of the babies in Bethlehem (Matt 2:17).[8] Besides these scriptures, Jesus explained to John the Baptist that his baptism was necessary in order to fulfill all righteousness (Matt 3:15).

> **EXPLORATION 4.1**
> **The Gospels on "Fulfillment"**
>
> The Greek word for "fulfill" is *plēroō* (πληρόω), which appears 86x in the New Testament, about half of which (42x) are in the Gospels. In the first paragraph earlier under the heading "Fulfilling Scripture," we saw the many verses in Matthew that use *plēroō* in reference to fulfilling Scripture, both Scripture in general and, especially, specific verses of Scripture, such as Isaiah 7:14 or Hosea 11:1. Aside from those verses, Matthew uses the word *plēroō* only one other time, in reference to "filling the measure of your fathers" (23:32).
>
> Mark uses *plēroō* only twice: the time is fulfilled (1:15), and scripture in general is fulfilled (14:49).

---

8. "Fulfill" is connected to specific OT scriptures 10x in Matthew: 1:22; 2:15, 17, 23; 4:14; 8:17; 12:17; 13:35; 21:4; 27:9. A very similar word (ἀναπληρόω, *anaplēroō*) is used in the same way in Matthew 13:14. "Fulfill" is also used in 26:54, 56 in regard to scripture in general.

> Luke uses *plēróō* 9x, each time with a different referent: scripture in general (24:44), scripture in particular (4:21), the words of Gabriel (1:20), the times of the Gentiles (21:24), and the Lord's Supper in the kingdom of God (22:16). A few times it simply means filled, as in valleys filled up (3:5), or a child being filled with wisdom (2:40). Once it refers to Jesus finishing speaking (7:1), and once it refers to accomplishing (finishing/filling) his upcoming departure (9:31).
>
> John uses *plēróō* 15x, and John's usage parallels Matthew's more closely than do the other Gospels. That is, John several times uses *plēróō* in reference to fulfilling specific passages of Scripture (John 12:38; 13:18; 15:25; 19:24, 36). He uses it also once to refer to fulfilling scripture in general (17:12), and a couple times in reference to fulfilling Jesus' own words (18:9, 32). Moreover, the word is used 4x in reference to joy (3:29; 15:11; 16:24; 17:13), the heart (16:6), Jesus' time (7:8), and a house being filled with a scent (12:3).
>
> In the rest of the New Testament, *plēróō* refers to the fulfilling of Scripture only three times: Acts 1:16; 3:18; James 2:23.

The word "fulfill" is sometimes used in a more mundane sense, like filling a net (Matt 13:48), or a valley (Luke 3:5). This usage might help us to think about what it means in reference to scripture. Jesus is "filling up" the scriptures, bringing them to completion, accomplishing them.

Jesus says that he has come to bring fulfillment, completion, to the Old Testament. This is an astonishing claim for a person to make. As Scot McKnight says, "Anyone who makes that claim thinks BC became AD when he was born."[9]

The Old Testament has a meaning in its own time in the context of ancient Israel. But not only do certain passages in the Old Testament point toward a coming Messiah (whether that term is used or not; e.g., Isa 11:1–10; Jer 23:4–5) but also other passages that were not thought to have anything particularly to do with the Messiah could be interpreted in this way by exploring patterns and typologies in the Scriptures. "These are my words that I spoke to you while I was still with you—that everything written about me in the Law of Moses, the Prophets, and the Psalms must be fulfilled" (Luke 24:44). So the scriptures that Matthew says have been fulfilled in Jesus (see esp. Jer 31:15 and Hos 11:1) had a meaning in their own time, and Jews who read those verses did not expect that anything in them still needed to be fulfilled. And yet, events in Jesus's life reflected these Old Testament statements in such a way that Matthew says Jesus filled up those statements—as if the meaning in its context in ancient Israel was not quite full (even if that fact was not realized at the time) and now we can recognize that Jesus fills up those statements with increased meaning. The Old Testament as a whole looks forward to the coming of one who would usher in God's kingdom, one who would defeat God's enemies, one who would suffer on behalf of the people. Jesus has not come to abolish such expectation rooted in Israel's Scriptures; he has come to fulfill these expectations.

But he has also come to "fill up" more things than just messianic prophecy. Immediately after this passage in the Sermon, Jesus will

---

9. Scot McKnight, *Kingdom Conspiracy: Returning to the Radical Mission of the Local Church* (Grand Rapids: Baker, 2014), 52.

cite various laws, starting with the Ten Commandments (Matt 5:21, 27), and he will explain how they need to be fulfilled (filled up). These laws aren't just about behavior, but they are about the heart. The command against murder has a broader application than just literally taking someone's life; it has to do with hatred. The command against adultery really encompasses the desire for adultery. In the same way, the verse in Hosea 11:1—despite initial appearances—is not just about ancient Israel coming out of Egypt but can also be applied to Jesus. In this way, the meaning of these verses becomes full.

Not One Jot or Tittle

The "jot" (the Greek word is *iota*, ἰῶτα) refers to the smallest letter of the alphabet, and the "tittle" refers to a small mark that distinguishes one letter from another, like the Hebrew letters *bet* (ב) and *kaf* (כ). Or think about the difference between a lowercase "f" and a lowercase "t," or a capital "R" and a capital "P."

Jesus emphasizes in Matthew 5:18 that so far from abolishing the law, he upholds the authority of every jot and tittle. This is Jesus's response to the question, "Is the Old Testament authoritative for a Christian?" His answer: yes, of course, every jot and tittle, until all is accomplished (= when heaven and earth pass away).

At the same time, we must recognize that the Old Testament is authoritative for us in a particular sense, not in every sense. In fact, we would say the same thing about the New Testament —not everything is directly binding upon us. You must take account of context and the purpose behind certain commands. That's usually what we say when we explain the passage about veils in worship services (cf. 1 Cor

11:1–16). We try to understand the "spirit" of the command, but we might practice that "spirit" in a different way than the first-century Christians.

What Jesus is about to do in the Sermon on the Mount resembles that line of reasoning, sort of. He seems to be saying in Matthew 5:21–48, "You have to understand the spirit behind the command against murder or the command against adultery or the divorce command, or the oaths command, etc." Now, we should recognize that Jesus will not say, "We obey the spirit behind the command against murder in a different way from ancient people, so it's okay for us to kill people because we're still following the spirit of the command." Jesus is not going to say that these commands in their literal application are irrelevant. No, they remain highly relevant, but there is a "spirit" or "meaning" behind the commandments that is even more crucial.

But according to Mark, at least, Jesus at one point offers some teaching that implies that the ancient food laws (Lev 11) are no longer directly relevant (Mark 7:19). Paul is going to insist sharply, especially in his letter to the Galatian churches, that the law regarding circumcision is irrelevant (more than that: harmful; Gal 5:1–4) for Gentile believers—circumcision is not the distinctive marker of God's people. Same thing for the Sabbath day (Col 2:16). On the other hand, we who walk by the Spirit and not by the flesh do fulfill "the righteous requirement of the Law" (Rom 8:4).

You can see how this subject can be confusing. We're not going to solve these problems in this chapter. We've seen that Christians have been struggling in this area for two thousand years. The two points we want to hold together are that (1) in Christ we are not under law and (2) we are not abolishing the law, but rather the Old Testament continues in some sense to be authoritative for

Christians. If you feel that these two points are in tension with each other, then here are two other points for you: (1) Christians throughout the ages have felt this same tension, and (2) this subject is merely one of several areas of tension in the Christian faith. Other areas of tension—such as whether Jesus was God or human, or what it means to say there is one God who is Father, Son, and Holy Spirit, or how faith and works are related in salvation—are at least as difficult to understand and hold together.

Within the Sermon on the Mount, Jesus does not give a treatise on how to understand this tension. To keep his point in context, we can say that Jesus insists that, despite appearances, he is not teaching people that the Law is irrelevant—quite the opposite. Here's how Scot McKnight puts it: "For Jesus the real Torah is permanent *as Jesus teaches it*, which is the point of 5:21–48."[10] Someone who teaches that it's okay to ignore the commandments will be called "least in the kingdom of heaven," which is not a way of saying you'll get the shabbiest throne in the kingdom. According to Jonathan Pennington,

> Being "least in the kingdom of heaven" is not a reference to ranking in the kingdom or getting in by the skin of one's teeth but rather is a poetically parallel way of saying one does *not* get in, as 5:20 makes clearer.[11]

---

10. McKnight, *The Sermon on the Mount*, 69.
11. Pennington, *The Sermon on the Mount and Human Flourishing*, (Grand Rapids: Baker, 2017), 178. McKnight (*The Sermon on the Mount*, 69) holds the same view, pointing to 7:21–23 and 8:11–12 as illustrative.

GREATER RIGHTEOUSNESS

Jesus isn't throwing out the Torah, but he is teaching something different from the other religious leaders. Jesus is teaching that strict obedience to the letter of the law is hardly pleasing to God, is in fact almost like breaking the law. Because the commandments are not aimed primarily at restricting people's behavior; they are aimed at shaping people's hearts. If your heart is not involved in keeping the commandments—if you're merely "going through the motions"—then you've missed the point.

Jesus contrasts this practice with that of the scribes and Pharisees (Matt 5:20). We should not read this statement as a blanket condemnation of the scribes and Pharisees. We in the twenty-first century value nuance enough to understand that Abu Ghraib does not define the American soldier, that *jihad* does not define every Muslim, and that Jimmy Swaggart does not define Christianity. In the days of Jesus, it was typical Jewish teaching to emphasize the love of God—they recited the Shema a couple times per day: "Hear O Israel, the Lord our God is one Lord. And you shall love the Lord your God with all your heart…" (Deut 6:5–6). Some religious leaders saw eye-to-eye with Jesus on this matter (Mark 12:28–34). But the scribes and Pharisees with whom Jesus came into conflict, of course, did not see eye-to-eye with him. Jesus identified the problem as one of emphasis; it's not that these scribes and Pharisees who disputed with Jesus did the wrong things or taught the wrong things (note Matt 23:2–3) but that they emphasized the technicalities of the law and failed to focus on the big picture. They emphasized tithing the tiniest spices but failed to emphasize justice and mercy and faithfulness (23:23). "Jesus clearly perceived the Pharisees as not centering the Torah in love but seeing love as merely *one* of the commandments."[12] But Jesus declared that love of God and love of neighbor was the basis for the entire Law and Prophets (22:37–40).[13]

Only when a person sees clearly the "spirit" of the commandments and embodies that spirit from the heart can he or she achieve the greater righteousness that Jesus mentions in Matthew 5:20. Remember that earlier in Matthew 1, Joseph's righteousness became manifest in his attempt to sever his relationship with pregnant Mary quietly, that is, with sensitivity and mercy toward her. This example provides another illustration of what righteousness looks like: it's not an emphasis on the letter of the law but on the spirit, "for the letter killeth, but the spirit giveth life" (2 Cor 3:6).[14] Jesus does not teach his disciples to ignore the precepts but to fulfill them with a greater righteousness than the scribes and Pharisees. The kingdom of heaven is characterized by righteousness from the heart. As Dietrich Bonhoeffer emphasizes in his discussion of this passage, disciples of Jesus need not worry about this lofty requirement: "the disciples' action surpasses that of the Pharisees in that it really is perfect righteousness, as opposed to the imperfect righteousness of the

---

12. McKnight, *Kingdom Conspiracy*, 57.
13. See also Rom 13:9; Gal 5:14.
14. I admit that Paul did not have in mind in 2 Cor 3:6 the significance I have given his words here; that is, I have misinterpreted his statement. For a helpful analysis of Paul's contrast between the "letter" and the "spirit," see Richard B. Hays, "A Letter from Christ," in *Echoes of Scripture in the Letters of Paul* (New Haven: Yale University Press, 1989), 122–53. On the other hand, see Keith D. Stanglin, *The Letter and Spirit of Biblical Interpretation: From the Early Church to Modern Practice* (Grand Rapids: Baker, 2018), particularly his comments on p. 215 and the footnote.

Pharisees. How can this be? The superiority of the disciples' righteousness is that Jesus stands between them and the law—he, who has completely fulfilled the law, and in whose community we live. Instead of a law not yet fulfilled, the disciples confronted a law which had already been fulfilled."[15]

Conclusion

The disciple of Jesus maintains the authority of the Old Testament because it is the word of God that reveals truth about God and about God's people. The disciple of Jesus looks to the spirit of Scripture, not desiring to do the least thing required to skate by but to obey God from the heart. After all, the greatest command is, "You shall love the Lord your God with all your heart..." (Matt 22:36-37).

---

15. Bonhoeffer, *Discipleship*, DBWE 4 (Minneapolis: Fortress, 2001), 119.

5

PERSONAL RELATIONSHIPS[1]
MATTHEW 5:21-48

Be perfect, therefore, as your heavenly Father is perfect. (Matt 5:48)

What is it like to be a disciple of Jesus? According to this passage (Matt 5:21–48), it entails fulfilling God's commandments in a deeper and more comprehensive way than usual. It involves total dedication from a person's entire heart, soul, and strength. It is a radical obedience, not a normal life.

The problem is that many of us Christians are content with a normal life. That's all we want: a nice, quiet, normal life. We would not use those terms to describe Jesus (nice, quiet, normal), and we claim to be followers of Jesus, but we don't want to follow him too closely. We're okay with being the type of disciples that are just okay at discipleship, though we wouldn't want that with our surgeons or our mechanics. (Thanks for that illustration, AT&T.)

---

1. I am deeply grateful to Kyle Crews for improving this chapter by his careful reading, especially in regard to Jesus' statements on retribution. Of course, Kyle would have written a much better chapter than I have done.

We want Nick Saban and Bryan Harsin to recruit only 4-star and 5-star guys, and then to challenge them to be even better. But we want to be 1-star disciples and go to a low-level program that provides no challenge. We don't like challenges.

Fortunately for us, Jesus is recruiting 1-star disciples (fishermen, tax collectors, etc.), but unfortunately, he's running an elite program full of challenges. He actually says in this section of the Sermon on the Mount that his disciples should not be just like everyone else—they should not be normal people. If you love people that love you back, well ... that's what everybody does (5:46). If you want to be a part of Jesus' elite team, you've got to imitate God; you've got to be perfect. This section of the Sermon tells us what that means.

> **EXPLORATION 5.1**
> **Note to Teachers**
>
> If I were teaching this material, I might take up the entire class time by doing the following four things:
>
> 1. Read Matthew 5:43–48
> 2. Discuss who our enemies are.
> 3. Discuss how we should love them.
> 4. Pray for them.
>
> The reason I suggest this approach is because the words of Jesus here are frequently debated and rarely enacted. As Richard Hays puts it: "One reason that the world finds the New Testament's message of peacemaking and love of enemies incredible is that

> the church is so massively faithless."[2] There are certainly some parts of Jesus' instructions that are worthy of discussion and contemplation, and some points of application are not obvious. Another discussion of the meaning of Jesus' words would be helpful, I think—but not as helpful as actually doing what he says. His words are straightforward enough that we don't need to wait until every problem is solved before we practice what he preaches. This will be hard and uncomfortable, but practice—not talk—makes perfect, and perfection is the goal (Matt 5:48).

Interpreting the Torah

Jesus now explains what it means to have "greater righteousness" (5:20) than the normal person who obeys the Torah, greater righteousness than even the Pharisee. The way you do that—have the greater righteousness—is by looking to the "spirit" of the commandments rather than merely the letter and obeying the intent of the commandments with your entire heart. Jesus here explains the intent of some important commandments.

This section of the Sermon on the Mount (5:21–48) is called by people today the Antitheses. Jesus makes some antithetical statements: "You have heard that it was said ... but I say to you ...." Jesus contrasts his teaching with previous teaching. We should not put too much emphasis on the word "but" separating Jesus' teaching from the previous teaching; in Greek it is not a big

---

2. Richard B. Hays, *The Moral Vision of the New Testament: Community, Cross, New Creation; A Contemporary Introduction to New Testament Ethics* (New York: HarperCollins, 1996), 343.

"but." This word (δέ, *de*) is a weak "but," and it can even sometimes be translated "and." In Matthew 5:21, this very word is translated first as "and" in the statement, "You shall not murder, and whoever murders will be liable to judgment," and then it's translated "but": "But I say to you…." Jesus does make a contrast, but the contrast is apparent in the sense of the two teachings and not in the use of the word *de*.

In each Antithesis, at least part of the previous teaching cited by Jesus is a verse of Scripture, always the Torah. Some commentators—Scot McKnight is an example, particularly in his comments on the retribution paragraph, 5:38-42—believe that at least in some of these cases Jesus is correcting the Torah or undoing it. I don't see it that way. I think that way of interpreting Jesus makes nonsense of the introduction to this section (cf. 5:18-19). It makes much better sense to say that Jesus is giving the proper interpretation of the Torah, correcting the interpretations that had grown up over the centuries, calling people back to true religion. I agree with James Dunn: "Several of the antitheses are best seen as a radicalization, not an abrogation, of the law."[3] McKnight is on point when he says, "in these antitheses we are given the original and full intent of God, which both was only partly revealed in Scripture and had been misread by some of Jesus' contemporaries."[4] In that sense, Jesus is doing what prophets before him had done. Jeremiah had spoken of a day when God's teaching would be written on people's hearts (Jer 31:33). Amos insists that external obedience is repulsive to God if not

---

3. J. D. G. Dunn, "Law," in *Dictionary of Jesus and the Gospels*, 2d ed., ed. Joel B. Green (Downers Grove, IL: IVP, 2013), 505–15, at 510.

4. McKnight, *The Sermon on the Mount*, Story of God Bible Commentary (Grand Rapids: Zondervan, 2013), 76.

accompanied by inner submission to God, obedience from the heart.⁵

Jesus is interpreting Torah, not casting it aside. This section could be called the Interpretations just as much as the Antitheses. His statements are antithetical to certain traditions and interpretations, not to the Torah itself.

THE AUTHORITY OF JESUS

At the end of the Sermon, the crowds who overhear it are amazed at the authority with which Jesus speaks. He does not talk like the scribes (Matt 7:28–29). I imagine if you were able to ask someone in the crowd that day, "What do you mean Jesus speaks with authority?" they would cite his statements here— "I say to you…." "What you have heard is wrong. I know the truth and I'll tell it to you." That's not how the scribes talked.

We have some idea of how the scribes talked because we have ancient rabbinic works from a couple hundred years after Jesus that preserve earlier teaching. These rabbinic works (the Mishnah is an example, and the Talmud) are filled with statements from Rabbis that go like this: "Rabbi Larry said in the name of Rabbi George: my teacher Rabbi Frank said such-and-such." It is rarer to read a statement in this literature that goes like this: "Rabbi Mark said: I tell you such-and-such." The Rabbis are always passing down the views of previous Rabbis. I don't really blame them. I talk the same way. If you ask me a difficult question about Scripture, I get uncomfortable just telling you what I think,

---

5. The whole book of Amos is on this topic but see especially ch. 2 and 5:21–24.

because…well, who cares what I think? I'd rather tell you what some ancient Christian writer thought, and what Luther and Calvin thought, and what Campbell and Lipscomb thought, and what Bonhoeffer thought. So, I don't mean to criticize the way the scribes in the first century talked; they were doing the best they could.

But Jesus didn't have to report what all the previous authorities had said. He carried his own authority. He didn't worry that he might get the answers wrong. "You have heard that it was said…, but I say to you…."

The Call to Perfection

Before diving into a (brief) discussion of the individual test cases explored by Jesus, let's jump to the end of the passage: "You therefore must be perfect, as your heavenly Father is perfect" (Matt 5:48). This kind of requirement is provocative, to say the least, and if it came from anyone but Jesus, we might even say it is blasphemous. How can we possibly be perfect like God is perfect?! Jesus came so that we wouldn't have to be perfect! But here is Jesus saying that we've got to be perfect. C. S. Lewis has a helpful way of looking at this verse.

> Some people seem to think this means "Unless you are perfect, I will not help you"; and as we cannot be perfect, then, if He meant that, our position is hopeless. But I do not think He did mean that. I think He meant "The only help I will give is help

to become perfect. You may want something less: but I will give you nothing less."⁶

And later in the same chapter:

> The command *Be ye perfect* is not idealistic gas. Nor is it a command to do the impossible. He is going to make us into creatures that can obey that command.

Let's also approach this call to perfection in another way. Obviously, we can't be perfect in every way, so we can attempt to understand this statement from Jesus by setting it in the context of this passage and trying to figure out what sort of "perfection" Jesus has in mind. First of all, we can notice that the structure of the statement—you shall be X as God is X—sounds a lot like some Old Testament verses, particularly Leviticus 19:2, "You shall be holy as God is holy."⁷ Jesus seems to be echoing this verse, but instead of holiness Jesus speaks of perfection. Possibly his audience associated the word "holy" with external actions, not necessarily involving the heart: purity laws, like washing hands (Matt 15:2) or avoiding the wrong sorts of people (Matt 9:11). And so by using the term "perfect," Jesus intended to summarize his whole prior teaching, that obedience to the Torah was inadequate unless it proceeded from "all your heart, all your soul, and all your strength" (i.e., perfection = wholeness). God is perfect in every way, but in this particular passage (Matt 5:43–48) he is perfect in

---

6. C. S. Lewis, *Mere Christianity* (New York: Macmillan, 1952), 157, at the beginning of the chapter called "Counting the Cost." Of course, the whole book is worth reading.

7. Similar at Leviticus 20:26; and "perfect" at Deuteronomy 18:13.

that he treats everyone the same, the righteous and the unrighteous. The problem for the Pharisees in Matthew's Gospel is not that they didn't practice what they preached but that they weren't pure in heart. Jesus encourages them to remember the words of Hosea 6:6—"I desire mercy and not sacrifice" (Matt 9:13; 12:7)—and Isaiah 29:13—"This people honors me with their lips but their heart is far from me" (Matt 15:8). Jonathan Pennington proposes the term *cardiographic reading*, a reading focused on the heart, to describe the way we ought to read Matt 5:48 and the entire Bible. In the Antitheses, Jesus is encouraging a *cardiographic reading* of the Torah.[8]

Six Test Cases

Jesus illustrates the greater righteousness expected of his followers by discussing six test cases. For each test case, he first quotes a passage of Torah, then he gives his explanation and some practical applications.

	Topic	Matthew Passage	Torah Passage
1	Murder	5:21–26	Exod 20:13 // Deut 5:17 (Sixth Comm.)

---

8. For the term *cardiographic reading*, see Jonathan T. Pennington, *The Sermon on the Mount and Human Flourishing: A Theological Commentary* (Grand Rapids: Baker, 2017), 82–83. On the idea that the Pharisees encountered in the Gospels weren't pure in heart, see pp. 79–80, 91–92. In contrast to this depiction of the Pharisees, note that later in the Sermon Jesus says that you can know people's hearts by their actions (7:16–20). See Pennington's ch. 3 for a discussion of "perfection."

2	Adultery	5:27–30	Exod 20:14 // Deut 5:18 (Seventh Commandment)
3	Divorce	5:31–32	Deut 24:1
4	Oaths	5:33–37	Lev 19:12 // Num 30:2 // Deut 23:21–23
5	Retribution	5:38–42	Exod 21:24 // Lev 24:20 // Deut 19:21
6	Enemies	5:43–48	Lev 19:18

1. Murder (5:21-26)

The main point of this first test case is pretty obvious: it's not about just whether you pull the trigger; even the anger that leads to the murder makes you guilty. As I've already argued, I don't think Jesus is saying the Ten Commandments are irrelevant or contrary to God's will. He's clarifying the intent of God when he gave the command.[9]

Jesus gives three examples of how you might become guilty: by becoming angry with your brother, by calling your brother "raca," or by calling him "fool." "Raca" is an Aramaic word that means "idiot." Some Bibles (e.g., the KJV) have the words "without cause" in v. 22: "Everyone who becomes angry with his brother without

---

9. The early second-century BC sage Ben Sira had gone some distance toward the interpretation of Jesus; see the deuterocanonical book Sirach 34:25–26, and see the discussion of David A. deSilva, *The Jewish Teachers of Jesus, James, and Jude: What Earliest Christianity Learned from the Apocrypha and Pseudepigrapha* (Oxford: Oxford University Press, 2012), 68–82.

cause...." Modern translations usually do not contain these words. The Greek manuscripts of the New Testament usually do contain these words, but the earliest Greek manuscripts seem to have omitted them.[10]

For instance, here is an image from Codex Sinaiticus, a fourth-century copy of the Greek Bible.[11] You can see that the Greek word EIKH (= εικη; meaning "without cause") has been written by someone in the right margin of this manuscript; it was originally omitted.

So, anyway, Jesus probably didn't give the exception "without cause." He probably just said you would be guilty if you get angry with your brother. That's pretty hardcore.

Bonhoeffer explains:

> Such words are an injury to a sister or brother, a thrust to the heart. They are intended to strike, wound, and destroy. But intentional words of derision rob sisters and brothers of their dignity in public. They intend to make other people despise them, as well. They aim in hatred to destroy another's internal

---

10. On this issue, see the online NET Bible on this passage, note 27.
11. Images of the manuscript are online at http://www.codexsinaiticus.org/en/.

and external existence. I pass judgment on another. That is murder. A murderer is handed over to judgment.[12]

Bonhoeffer concludes his chapter on this paragraph with these words:

> Service to sisters and brothers which satisfies them and respects their rights and life is the path of self-denial, the path to the cross. No one has greater love than those who lay down their lives for their friends. That is the love of the crucified one. Thus, this commandment is fulfilled solely in the cross of Jesus.[13]

Jesus himself got angry on occasion (cf. Matt 21:12–13), and of course the Bible not infrequently presents God as angry, in the Old Testament and in the New Testament (e.g., Col 3:6). We could interpret Jesus' condemnation of anger, then, as hyperbole. I like McKnight's view that Jesus is not being hyperbolic, but he's proclaiming a way of life characteristic of the kingdom of God, and when the kingdom of God fully comes, anger will cease to exist.[14] Disciples of Jesus should be people who live according to the kingdom of God now, since we are already in the kingdom.

In the world in which we live, perhaps anger will at times be appropriate, but in general we should be a people who is hard to offend, who promote reconciliation. McKnight narrates some powerful examples of reconciliation, but he goes on to encourage

---

12. Bonhoeffer, *Discipleship*, DBWE 4 (Minneapolis: Fortress, 2001), 122.
13. Bonhoeffer, *Discipleship*, 125. I have corrected the typo ("that" for "than") in the English translation in the second quoted sentence.
14. McKnight, *The Sermon on the Mount*, 81–82.

us to contemplate "the ordinariness of Jesus' examples: immediately suspending what we are doing to find peace with our own relations."[15] These examples are given by Jesus in verses 23–26, and they help us to picture how we need to make reconciliation a priority in our lives.

2. *Adultery (5:27-30)*

The point of this Antithesis is very similar to that of the previous paragraph: obedience not only to the letter but more especially to the spirit of the Law is what pleases God.

The Old Testament pronounced death for adultery (Deut 22:22). Jesus extends guilt to the desire for adultery. Even this desire, lust, will send a person to hell. The examples Jesus uses of cutting off a hand and gouging out an eye (vv. 29–30; cf. 18:8–9) suggest that we should take this teaching pretty seriously, but, of course, the problem of lust does not exist in the eye or the hand but in the heart.

There is no doubt that in our day it is easier to harbor lust in your heart than at any other time in history, and this is by-and-large a male problem, and that's certainly how Jesus addresses it. As McKnight says, "The problem in our text is male desire."[16] Most men look at porn frequently; most Christian men look at porn frequently; most Christian preachers have struggled with porn.[17]

The words of Jesus are more relevant now than ever. Avoid not just the illicit sex that you do with your body but the lust that you do with your heart.

---

15. McKnight, *The Sermon on the Mount*, 83.
16. McKnight, *The Sermon on the Mount,* 88.
17. https://www.barna.com/the-porn-phenomenon/#.Vp5-fzb6fNU.

3. Divorce (5:31-32)

See the next chapter.

4. Vows (5:33-37)

The main point of this Antithesis is that people need to be honest. Jesus teaches about oaths also at 23:16-22, and his brother James echoes his words at James 4:13-17. All of these passages oppose oaths.

The problem with oaths is that they assume that people are basically dishonest. As Bonhoeffer says, "The oath is proof of the existence of lies in the world."[18] The ancient Jewish philosopher Philo agrees: "Next to not swearing at all, the second best thing is to keep one's oath; for by the mere fact of swearing at all, the swearer shows that there is some suspicion of his not being trustworthy" (*On the Decalogue* 84). Both Josephus and Philo report that the Essenes avoid swearing altogether.[19] The Law of Moses includes some regulations concerning oaths (e.g., Lev 5:4-6; Deut 23:21), but there is no requirement to make an oath (or a prohibition from making one). The Bible contains some examples of disastrous oaths: Jephthah in Judges 11:30; Herod at Mark 6:22-23.

Jesus prohibited oaths. How far should we press this teaching? Is it okay to swear on a Bible in a courtroom? Bonhoeffer thinks that's fine,[20] but McKnight has a different view: "I would argue, then, that followers of Jesus are to tell a judge who requests an oath

---

18. Bonhoeffer, *Discipleship*, 129.
19. Josephus, *Jewish War* 2.135; Philo, *Every Good Man Is Free* 84.
20. Bonhoeffer, *Discipleship*, 130.

that they are bound by Jesus not to use oaths because their words are honest."[21] I think Bonhoeffer's view makes more sense. By taking an oath in court, we are not implying that the absence of such an oath means that all bets are off, that we can lie as much as we want. The court requires the oath; giving the oath or not giving it does not affect our own honesty. We are always honest because we are disciples of Jesus.

At any rate, we shouldn't get caught up in these sorts of possible exceptions to the words of Jesus. We should rather make every effort to put into practice what Jesus says: be honest. No matter what. Don't bend the truth. Don't look for ways to hide something from others. Be honest.

5. RETRIBUTION (5:38-42)[22]

The main point of this Antithesis is—don't seek retribution but get as far from that as possible by handing over more than an evildoer demands of you.

Here Jesus quotes the *lex talionis*. The Latin word *talionis* means "of retaliation," and *lex* means "law," so *lex talionis* = "law of retaliation." In the Old Testament it is found in Exodus 21:24; Leviticus 24:20; Deuteronomy 19:21.[23]

---

21. McKnight, *The Sermon on the Mount*, 119.

22. This hard saying of Jesus has been interpreted variously, as a pacifist manifesto, or as something else. See, for instance, Dorothy Jean Weaver, "Transforming Nonresistance: From *Lex Talionis* to 'Do Not Resist the Evil One'," in *The Love of Enemy and Nonretaliation in the New Testament*, ed. Willard M. Swartley (Louisville: WJK, 1992), 32–71, esp. 32–36.

23. Other cultures had similar laws: see Ulrich Luz, *Matthew 1–7: A Commentary*, Hermeneia (Minneapolis: Fortress, 2007), 275n41. There were ancient Jewish discussions on how literally to take the *lex talionis*;

There are several issues we need to discuss here.

Is Jesus repealing this Old Testament command? Well, here more than other places, it sounds like Jesus is saying the *lex talionis* should not apply, is no longer in effect, so don't follow that commandment. McKnight argues strongly for this view. I myself am not at all convinced that Jesus is setting aside the original intent of the law. I am led to question this idea partly because it's hard for me to think about Jesus in this context telling his audience, "Don't pay attention to the Torah." It's much easier for me to imagine him saying, "Let me tell you what the Torah was talking about." The other reason I'm unpersuaded that Jesus is repealing the *lex talionis* here is based on the context of that law within the Old Testament.

Here's the relevant paragraph in Exodus:

> When men get in a fight and hit a pregnant woman so that her children are born prematurely but there is no injury, the one who hit her must be fined as the woman's husband demands from him, and he must pay as the judges determine. If there is an injury, then you must give life for life, eye for eye, tooth for tooth, hand for hand, foot for foot, burn for burn, bruise for bruise, wound for wound. (Exod 21:22–25).

Look at the passage in Leviticus:

> If a man kills anyone, he must be put to death. Whoever kills an animal is to make restitution for it, life for life. If any man inflicts a permanent injury on his neighbor, whatever he has

---

see James G. Crossley, *The New Testament and Jewish Law: A Guide for the Perplexed* (London: T&T Clark, 2010), 76–81.

done is to be done to him: fracture for fracture, eye for eye, tooth for tooth. Whatever injury he inflicted on the person, the same is to be inflicted on him. (Lev 24:17–20)

What is the social context where this retributive justice is carried out, according to these passages? The Exodus passage makes it explicit with its mention of "judges" (v. 22). The setting is the court. The passage in Deuteronomy is the same; it actually introduces the *lex talionis* by talking about the problem of false witnesses in a courtroom (19:16–20). This retaliation is not carried out by the injured party but by officers of the court. These *lex talionis* texts in the Old Testament do not say: if someone puts out your eye, then you put out his eye right back. It's more like: if someone puts out your eye, then that person will be punished in like measure by the (God-ordained) court. In fact, as it is presented in the Old Testament, the *lex talionis* is opposed to personal vendettas. As the Proverb says: "Don't say, 'I'll do to him what he did to me; I'll repay the man for what he has done'" (Prov 24:29).

Taking note of this Old Testament context assists greatly in understanding what Jesus is up to. In Matthew 5:38–42, he is telling his disciples that the *lex talionis* does not apply to their personal relationships. I cannot believe that Jesus is saying that the original intent of the *lex talionis* in the Old Testament should be abandoned; how would courts function in that case? Judges would convict criminals of wrongdoing and then sentence them to … nothing? No, Jesus is not talking about how courts ought to function, he's talking about how his disciples ought to interact with other people, and he's telling them that the *lex talionis* was not intended to apply to that situation.²⁴ "What Jesus rejects is vengeance executed on a personal level."²⁵

Now that we've dispensed with that distraction about whether Jesus was contradicting the Old Testament (he was not), we can dive into the difficult teaching that he presents here.

Bonhoeffer compares Jesus's words here to the third beatitude, "Blessed are the meek, for they will inherit the earth." Jesus wants his disciples to be meek in the way they deal with everyone, even evildoers, and our Lord himself provides the example. As Bonhoeffer says, "just retribution takes place only in not resisting" evil.²⁶

Now, when we hear something like this, our mind immediately starts searching for extreme scenarios—what about...Hitler? Especially do we think about Hitler when we read Bonhoeffer on this subject, since Bonhoeffer was executed for his role in a plot

---

24. McKnight disagrees: "Jesus overtly ends the Mosaic command to 'show no pity' in the appropriation of the *lex talionis* and in its place orders his followers to be merciful" (McKnight, *The Sermon on the Mount*, 124, italics removed). But the command to "show no pity" wasn't directed at the disciples, it was directed at judges in a court, and Jesus does not tell judges to ignore the *lex talionis*. Later: "the *lex talionis* antithesis is a public (not private) framework, and that is what Jesus is stopping" (p. 129). I don't see the polarity as public vs. private but as personal vs. communal/state. McKnight cites plenty of scholars (p. 129) who oppose his view. I agree with Dunn ("Law," 510): "The one antithesis that seems to 'abolish' a law (Mt 5:38-42), the *lex talionis* [....], is again better heard as pressing behind the law to reinforce the social principle behind it."

25. W. D. Davies and Dale C. Allison, *Matthew 1-7*, ICC (London: T&T Clark, 1988), 540.

26. Bonhoeffer, *Discipleship*, 132.

against Hitler.[27] It seems that he did not necessarily think that the best way to requite the evil presented by Hitler was by non-resistance. Here, Bonhoeffer's thought is complex. His English-language editors have offered this summary: Bonhoeffer "was not, as history and statements from his *Ethics* have shown, uncompromising about using violence to prevent the greater evil of war and genocide. But even in the matter of the political conspiracy, he associated the well-intentioned acts of violence against the evil government of Adolf Hitler with sin, guilt, and the need for repentance."[28]

I fear this line of thought leads us down some unhelpful paths by taking us away from the point Jesus was making. I mean, sure, I guess it's not impossible that we'll find ourselves in Bonhoeffer's shoes. After all, Hitler is not exactly unique in world-history: even in the 20th century, we can think of other world leaders who slaughtered millions of their own people, so, yes, maybe we will face situations in which we will have to make a choice about what it means to follow Jesus in the face of a madman who has power over a nation. But—Jesus' examples are not about that: "when a national leader starts shoving millions of people into ovens or gas chambers…."

Jesus is not talking about the grand situations faced by few, he's talking about the ordinary situations faced by everyone, not once in a century but once in a week. How do you handle someone who

---

27. This is the 20 July Plot. For Bonhoeffer's role, see Victoria J. Barnett, "Bonhoeffer and the Conspiracy," in *The Oxford Handbook of Dietrich Bonhoeffer*, ed. Philip G. Ziegler and Michael Mawson (Oxford: Oxford University Press, 2019), 65-76.

28. Geffrey B. Kelly and John D. Godsey, "Editors' Introduction to the English Edition," in Bonhoeffer, *Discipleship*, 15.

wrongs you on a personal level? "Do not resist him who is evil." A similar teaching can be found on the lips of Socrates, who taught "that it is never right to do wrong or to requite wrong with wrong, or when we suffer evil to defend ourselves by doing evil in return."[29]

Jesus gives four examples: turning the other cheek, giving your shirt and coat, going the extra mile, and giving to anyone who asks. Jesus himself had his clothes confiscated (Matt 27:35) and he was struck (26:67), and these are the kinds of things that had been spoken about Isaiah's Servant of the Lord (Isa 50:4–9). He imagines that his disciples will face similar abuse (Matt 5:10–12).

EXPLORATION 5.2

BONHOEFFER ON TURNING THE OTHER CHEEK

These quotations are collected from Bonhoeffer's section called "Retribution" in *Discipleship*, with page numbers in parentheses after each quotation. The quotations are presented here for your reflection.

The overcoming of others now occurs by allowing their evil to run its course. The evil does not find what it is seeking, namely, resistance and, therewith, new evil which will inflame it even

---

29. As quoted by Plato, *Crito* 49D, in the translation of Harold North Fowler, Loeb Classical Library (Cambridge, MA: Harvard University Press, 1914), 173. Already in the second century, the pagan critic of Christianity, Celsus, pointed out the similarity between the teaching of Jesus and the passage in Plato; see Origen, *Against Celsus* 7.58.

> *more. Evil will become powerless when it finds no opposing object, no resistance, but, instead, is willingly borne and suffered. (133)*
>
> *A disciple should not resist when challenged by evil that cannot be justified at all. Instead, by suffering, the disciple will bring evil to its end and thus will overcome the evil person. Suffering willingly endured is stronger than evil; it is the death of evil. (134)*
>
> *[T]he one speaking here about overcoming evil with suffering is he who himself was overcome by evil on the cross and who emerged from that defeat as the conqueror and victor. There is no other justification for this commandment of Jesus than his own cross. Only those who there, in the cross of Jesus, find faith in the victory over evil can obey his command, and that is the only kind of obedience which has the promise. Which promise? The promise of community with the cross of Jesus and of community with his victory. (136)*
>
> *How will our preaching of the passion of Jesus Christ become visible and credible to the world if the disciples avoid this passion for themselves, if they despise it in their own bodies? (136)*

We cannot achieve victory over evil except through the cross. The question should be not how we can resist this evil, but how we can overcome it, and the only way is through the cross.

There are some great examples of what this looks like. First of all, Jesus. Then there are the martyrs of faith.[30] In the 20th Century, we think of Gandhi and MLK. I'm not saying that it is obvious that these people followed the best course of action, but they provided examples of acting in an unusual way that is close to the behavior Jesus recommends here, and their examples are worthy of our contemplation. In fact, MLK did not call his own method "non-resistance" but rather "non-violent resistance." He apparently would have said that he was trying to resist him who is evil. I would say the same thing for Atticus Finch.[31]

Jesus is talking about personal relationships. If the situation moves beyond personal relationships, it's a little harder to know how this paragraph applies.[32] Bonhoeffer's section on this paragraph is very good and challenging, but he never addresses a situation where a Christian looks on at someone else being abused. In that situation, do the words of Jesus apply? If a gunman comes into our church building, what is the godly response? What about war? What would Jesus do?

Since Jesus does not address this particular situation, I don't think we can arrive at any easy answers. The way forward, I think, is by following these steps:

---

30. There are some wonderful stories of Jewish martyrs in 2 Maccabees 6–7. An ancient story of a Christian martyr is the *Martyrdom of Polycarp*. These stories can easily be found online.

31. I'm especially thinking of the moment when Bob Ewell spits in Atticus' face. If you don't remember how this goes in the movie *To Kill a Mockingbird*, it would be worth your time to find the scene on YouTube.

32. For instance, see Jeremy Weber, "No Cheeks Left to Turn," *Christianity Today* (Oct 19, 2018).

> Prayer
> Study
> Discussion with faithful Christians (Bible class)
> Meditation
> Prayer

There are no easy answers and there are no completely satisfying solutions to terrible situations. We humbly arrive at "what we would do" in the assurance that God loves us and will guide us into truth if we seek it, and that God is fully aware of our faults, including our faulty reasoning, and he loves us and saves us anyway. We want to imitate Jesus as closely as possible, to carry out his teaching as far as possible, to show love to people as perfectly as possible, and we can be confident (just as God is confident) that we will fail to do this in many ways. Of course, that doesn't mean we should try to fail, that we can be flippant about this teaching of Jesus, to just say that it is impractical and ignore it. This is Jesus—it's supposed to be hard; it's supposed to be not normal, and Jesus himself lived it out. If it's not a struggle, then we're probably missing something.

Many people have seen and continue to see pacifism as the direct consequence of Jesus' teaching here.[33] Pacifism was a very common position among Christians in the second and third

---

33. For a simple, recent discussion going in this direction, see McKnight, *The Sermon on the Mount*, 130–38. When you're ready for something meatier, see Hays, *Moral Vision of the New Testament*, 317–46.

centuries (= before Christians took over the government),[34] and pacifism has deep roots in churches of Christ. Alexander Campbell, David Lipscomb, and H. Leo Boles all published strong stances favoring pacifism,[35] and all took heat for opposing Christian participation in the wars of their eras (especially the Civil War and World War I). The Sermon on the Mount routinely features in these discussions. Pacifism was in fact a very common position in churches of Christ up until around ... oh, I'd say, December 7, 1941. Since then, not so common.[36] Knowing this history should caution us from thinking that our positions on these issues are so obvious that any thinking person would agree with us. History should engender humility.

This is a tough issue, especially for people who want to hold together two principles: it seems intuitive that physical resistance to evil is sometimes necessary, and we like to cite book, chapter,

---

34. See Everett Ferguson, *Early Christians Speak: Faith and Life in the First Three Centuries*, rev. ed. (Abilene: ACU Press, 1987), ch. 18, "Christians and Military Service."

35. David Lipscomb, *Civil Government* (Nashville, 1887); H. Leo Boles, *The New Testament Teaching on War* (Nashville: Gospel Advocate, 1923). Part of Alexander Campbell's "An Address on War" (1848) is excerpted in Michael G. Long, ed., *Christian Peace and Nonviolence: A Documentary History* (Maryknoll, NY: Orbis, 2011), 122–23, but you're probably talented enough at the internet to find the whole thing. On Campbell's lifelong pacifism, see Harold L. Lunger, *The Political Ethics of Alexander Campbell* (St Louis: Bethany, 1954).

36. For a brief account of the history of the issue in Churches of Christ, see Michael W. Casey, "From Religious Outsiders to Insiders: The Rise and Fall of Pacifism in the Churches of Christ," *Journal of Church and State* 44 (2002): 455–75. For more from Casey, see the forthcoming collection of his essays, Kyle Crews, ed., *Pacifism and Politics in the Churches of Christ: The Collected Essays of Michael W. Casey* (Eugene, OR: Pickwick).

and verse for our theological positions, especially when we're trying to come up with a way of ignoring something Jesus said. What I mean is, if we think there are times that Jesus' teaching here does not apply, it'd be nice if we could cite a balancing Scripture that presents the other side of it. So, where are those balancing Scriptures that say Christians might need on occasion to take up the sword?

Anyone? Anyone?

Oh, yes, there's Romans 13. And that might do it. It seems to say that humans might play a legitimate role at times in carrying out the judgment of God (Rom 13:4), and perhaps Christians could be those humans. Not everyone agrees with that reading of Romans 13,[37] but there's certainly room for debate. And then there are all the soldiers in the New Testament, soldiers like Cornelius (Acts 10) and those guys who question John the Baptist (Luke 3:14–15)—none of whom are told to stop being soldiers. It is this example of soldiers that Richard Hays says "provides the one possible legitimate basis for arguing that Christian discipleship does not necessarily preclude the exercise of violence in defense of social order or justice."[38] Presumably it was texts like these that helped C. S. Lewis draw a distinction between personal violent actions and violent actions of the state: "It is, therefore, in my opinion, perfectly right for a Christian judge to sentence a man to death or a Christian soldier to kill an enemy. … War is a dreadful

---

37. E.g., John Howard Yoder, *The Politics of Jesus: Vicit Agnus Noster*, 2d ed. (Grand Rapids: Eerdmans, 1994), ch. 10: "Let Every Soul Be Subject, Romans 13 and the Authority of the State."

38. Hays, *Moral Vision of the New Testament*, 335–36. Hays later (p. 337) says that these examples of soldiers "weigh negligibly" in the New Testament's overall depiction of the Christian's use of violence.

thing, and I can respect an honest pacifist, though I think he is entirely mistaken."³⁹

Let me reiterate that we should not let this discussion distract us from the heart of the issue. No one would doubt that Jesus, in this passage, forbids his disciples from seeking retribution in personal relationships. So far from retribution, Jesus commands his disciples to actively do good to people who do not seek their good. What Jesus would counsel us is: Think of people who want to do harm to you, and think of ways of doing good to them.

6. *Enemies (5:43-48)*

The main point here is similar to that of the previous Antithesis: actively do good to people who don't seek your good. Love your enemies. Love in the way God loves his enemies, by giving them gifts (rain and sunshine). In this way, you will be perfect (complete, whole) in the way that God is perfect.

Not everyone in Antiquity thought like Jesus (of course). The ancient sage known as Ben Sira in the early second century BC gave his students the following advice.⁴⁰

> Give to the devout, but do not help the sinner.
> ⁵Do good to the humble, but do not give to the ungodly;
> hold back their bread, and do not give it to them,
> for by means of it they might subdue you;
> then you will receive twice as much evil
> for all the good you have done to them.
> ⁶For the Most High also hates sinners

---

39. Lewis, *Mere Christianity*, 91–92, in book 3, ch. 7, "Forgiveness."
40. The Book of Sirach (a.k.a., Ecclesiasticus) is one of the deuterocanonical books (sometimes called Apocrypha).

and will inflict punishment on the ungodly.
⁷Give to the one who is good, but do not help the sinner.
(Sirach 12:4–7)

The advice of Ben Sira is pretty reasonable, and I think I've heard Christians offer the same sort of advice in the modern day. But the words of Jesus at the end of Matthew 5 stand directly contrary to the words of Ben Sira.

Jesus quotes the second greatest commandment at Matthew 5:43 (Lev 19:18; cf. Matt 22:34–40) and adds an element to it not contained in the Old Testament: hate your enemies.[41] This additional element is apparently a way that some ancient Jews interpreted the commandment: strictly speaking, God tells us to love only our neighbors, so he doesn't require us to love the people who are not our neighbors, so we should hate them. They may have even thought this was a godly approach—we are hating the people who profane God's law; we are hating God's enemies.[42]

But if we follow this reasoning, Jesus says, we are just like normal people, or worse, tax collectors and Gentiles. Even they love people who love them in return. The greater righteousness that Jesus requires is manifest only when we love our enemies alongside our neighbors, when we see our enemies as our neighbors. Bonhoeffer: "The actions of the disciples should not be determined by the human actions they encounter, but by Jesus

---

41. In fact, at least one Old Testament passage encourages praying for an enemy (Jer 29:7; also, in the deuterocanonical book of Baruch 1:11). There are also some OT passages that counsel doing good to enemies, as quoted by the apostle Paul in Romans 12.

42. The community at Qumran attests this line of thinking, as seen in their *Community Rule* (1QS 1.10–11).

acting in them. The only source of the disciples' action is the will of Jesus."[43]

Or listen to Paul:

> Friends, do not avenge yourselves; instead, leave room for God's wrath, because it is written, Vengeance belongs to me; I will repay [Deut 32:35], says the Lord. But, if your enemy is hungry, feed him, if he is thirsty, give him something to drink. For in so doing you will be heaping fiery coals on his head [Prov 25:21-22]. Do not be conquered by evil, but conquer evil with good. (Rom 12:19-21)

Once again, Jesus provides the example of how to live out these difficult words, for he prayed for his enemies (Luke 23:34) and showed them love (Rom 5:8-10).

Bonhoeffer again:

> Faced with the way of the cross of Jesus Christ, however, the disciples themselves recognize that they were among the enemies of Jesus who have been conquered by his love. This love makes the disciples able to see, so that they can recognize an enemy as a sister or brother and behave toward that person as they would toward a sister or brother. Why? Because they live only from the love of him who behaved toward them as toward brothers and sisters, who accepted them when they were his enemies and brought them into communion with him as neighbors. That is how love makes disciples able to see,

---

43. Bonhoeffer, *Discipleship*, 139.

so that they can see the enemies included in God's love, that they can see the enemies under the cross of Jesus Christ.[44]

And McKnight: "Until we name our enemies, we can't live these words of Jesus. Until we invite them into our home, or treat them as our neighbor, or love them as we love ourselves, we do not live these words."[45]

Conclusion

At the end of this protracted discussion of the Antitheses—but it easily could have been much longer! —we return to the main point. The disciples of Jesus cannot have the goal of being normal people, of fitting neatly into a society dominated by sin. Jesus was far from normal, and in these test cases he explains in some very practical ways how his disciples should, must, avoid being normal, as well. They shouldn't do just enough to say that they are obeying the letter of the Torah; rather, they must reflect on God's will and pursue a greater righteousness.

---

44. Bonhoeffer, *Discipleship*, 141.
45. McKnight, *The Sermon on the Mount*, 147.

6

MARRIAGE AND DIVORCE

[Christians] marry, but their marriage will look different from that of the world. Their marriage will be "in the Lord" (1 Cor. 7:39). It will be sanctified through being in the service of the body of Christ, and it will be subject to the discipline of prayer and abstinence (1 Cor. 7:5). In this, Christian marriage will become a parable of Christ's self-sacrificial love for his church-community. Indeed, their marriage will itself be a part of the body of Christ. It will be church (Eph. 5:32). —Dietrich Bonhoeffer[1]

And there ain't no nothing we can't love each other through. —*Family Ties*[2]

I watched *Family Ties* growing up. It was my favorite show, and I had an odd, exaggerated affection for Alex P. Keaton and the

---

1. Bonhoeffer, *Discipleship*, DBWE 4 (Minneapolis: Fortress), 249.
2. From the song "Without Us," written by Jeff Barry and Tom Scott, the song that played during the credits for the 1980s sitcom *Family Ties*.

values he represented. Only now as an adult re-watching the show do I realize how his conservative values and his greed were played for laughs, not for imitation. But *Family Ties* wasn't all about humor; it was on TV back when sitcoms could sometimes have very special episodes, back before *Seinfeld* killed that idea. And looking back at *Family Ties* now, I realize how fortunate I was to grow up with a show like that, a show that represented a nuclear family as the most normal thing in the world—a mom and dad and kids who had their problems but always worked them out (usually within thirty minutes, but sometimes they needed a double-episode). This family was committed to one another. There wasn't anything they couldn't love each other through.

In season 5, there was one of those double episodes, called "Oh, Brother."[3] The plot revolves around a visit from Uncle Rob (Steven Keaton's brother) during which he reveals that he has left his wife. If this were the basis for a sitcom plot today, how would the Keatons have received such news of the divorce of their family member? With a shrug? With a pat on the back and an "I'm sorry, better luck next time"? I don't know, it's hard to imagine. In 1986, the Keatons were devastated, so much so that their working through their own grief about the divorce of a family member became the basis for two entire episodes. Part of what made it so hard on the Keatons was that Rob didn't really seem to have a very good reason for leaving his wife; it's not that he didn't like her, it's not that she had cheated on him, it's just that he didn't want to be married any more. Uncle Rob explains: "I'm on the right path. For the first time in my life I have a good shot at finding out who I am."

---

3. These two episodes are numbers 13 and 14 in season 5, and they originally aired in January, 1986.

That sounds like the type of thing you might hear someone say today to explain his or her divorce (or other selfish decision), but what is so odd about watching this show from the 1980s is seeing how much trouble he had convincing his family to stop trying to talk him out of it.[4] I think that kind of reaction still happens today in some families, but I don't think we'll ever see it again on TV.

No matter what our culture promotes, though, people who regard the New Testament as a guide for life will still think of divorce as devastating, just like the Keatons.

> [All Christian churches] regard divorce as something like cutting up a living body, as a kind of surgical operation. Some of them think the operation so violent that it cannot be done at all; others admit it as a desperate remedy in extreme cases. They are all agreed that it is more like having both your legs cut off than it is like dissolving a business partnership or even deserting a regiment. What they all disagree with is the modern view that it is a simple readjustment of partners, to be made whenever people feel they are no longer in love with one another, or when either of them falls in love with someone else.[5]

We're talking about marriage and divorce because Jesus talked about marriage and divorce in the Sermon on the Mount (Matt

---

4. Uncle Rob comes back for another double episode (episodes 12–13, titled "Father Time") in the following season, in which the plot revolves around the strained relationship between Uncle Rob and his teenage daughter following the divorce. In these episodes, Steven is much more supportive of his brother's decision to have gotten a divorce.

5. C.S. Lewis, *Mere Christianity* (New York: Macmillan, 1952), 82, in book 3, ch. 6, "Christian Marriage."

5:31–32). Before we dig into the context and try to understand what Jesus' teaching may have meant to his initial audience, let's get something straight. The main point Jesus wants to make is:

Stay married.

That's it. That's his big marriage advice. Be faithful. Be committed. Be a disciple of Jesus—and a disciple has discipline, and that means you don't seek to fulfill your own desires, but you seek to please others. And, yes, sometimes that's hard. But, after all, Paul encourages us to have the mind of Christ, who emptied himself on behalf of us, who became a slave, who died for others (Phil 2:5–8). Inasmuch as it depends on you, be at peace with all people (Rom 12:18), including your spouse.

And now let's get to what Jesus does not say. If you're in an abusive relationship, he does not tell you to stay in that relationship. If there's a wife getting pounded on by her husband, Jesus does not expect her to "empty herself" and stay in that marriage. She should get out of the house and take her kids with her. Too often this teaching by Jesus has been misapplied to perpetuate abuse, and I guess it's been preachers and elders that have been guilty of that. Let's stop doing that.

I know your next question is, how do we define abuse, and is emotional abuse an okay reason to divorce, and what about other forms of abuse? Look, there are a lot of hard issues here, and we'll try to parse some of them out as this chapter proceeds, but let's remember that we're interpreting the Sermon on the Mount, which means that it's going to be hard. Everything in the Sermon is tough; this is not a Sermon for people that want an easy life of wish-fulfillment. There are going to be things in here that we find hard to live out in practice—like, basically, everything Jesus says. So, I'm not about to tell you that there are all kinds of reasons you might get divorced and it's okay to get remarried after that. Neither am I going to tell you to get out of a marriage that you're in. What I'm going to tell you is what Jesus tells you.

Stay married.

There are a few more preliminaries before we begin. I feel it necessary to admit upfront that I have basically no experience with divorce. I am neither a divorcee nor the son of a divorcee (nor the father of a divorcee—my kids are too young to get married). I've been married for two decades; my parents have been married going on five decades. That's my experience, and I admit that it's limited, and I'm sure that some more personal experience with divorce would give me a different perspective on some things. Despite my limited experience, I'm doing the best I can to interpret the words of Jesus, a man who was never married, so far as we know.

What I'm Going to Say

Let me go ahead and tell you what you want to know: what I think Jesus says about these issues. Here you go:

- Jesus teaches that you ought to stay married.
- Jesus teaches that if you get divorced and then remarried, you have committed adultery.
- The way Jesus words the prohibition here (Matt 5:31–32) and in Matthew 19:1–9 and in Mark 10:1–12 and in Luke 16:18, the "adultery" comes in at the time of the remarriage, not the time of the divorce.
- You might be in a situation in which you should stay single, in which Jesus would counsel you to stay single. Singleness is not a punishment. Jesus was single.

- Jesus includes one exception here (Matt 5:31–32) and in Matthew 19:9—fornication committed by the other spouse. In that situation, a person who divorces and remarries does not sin.

SINGLENESS

The church has recently undervalued singleness. We can't say that the church has historically undervalued singleness, because there is a very strong tradition within Christianity promoting the high value of celibacy for both men and women (think: monks, and priests, and nuns, and such). But in my own experience of Christianity, there is an extreme emphasis placed on attracting young families into our churches, and on emphasizing the value of marriage. I am married and I think marriage is valuable, but perhaps the pendulum has swung too far? What are the chances that an unmarried twenty-something at our churches will be asked sometime during a given month whether he or she has any marriage prospects? My guess is, pretty good. I mean, after all, "it is not good that the man should be alone" (Gen 2:18), which means people need to get married. A single person is an incomplete person.

I hope that last sentence makes you uncomfortable. I wrote it very much tongue-in-cheek. Do we not worship a Savior who was single?[6] Did that make him incomplete? Was not the apostle Paul (so far as we know) single? Was he incomplete? Was there

---

6. For a reasonable, historical approach to this issue, see Anthony Le Donne, *The Wife of Jesus: Ancient Texts and Modern Scandals* (London: Oneworld, 2013).

something wrong with Jesus and Paul, that they weren't married? Paul actually argues just the reverse, that the single lifestyle is the superior lifestyle, the lifestyle that allows for greater attention to spiritual matters as opposed to fleshly concerns, but that marriage is okay if you need that sort of thing (1 Cor 7). (I am aware that some people try to get 1 Corinthians 7 to say that marriage and singleness are equal, or that marriage is even superior to singleness,[7] but I haven't figured out how they can get this particular passage to say that.) So, let's stop saying singleness is some sort of inferior existence, some sort of punishment. I believe the truth of Gen 2:18, that it is not good for people to be alone, but that's what the church is for. People in the church are family (Mark 3:31–35); they are not alone.[8]

Paul does say that singleness is a gift that some people have, and others don't (1 Cor 7:7), but he seems to think that a good deal more people have the gift than have realized it.

Sometimes people who write about divorce—in an attempt to be compassionate to divorced people—say some inadvertently negative things about singleness, implying that single people are broken or companionless or even haven't experienced the fullness of God's grace.[9] Especially in this day and age, with the marriage

---

7. Rubel Shelly, *Divorce and Remarriage: A Redemptive Theology* (Abilene, TX: Leafwood, 2007), 118. See also the statement on p. 138, marriage "is not a concession to human weakness," which is the exact opposite of what Paul says at 1 Corinthians 7:9.

8. For more on this way of looking at the matter, see Christina S. Hitchcock, *The Significance of Singleness: A Theological Vision for the Future of the Church* (Grand Rapids: Baker, 2018).

9. See, for instance, the comments in Shelly, *Divorce and Remarriage*, 109, and the comment at p. 110 that is repeated from p. 37. Shelly does finally say something positive about single people at p. 136.

rates (and divorce rates) like they are, the church needs to get out of its 1980s mindset and bring more balance to conversations about marriage and singleness. The church needs to reemphasize the godly, single life. We need to recognize how valuable single people are in our midst. We need to hold up single people as models, as images of Christ, who was himself a single person. We need to recognize in single people a foretaste of the resurrection life, "for when they rise from the dead, they neither marry nor are given in marriage, but are like angels in heaven" (Mark 12:25).

To take an example from a roughly parallel situation but one that, I think, will be a little clearer to some of my readers: when someone comes to you and asks whether as a homosexual he or she can ever find true happiness, what are you going to tell that person? If you are a traditionally minded Christian, aren't you going to advise that person to remain single? Wouldn't it be easier to give that sort of advice if you were already doing so more generally, if you were already talking about both marriage and singleness as good, godly options, and not encouraging people to disparage one option as a punishment and magnify the other option as a higher gift of God's grace?

Marriage is good because a good marriage represents Christ and the church (Eph 5:21–32). Singleness is good because a faithful, single person represents to us both Christ, who was single, and the resurrection life.

So, if it turns out that you're in a situation in which you should stay single in order to avoid the sin condemned by Jesus in Matthew 5:31–32 and 19:9, then, what should we say? Rejoice that God allows you to represent him in the way that he does. Yeah, I know that might be a hard thing for some people to hear. I don't know that it's any harder than what Jesus has already said in the

Beatitudes, about rejoicing in persecution (5:12). I don't know if it's any harder than what he says about taking up a cross (16:24). But it is a hard thing in its own right.

COMPLEXITIES AND VIEWS

I don't have to tell you that divorce is a sensitive topic, and a difficult one. At first glance, it looks like the biblical teaching—or, at least, the New Testament teaching—is pretty simple and straightforward, and maybe it is. But people are not simple and straightforward; they get themselves into all kinds of complicated situations, and it is not easy to figure out how to apply a simple and straightforward teaching to a messy situation. And while the general emphasis of the New Testament on the permanence of marriage is pretty clear, there are some legitimate debates on certain points, as we will see.

One can get lost in the debates on the biblical teaching on divorce, but we should not lose sight of the fact that this discussion has very real implications for real people, people that we know and love. James gave a warning that not many people should become teachers, because they'll face a stricter judgment (3:1). I think he was talking about subjects like this. We are obligated to present what the Bible says about all things, and especially about things that really affect people's lives, because God wants to use us teachers to help mold his people into more perfect representatives of Jesus. But particularly when we're talking about issues that really affect people's lives, we need to be careful and sensitive to the situations people are in. And we need to be humble, recognizing that we always have more to learn, and maybe some people in our class can teach us.

There are all kinds of books available from Christian writers on the topic of divorce, sometimes specifically on trying to make sense of the biblical teaching, sometimes dealing more with modern issues of church practice. This chapter will focus more on issues of biblical interpretation without completely ignoring modern church practice. While the Bible doesn't say a whole lot about divorce—we'll be able to cover here the main passages of the New Testament—the need to place the biblical teaching in a proper ancient context (Old Testament teaching, rabbinic discussion, Greco-Roman practice, etc.) has led to the writing of many books taking many different views.

To cite an example, Gordon Wenham and William Heth wrote a book (first published in 1984) arguing that the New Testament does not permit remarriage after divorce for any reason.[10] But in 2002, Heth wrote an essay chronicling why he had changed his mind about his earlier conclusions; he now believes that remarriage is permitted after divorce if the divorce was caused by adultery or abandonment.[11] Both authors (Wenham and Heth) have essays in a book presenting different views of the matter, as to whether the New Testament permits no remarriage after divorce (Wenham), remarriage after divorce resulting from adultery or abandonment (Heth), or remarriage after divorce resulting from adultery, abandonment, or abuse (Craig Keener).[12]

---

10. Gordon J. Wenham and William E. Heth, *Jesus and Divorce: The Problem with the Evangelical Consensus* (Carlisle, UK: Paternoster, 1984).

11. Williams A. Heth, "Jesus on Divorce: How My Mind Has Changed," *The Southern Baptist Journal of Theology* 6 (2002): 4–29; google it and you'll find it online.

12. Mark L. Strauss, ed., *Remarriage after Divorce in Today's Church: 3 Views* (Grand Rapids: Zondervan, 2006). Notes from this book are

Within churches of Christ, what we might call the more progressive preachers have started to promote the view—okay, it's been a few decades now—that it is always sinful to get a divorce but it is (almost) never sinful to enter into a marriage. An example is Rubel Shelly's book, already mentioned.[13] The view I grew up with (I guess; it's hard to remember) and certainly learned at college can be found in various places but is well-represented by an essay by Earl Edwards, arguing that marriage after a divorce that did not result from adultery of the other spouse is an unscriptural marriage and should be dissolved.[14]

The point I'm making now is that this is a complicated discussion that requires a lot of background information, which we will introduce in this chapter, but we can't possibly do justice to the various issues here. This chapter is a beginning point.

And let's begin with the history of the discussion.

THE HISTORY OF THE QUESTION

It may surprise you to learn that the early church—by which I mean the church from the second century to the fourth or fifth century—took a very rigid position on whether a Christian could remarry after a divorce. They basically said "no"; there was no situation in which a person could remarry after a divorce.[15] For

available online; google "divorce and remarriage book summary guide," and look through the hits.

13. Shelly, *Divorce and Remarriage*.

14. Earl D. Edwards, "What about Matthew 19:9?" *The Spiritual Sword* 41.3 (April 2010): 26–29.

15. This material is surveyed and emphasized in the book by Wenham and Heth mentioned above, who share with the early church the view that all remarriage after divorce is prohibited (though, again, Heth has

example, according to the second century document known as the *Shepherd of Hermas*, divorce after a spouse commits adultery does not allow the innocent party to remarry. Instead, the innocent party must remain single or be reconciled to the first spouse (*Mandate* 4.1.6 [29.6]). If, on the other hand, a spouse dies, then the surviving partner may remarry without sin but remaining single "gains for oneself greater honor and great glory with the Lord" (*Mandate* 4.4.2 [32.4]). In fact, some early Christians prohibited a second marriage even after the death of the first spouse: "for he who deprives himself of his first wife, even though she be dead, is a cloaked adulterer, resisting the hand of God, ... and dissolving the strictest union of flesh with flesh" (Athenagoras, 2nd century, *Plea for the Christians*, ch. 33).

But we might be somewhat suspicious of early Christian teaching on this issue because they often seem to have harbored a bias against marriage. That is, early Christians often promoted an ascetic brand of Christianity that favored celibacy over marriage, so naturally any second marriage would be frowned upon if even first marriages were somewhat frowned upon.[16] So, even though early Christians were much closer to the time of Jesus than we are, their own ideology of marriage may have obscured for them what the New Testament teaches on the subject.

The Roman Catholic Church has traditionally taken a very rigid position on this issue (no remarriage after divorce). The usual

---

changed his mind). For a very convenient presentation of the early Christian evidence, see Everett Ferguson, *Early Christians Speak: Faith and Life in the First Three Centuries*, vol. 2 (Abilene, TX: ACU Press, 2002), 281–305.

16. On asceticism in the ancient church, see Ferguson, *Early Christians Speak*, vol. 2, ch. 13.

Protestant view—marriage is permitted after a divorce in some limited cases—was popularized at the time of the Protestant Reformation (sixteenth century), most notably by Erasmus.

DIVORCE IN THE GOSPELS

All three Synoptic Gospels include teaching from Jesus on divorce. The major passage is Matthew 19:1-12 and its parallel in Mark 10:1-12. The Sermon on the Mount contains an Antithesis concerning divorce (Matt 5:31-32). Luke includes a single verse on the issue (Luke 16:18). The main point of all these presentations of Jesus on divorce is to discourage serial monogamy, to promote strong and lasting marriages. In order to do this, Jesus says that remarriage after a divorce basically amounts to adultery,[17] because simply delivering a divorce certificate does not sever the bond uniting the husband and wife.

To say it again, the way Jesus words the statement, the problem (the adultery) really comes in at the point of the remarriage. That seems odd, because it seems like the problem ought to be the divorce, not a subsequent marriage. Marriage is a happy occasion, divorce is awful. It's the divorce that should be the sin. In fact, some writers go ahead and make Jesus say what they think he ought to have said.

---

17. This wording implies uncertainty regarding how literally to take Jesus' statement. Is the second marriage actually and in fact "adultery," or is it "tantamount to adultery"? After all, some of Jesus' other statements in the Sermon seem like they might be a bit exaggerated, or somehow not to be taken with extreme literalness (5:29-30). This is also a point that Shelly raises (*Divorce and Remarriage*, 83-87): "This is hyperbole. It is obvious exaggeration for the sake of emphasis" (92).

> In Mark's account...Divorce—whether remarriage ever occurs or not—is adultery (i.e., covenant-breaking, faithlessness). ...there is no prohibition against [divorced people remarrying].[18]

The problem is, Jesus didn't actually say that, did he? He gives the label "adultery" to the subsequent marriage after a divorce. And if we think just a moment, we can see why. When a man divorces his wife, Jesus wants to say that they are actually still married in some way; "what God has joined together let man not separate." So, he says that if the guy gets married to some other woman, then it's like committing adultery against his first wife. As Susan Hylen says:

> Instead of simply prohibiting divorce, these verses suggested that divorce accompanied by subsequent remarriage constituted adultery. In doing so, they reinforced the culture's value of a single marriage.[19]

It seems like to me that the implication of Jesus' words is that a man who divorces his wife and remains single (and, of course, celibate) does not fall under the condemnation voiced by Jesus in these instructions; he is not committing the adultery. He no doubt falls under some other condemnation, like breaking his vows to his wife, a clear failure in faithfulness, but he has not committed the adultery of Matthew 5:32 and 19:9.

In this discussion, we should also talk about repentance. When divorce happens, when remarriage happens, repentance is

---

18. Shelly, *Divorce and Remarriage*, 106.
19. Susan E. Hylen, *Women in the New Testament World*, Essentials of Biblical Studies (Oxford: Oxford University Press, 2019), 88 (and see p. 62).

necessary. Repentance is never easy, but, well...see Luke 13:3. Fortunately for us, the Bible talks a lot about repentance, and gives a lot of examples of repentance. The theme is especially prominent in the Gospel of Luke: see the advice of John the Baptist (Luke 3:10-14), or the example of Zacchaeus (Luke 19:8)—not easy, to be sure, but necessary. Or think about the Prodigal Son (15:17-21). Think about what a brave decision it was to get up out of that pig pen and decide to look his father in the eye again. Think about how much he probably dreaded to see all the people of his hometown, who all knew how he had blown through his inheritance. Think about how much he dreaded to see his older brother again. Not easy, but necessary. If you have hurt your former spouse, if you have sinned against him or her, you've got to repent. If you've done what our Savior condemns, you've got to repent. At the very least, that means apologizing for the harm you've caused. Depending on your situation, it might mean much more than that. Talk to your church leaders for help through this process.

This is where we should again emphasize the value and nobility of the single life. It is in no way inferior in God's eyes, though in some ways it may be harder. Then again, in some ways it's going to be easier; after all, divorce does frequently happen (i.e., marriage is not easy). If you find yourself in a situation in which entering a marriage would be condemned by Jesus, then don't enter a marriage. Stay single. We need faithful single people in the church and in the world.

Whereas Luke's brief mention (16:18) of the issue jumps straight to the conclusion (remarriage after divorce = adultery), the other passages interact explicitly with the single Old Testament passage that talks about the divorce certificate, Deuteronomy 24.

Let's take a look at this passage before considering how it was interpreted in the days of Jesus.

Deuteronomy 24

This chapter in Deuteronomy covers a lot of different topics; we're only concerned with the first four verses, on the divorce certificate, or "bill of divorcement." It is important to note the nature of this law.[20] The passage starts with an "if," and we don't get the "then" until v. 4, which means that the first three verses are just setting up a scenario, and verse 4 is the real point of the law. You might need to confirm this point by looking at different translations. Some English translations obscure the point I'm making by breaking up the sentence into smaller units. But in Hebrew the whole command, all of verses 1–4, is a single sentence, with a "then" delayed until the start of v. 4.

So, let's cut to the chase and see what v. 4 says: "the first husband who sent her away may not marry her again after she has been defiled." This woman is defiled, as we see in the first three verses, because after getting divorced from her first husband she went and married someone else. This subsequent marriage defiled her—it did not defile her completely, just in reference to one particular man, her first husband. With regard to him, she is defiled, but not with regard to any other men. The basic idea of the law is that when a marriage breaks up and the spouses marry other people— I'm being egalitarian here, to include both spouses; the Bible actually just talks about the woman—and then their second

---

20. For an essay by a Jewish writer on this matter, see https://thetorah.com/when-is-a-man-allowed-to-divorce-his-wife/.

marriages break up, they cannot get back together with the first spouse. They have been defiled through the subsequent marriage.

Let's notice some further points in this law.

- This is not primarily a law about when it's okay to get a divorce. That issue is sort of addressed, but very obliquely. Verse 1 says that husbands sometimes divorce their wives when there is something about the wives that the husbands don't like. The thing that the husbands don't like is called here "something indecent," and the Hebrew term is *ervat davar* (עֶרְוַת דָּבָר). There is today much debate on what this phrase means, just as there was in antiquity. Does it include adultery only, or also other things? Usually these discussions have to do with what sort of permission this passage grants for a divorce: what is the "something indecent" for which a man may divorce his wife? But, again, this passage is not about that. This passage does not grant permission at all for a divorce. It merely says when divorce happens—and divorce usually happens because the spouses don't want to be married anymore (they regard marriage to the other person as indecent, distasteful)—then certain things need to be kept in mind. It is not a passage about how to write a divorce certificate or when to give it. The point of the command is: previously married people cannot get back together once they have been married to someone else.
- This passage assumes the existence of divorce.
- The law assumes that a husband divorcing his wife would give her a divorce certificate. We have examples of such certificates from around the first century (see below).

These certificates make it clear that the wife is not bound to a husband and is free to marry.

I want to point out one more thing about the Old Testament on divorce, not Deuteronomy 24 specifically. There's a verse in Malachi that mentions divorce (2:16), and the traditional English rendering says that God hates divorce. I'm pretty sure that God does hate divorce, but the translation of this particular verse is difficult and contested and so translations differ. I don't have the answer to this problem, but ancient people did disagree on how to understand this verse.[21]

Rabbinic Disputes

Despite the focus of the law in Deuteronomy 24, ancient Jewish teachers redirected the aims of the law in order to address legitimate causes for divorce.[22] They focused on that phrase *ervat davar*, "something indecent," as if it might provide a clue as to when, under what circumstances, God might allow divorces. It is somewhat understandable why they took the passage in this way,

---

21. See John J. Collins, *What Are Biblical Values? What the Bible Says on Key Ethical Issues* (New Haven, CT: Yale University Press, 2019), 92–93.

22. This material is most helpfully covered by David Instone-Brewer, *Divorce and Remarriage in the Bible: The Social and Literary Context* (Grand Rapids: Eerdmans, 2002). For an online summary of Instone-Brewer's book, see https://www.douglasjacoby.com/wp-content/uploads/Instone-Brewer-on-Divorce-Remarriage-1.pdf. Instone-Brewer has himself summarized his work in his article "Divorce," in *Dictionary of Jesus and the Gospels*, 2d ed., ed. Joel B. Green (Downers Grove, IL: IVP, 2013), 212–16.

since Deuteronomy 24 is the only passage in the Hebrew Bible that comes close to giving permission for divorce (though, again, that's not what it was trying to do).

We don't have a record of these ancient debates from the exact time of Jesus, but we do have a record from a little bit later, contained in the Mishnah (from around AD 200), and this record talks about the debate in terms of Rabbis that did live around the time of Jesus. So, the Mishnah probably gives us a pretty good idea of how Jewish leaders thought about divorce in the time of Jesus.

The most well-known passage is from the part (tractate) of the Mishnah called *Gittin* (= "divorce certificates" in Hebrew). Shammai and Hillel were both famous Rabbis from the time when Jesus was a kid. They were so famous that they attracted a lot of disciples, called here "schools."

> The School of Shammai say: A man may not divorce his wife unless he has found unchastity in her, for it is written, *Because he hath found in her indecency in anything*. And the School of Hillel say: [He may divorce her] even if she spoiled a dish for him, for it is written, *Because he hath found in her indecency in anything*. Rabbi Akiba says: Even if he found another fairer than she, for it is written, *And it shall be if she find no favour in his eyes*....[23]

Here are the main lines of debate. Shammai says the only legitimate reason for a divorce is "unchastity," that is, fornication. In the *ervat davar*, "indecency in anything" (= something

---

23. Translation in Herbert Danby, *The Mishnah* (Oxford: Oxford University Press, 1933), 321. See also Mishnah *Ketuboth* 5.5–8 (= Danby, pp. 252–53) and 7.2–10 (= Danby, pp. 254–55).

indecent), Shammai emphasizes the word *ervat*, indecency, which in his mind points toward sexual sin.[24] But Hillel says the husband can divorce his wife for basically any reason in the world, for ruining supper. In the phrase *ervat davar*, "indecency in anything," Hillel emphasizes the word *davar*, "in anything." One of Hillel's disciples, Rabbi Akiba, supports Hillel's interpretation by pointing to another part of Deut 24:1, "if she finds no favor in his eyes," a phrase that Akiba understands as meaning that the husband thinks the wife is ugly, or at least less pretty than some other woman.

Hillel was a much more influential rabbi than Shammai, so that his views generally won the day. In rabbinic literature, the potential causes for divorce are pretty wide open.[25] Josephus, the first-century Jewish historian, says that he divorced his first wife (after she bore him three children) because he wasn't pleased with her behavior.[26]

On the other hand, one of the Dead Sea Scrolls, called the Temple Scroll, prohibits divorce altogether.

> But only from the house of his father shall he take a wife for himself, (that is,) from the family of his father. And he shall not take another wife besides her, for she alone shall be with him all the days of her life

---

24. At least, according to this particular Mishnah passage, Shammai accepted only adultery as legitimate grounds for divorce. But he was open to a few other causes of divorce, based on Exodus 21:10–11; see Instone-Brewer, *Divorce and Remarriage*, 111–12.

25. Charles Quarles, *Sermon on the Mount: Restoring Christ's Message to the Modern Church*, NAC Studies in Bible & Theology (Nashville: B&H, 2011), 125–26.

26. Josephus says this in his autobiography (*Vita*), at the end (§426 in modern divisions).

(ולוא יקח עליה אשה אחרת כי היאה לבדה תהיה עמו כול ימי חייה). And if she should die, then he may take for himself another from the house of his father, (that is,) from his family. (11Q19 57.16–19)[27]

Obviously, this very strict view did not become the dominant view in ancient Judaism,[28] but it does illustrate that not everyone was thinking the same way on this issue. Sorta like today.

Divorce Certificates

As mentioned earlier, we have some examples of ancient divorce certificates.[29] The Mishnah says this:

> The essential formula in the bill of divorce is, 'Lo, thou art free to marry any man'. R. Judah says: 'Let this be from me thy writ

---

27. James H. Charlesworth, ed., *Temple Scroll and Related Documents*, PTSDSSP 7 (Tübingen: Mohr Siebeck; Louisville: WJK, 2011), 149, with the Hebrew on p. 148.

28. It can be argued that this strict view is not carried through consistently in the Dead Sea Scrolls, or even in the Temple Scroll; see James G. Crossley, *The New Testament and Jewish Law: A Guide for the Perplexed* (London: T&T Clark, 2010), 73–74.

29. See Scot McKnight, *The Sermon on the Mount*, Story of God Bible Commentary (Grand Rapids: Zondervan, 2013), 98–99. His examples are also given below, except for 5/6Hev 10. Further examples are given in a couple of articles written by Instone-Brewer, "1 Corinthians 7 in the Light of the Graeco-Roman Marriage and Divorce Papyri," *Tyndale Bulletin* 52 (2001): 101–16; "1 Corinthians 7 in the Light of the Jewish Greek and Aramaic Marriage and Divorce Papyri," *Tyndale Bulletin* 52 (2001): 225–43. Both of these articles are available at Instone-Brewer's academia.edu page.

of divorce and letter of dismissal and deed of liberation, that thou mayest marry whatsoever man thou wilt'. (*Gittin* 9.3)[30]

Here is another example that was found in relation to the Dead Sea Scrolls in a document labeled by scholars XḤev/Se 13 and dated to AD 134/35:

> In the month of Siva, day 20, in 134/35 AD, I acknowledge—I Shelamṣion daughter of Yehosef from Ein Gedi—I acknowledge that you, my former husband—Eleazar son of Hananiah—don't owe me anything from the divorce.[31]

This divorce certificate was written by a woman, acknowledging that her former husband owes her no money. It confirms that a woman could initiate a divorce, as the Mishnah also allows.[32] The

---

30. Danby, *Mishnah*, 319.

31. This is my paraphrase of the translation appearing in DJD 27 (1997), p. 67, which actually runs as follows:

> On the twentieth of Sivan, year three of the freedom of Israel in the name of Shim'[o]n son of Kosibah, the pr[in]ce of Israel, [...] ... [I admit that ... I] do not have, I, Shelamṣion daughter of Yehosef *Qbšn* from Ein Gedi, with you (= you don't owe me), you 'El'azar son of Ḥanania[h] who had been her/my husband from before, th[at (one)] from whom you had (received)/who had (received/receives) from me a document of divorce and expuls[ion ...,] [a wo]rd of notice (that cancels in advance) I do not have with you (= you do not owe me), y[ou,] 'El'azar, concerning a matter of anything. It is confirmed by her/by me I, Shelamṣion daughter of Yehosef, for herself, borrows the writing. Mattat so[n] of Shim'on, at her word. ... son of Shim'on, witness; Masabalah son of Shim'on, witness.

32. See Mishnah *Arakhin* 5.6 (= Danby, *Mishnah*, p. 548); see discussion in Crossley, *New Testament and Jewish Law*, 74–76.

duties of a man toward his wife are spelled out in Exodus 21:10–11 (providing food, clothing, "marital rights"); if a husband neglects these, the wife could pursue a divorce. This evidence corrects the common view held today that in ancient Judaism only a husband could initiate a divorce.[33]

A Brief Word on the Greco-Roman Law

Marriage laws in the Roman world were actually fairly conservative from our modern standpoint. The Roman emperors, starting with Augustus, promoted "traditional family values," as we might call them, though they did not always live out those values themselves (to say the least). But the paperwork was also different from our own day, and different from the situation in Judaism. In fact, there was no paperwork. According to Roman Law in the first century, a married couple was divorced when they no longer wanted to be married. This lack of paperwork makes it difficult for us to determine how frequent divorce was, since they didn't leave a paper trail.[34] Roman law also required divorce in certain situations, such as adultery committed by a wife. "A husband who retained an adulterous spouse could be charged as a

---

33. This view is assumed, for instance, by J. D. G. Dunn, "Law," in *Dictionary of Jesus and the Gospels*, 2d ed., ed. Joel B. Green (Downers Grove, IL: IVP, 2013), 505–15, at 509; Shelly, *Divorce and Remarriage*, 171n19, 98. For a nuanced discussion of the evidence, see John J. Collins, "Marriage, Divorce, and Family in Second Temple Judaism," in *Families in Ancient Israel*, ed. Leo G. Perdue et al. (Louisville: WJK, 1997), 104–62, at 119–21. Hylen, *Women*, points out that both Jesus (p. 88) and Paul (p. 89) share the assumption that women could initiate a divorce (see also p. 81).

34. Hylen, *Women*, 80.

pimp."[35] Jews did not necessarily follow Roman law in these respects; in fact, while polygamy was forbidden under Roman law and was uncommon in Judaism of the first century, it is attested among some Jews at this time.[36]

MATTHEW 19 // MARK 10

The Pharisees approached Jesus with a question about divorce. Matthew (19:3) and Mark (10:2) say that their intent was to test Jesus. Perhaps they were aware of his teaching on divorce (Matt 5:31–32) and considered this subject a good one to get him in trouble.[37] Perhaps they were thinking about how John the Baptist got in trouble with regard to this same subject (Matt 14:3–4), though John was probably interpreting not Deuteronomy 24 but rather Lev 18:16; 20:21.[38]

(By the way, Hillel was most likely a Pharisee. Same for Shammai. For the most part, it seems that the Pharisees were the forerunners of the later rabbis that wrote the Mishnah. So, we could probably say that the debate we noticed earlier between the School of Hillel and the School of Shammai is a debate between two groups of Pharisees.)

These Pharisees are wondering what Jesus' take was on the *ervat davar*, "something indecent," in Deuteronomy 24:1. But they don't ask that specifically; they just say, what's the reason that a man can

---

35. Hylen, *Women*, 80–81, citing Thomas A. J. McGinn, *Prostitution, Sexuality, and Law in Ancient Rome* (Oxford: Oxford University Press, 1998), 171–72.
36. See again Hylen, *Women*, 76–77.
37. Hays, *The Moral Vision of the New Testament*, 350.
38. N. T. Wright, *Simply Jesus* (New York: HarperCollins, 2011), 103.

divorce his wife? The implication: do you agree with Shammai, or Hillel, or with some other opinion, like the one in the Temple Scroll? The answer Jesus gives resonates more with the Temple Scroll than with the others. He doesn't offer an interpretation of Deuteronomy 24, because that's not the relevant passage of Scripture to answer the question about legitimate grounds for divorce. The relevant passage of Scripture, Jesus says, is Genesis 2:24— "the two will become one flesh." "Therefore, what God has joined together, let no one separate" (Matt 19:6, Mark 10:9).

But the Pharisees think that Moses has specified grounds for divorce in Deuteronomy 24, so they ask about that passage specifically (Matt 19:7, Mark 10:4). Jesus corrects their understanding of the passage. This law in Deuteronomy 24 is not about how divorce is okay. It's a law that regulates divorce, but divorce itself arises only because of hard hearts. Again, Deuteronomy 24 attempts to bring some order to a hard-hearted practice that people were already doing. So, if the question is, "how should we go about doing divorce," Deuteronomy 24 has something to say about that. But if the question is, "should we be doing divorce," Jesus points us to Genesis 2 as providing the relevant teaching. The man and the woman are one flesh; they should not separate.

Jesus is not the only Jew at this time who would point people to creation as providing the correct view of marriage and divorce. Another passage from the Dead Sea Scrolls, in a work called the Damascus Document, criticizes people who engage in fornication, which includes "taking two wives in their lifetimes, although the principle of creation is male and female he created them [Gen 1:27]."[39]

SERMON ON THE MOUNT

Jesus' teaching in the Sermon is essentially a summary of his more extended teaching in Matthew 19. But here in the Sermon he cites Deuteronomy 24:1—well, he doesn't cite the text so much as he cites the way people often read the text, as permission for divorce, as if the point of the law was that when a man wants to divorce his wife he needs to provide her with a divorce certificate. Of course, that's not what the law of Deuteronomy 24 is about, and Jesus dismantles this incorrect understanding by highlighting the indissolubility of marriage. Serial monogamy is just another way of committing adultery.

As Instone-Brewer says:

> In Roman law adultery could be committed only against the husband, though in Jewish law adultery was committed when either a husband or a wife slept with someone other than their marriage partner.[40] By saying that a 'divorced' person was

---

39. CD 4.21; translation in Michael Wise, Martin Abegg Jr., and Edward Cook, trans., *The Dead Sea Scrolls: A New Translation* (San Francisco: HarperSanFrancisco, 1996), 55–56. See also Tobit 8:4–9, where Adam and Eve are the model for marriage. And the apostle Paul twice quotes the same passage as Jesus does, Genesis 2:24 (cf. 1 Cor 6:16; Eph 5:31).

40. For a different interpretation of the situation in Judaism, see Hays, *The Moral Vision in the New Testament*, 352.

committing adultery, Jesus was declaring that they were still married to their original partner.[41]

In the words of Bonhoeffer, disciples of Jesus "maintain their sole allegiance to Christ even in their marriage by practicing discipline and self-denial."[42]

As is the case for all the Antitheses (Matt 5:21-48), "The teaching [in Matt 5:31-32] is one of several examples that illustrate how the disciples are to go beyond the formal requirements of the Law to fulfill its deeper intent."[43]

THE EXCEPTION

In both Matthew 5 and Matthew 19—but not, interestingly, in the parallel passages Mark 10 and Luke 16:18—Jesus makes an exception to the universal prohibition of divorce. It's worded a little bit differently in the two passages, but most scholars think it basically means the same thing. If the divorce had taken place as a result of "fornication," then remarriage is permissible.

Of course, this exception itself creates all kinds of questions, probably more questions than would have been the case had Jesus simply prohibited divorce altogether. Some people wonder what "fornication" (Greek *porneia*) means, but that's pretty straightforward.[44]

Is this the only exception—was Jesus being exhaustive, or just

41. Instone-Brewer, "Divorce," 215.
42. Bonhoeffer, *Discipleship*, 127.
43. Hays, *The Moral Vision in the New Testament*, 357.
44. Instone-Brewer, "Divorce," 215; more in Luz, *Matthew 1-7*, 253-55.

throwing out an example? Well, that's a tough one. Of course, this passage doesn't tell us. But Paul has something to say about it (see below).

Does this exception apply only to the "innocent" party or also to the party guilty of the fornication? Again, the passage doesn't really say, but it seems to me the only reasonable reading is that the "innocent" party is the one to whom the exception applies.

What about Paul?

Paul talks about marriage and divorce in 1 Corinthians 7. We're going to concentrate here on verses 10–16. First of all, it looks like Paul is familiar with Jesus' teaching on the topic, because he cites "the Lord" as saying that "a wife is not to leave her husband" (1 Cor 7:10), which sounds like what we've been reading in Matthew 5 and 19. A woman who leaves her husband, then, should remain single or be reunited with her husband.

But then Paul addresses a situation that would not have applied in Jesus' context. What if there is a believer married to an unbeliever (a pagan)? This would be a very conceivable situation in the cities where Paul is preaching, if one spouse comes to faith and the other one doesn't. Paul says that the believer should remain faithful to his or her marriage vows (vv. 12–13). But it's not always up to the believer; what if the unbeliever wants a divorce? According to Paul, in such a situation the believer "is not bound" (v. 15).

There has (of course) been disagreement about what exactly Paul means here. It seems, from my reading, that most people think "not bound" means not bound to the marriage and therefore free to remarry. That is, from what I have read, most people seem to think that Paul is adding an additional "exception" to the complete prohibition of divorce. Jesus gave the exception about fornication, and Paul gives the exception about abandonment or desertion. If your spouse leaves you, then you are free to remarry, says Paul.

I should acknowledge that this is not a view I have encountered very often in the churches of Christ of the Tennessee Valley. The view that I have encountered in these churches of Christ most frequently is that Jesus gives the only exception, and Paul simply means that a believer is "not bound" to try to save the marriage, but Paul does not mean that the believer is free to remarry.

The main point that Paul is making, though, is not about how to get out of an unhappy marriage, but about how to be faithful in all aspects of your life, including in your marriage. N. T. Wright (who favors the view that "not bound" = free to remarry) characterizes the passage this way:

> In other words, within the one family (i.e. of the *ekklēsia*), divorce and remarriage will count as adultery. However, when the issue between spouses is that one partner is a 'believer' and the other is not, the believer is 'not bound' if the unbeliever wishes to separate. That, I take it, means that the abandoned believing spouse is free to remarry— 'only in the Lord', as when one is widowed [7:12–16, 39]. This is a remarkably careful distinction of cases. The underlying principle which makes sense of it is that the new community, the single family, which is the central symbol of Paul's worldview, is the primary thing that matters. The behaviour of 'individuals' [...] is to be aligned with the vocation of that community. And the point Paul is making throughout 1 Corinthians, and indeed elsewhere, is that this community is to be the new genuine

humanity. In this humanity, the programme of Genesis 1 and 2 is at last to be realized: one man, one woman, for life. That vision of true humanity is what drives Paul's entire thinking on this and related subjects.[45]

So What Do We Do?

First and foremost, we encourage people to stay married. As McKnight says, "divorce is wrong. We are to hold fellow followers of Jesus to that standard."[46] Through difficulties, show faithfulness. Recognize your relationship with your spouse as no less important than your relationship to your enemies, whom you are supposed to love and treat with kindness, according to Jesus. Our behavior here is part of what it means to follow Jesus. Following Jesus means we sacrifice for others, most especially those whom we see every day, most especially the people we live with. In this vein, Richard Hays exhorts us to "recover the New Testament's vision for marriage as an aspect of *discipleship* and as a reflection of God's unbreakable *faithfulness*."[47]

If we cannot be faithful when we have literally made vows in front of a room full of witnesses ... well, that doesn't bode well for our understanding of what it means to follow Jesus.

So, the church needs to encourage faithfulness in our marriages just as in all aspects of our lives. That's certainly the emphasis of Jesus in our passage and of Paul in 1 Corinthians 7.

---

45. N. T. Wright, *Paul and the Faithfulness of God* (Minneapolis: Fortress, 2013), 446.
46. McKnight, *The Sermon on the Mount*, 106.
47. Hays, *The Moral Vision of the New Testament*, 372. Hays (p. 350) says something similar about Mark's inclusion of Jesus' teaching in a context of discipleship.

EXPLORATION 6.1
Marriage Tips

If you're just entering into a relationship, or if you're trying to figure out how to right the ship, maybe these tips will prove helpful. Some of them are written from the husband's perspective because I've never been a wife. Let me say again that these tips are not intended for a spouse in an abusive relationship. If you're in that kind of relationship, get out of the house and take your kids. The following ideas do not apply to you.

- Take responsibility for your marriage. Don't leave it up to your spouse to resolve conflicts.
- Be more committed to the marriage than you are to your spouse. Shirley Jones sings in *The Music Man* that she'd like to find a man "more interested in me than he is in himself, and more interested in us than in me." The marriage was ordained and instituted by God. Shall I quote Jesus again? "What God has joined together, let man not separate." You might find at some point that you don't like your spouse very much. But you're in a marriage, ordained by God. Be committed to the marriage. Hold up in honor those people who have been married for five or six or seven decades. Make it your goal to reach those milestones. Your commitment to your spouse is part of your commitment to God. After all, God joined you together. Be faithful.
- Take responsibility for your marriage. Don't leave it up to your spouse to resolve conflicts.

- Let your spouse vent. Don't take it personally. Be quiet and listen.
- Don't do things that make your spouse uncomfortable. If you're not sure, ask your spouse how he/she feels about it. And look for the clues that when your spouse says "oh, it's fine, go ahead and do it," he/she doesn't really mean it. And then don't blame your spouse when he/she is bothered by it even though he/she said he/she wouldn't be. You knew he/she would be.
- Take responsibility for your marriage. Don't leave it up to your spouse to resolve conflicts.
- Husbands, there are some things that will make your wife uncomfortable no matter what she says: (1) having lunch with a woman who is anywhere close to your age, or younger than you but older than, let's say, ten years old. I think if it's a woman who is forty years older than you, you're probably safe, but you should probably ask, anyway. Is that an unreasonable rule? Well, a lot of affairs have started over lunch. (2) Texting another woman. If it's a group text and there are guys in on the group, that's probably fine. If it's just you and the woman, not fine—especially if y'all are discussing (even innocent) personal matters rather than business. Add your wife to the texts. If the other woman thinks that's weird, who cares? You're not married to her. You want to make your wife comfortable.
- Take responsibility for your marriage. Don't leave it up to your spouse to resolve conflicts.
- Look for ways to honor your spouse.

> - Husbands, do not sit on the couch while your wife is working around the house. That's just lazy. She's not your servant. Get off the couch and do something.
> - Take responsibility for your marriage. Don't leave it up to your spouse to resolve conflicts.
> - Go to bed at the same time as each other. You can get up at different times but go to bed at the same time. Have a nightly routine.
> - Eat ice cream every night together. It's hard to hate someone when you eat ice cream with them every night.
> - Take responsibility for your marriage. Don't leave it up to your spouse to resolve conflicts.
> - Husbands, just recognize that you need her more than she needs you, which means that you need to be looking for some job security in your marriage. You need to treat her in such a way that it would never enter her mind that she might be better off with some other guy.
> - Take responsibility for your marriage. Don't leave it up to your spouse to resolve conflicts.

But, as I said earlier, people get themselves into all kinds of messes. Moses had to offer some instruction about how to go about doing divorces because people had hard hearts and they were going to get divorces. This has not changed in our day. I love McKnight's pastoral reflections.[48] He recognizes that there are different views on this issue, different historical views, and that the answers we Bible teachers give carry much weight. He says we can't leave these questions to individuals to figure out on their own. There is a great

---

48. McKnight, *The Sermon on the Mount*, 104–9.

responsibility to the church, here, not only in teaching but in standing with people. McKnight recognizes that the more rigorous the view, the more obligation the church has to help people through marriage problems.

Some people add a third "exception" to the divorce prohibition: abuse. This one is not exactly spelled out in Scripture, but McKnight sees it hinted at in Exodus 21:10–11.[49] There are several things to say about this. First, a person in an abusive relationship ought to get out of that relationship, and the church should offer aid to victims in these situations. No thinking person would say that a battered wife ought to stay with her husband.[50] Second, I think it's a fine thing to question and discuss whether Jesus and Paul intended to list every legitimate ground for divorce. It's a good discussion to have. But, third, if we're interpreting scripture according to our own cultural context, then I would say that in our current 21st-century American context, we are not in a culture in which women need to get married in order to be supported. It is a perfectly legitimate lifestyle today for people to stay single. (Of course, it always has been—1 Cor 7:11, 34—but now more than ever.) I'm not sure that in the day we live in we can say that a divorced person needs to get remarried, or that by disallowing remarriage that we thereby enable an abuser. In our society, you could make the argument that illegitimate marriages ought never to happen among Christians because women are empowered and independently wealthy (= they have jobs). The same pressure to

---

49. McKnight, *The Sermon on the Mount*, 107–8.
50. Of course, some people don't think; see the case study in Shelly, *Divorce and Remarriage*, 9–10.

marry—economic and social—is not there as it was in the first century.

I think one of the solutions to the messed-up marital situation of 21st-century America is for the church to highlight singleness as a noble lifestyle, in imitation of both Jesus and Paul and as a foretaste of resurrection life (Matt 22:30).

If we do find ourselves in a situation condemned by Jesus, if we have committed the adultery that Jesus warns about, then, as with every other sin, we must repent. What exactly repentance in these situations looks like is not precisely spelled out in Scripture—should we end the second marriage? or would that be a case of two wrongs not making a right? If we end the second marriage, should we get married to our first spouse, a case condemned as an abomination to the Lord in Deuteronomy 24? These are questions that deserve careful reflection by the church as we seek to help people become faithful disciples of Jesus. I'm not going to give you an answer here. I do have my own thoughts, but for this discussion I think it's important for people to recognize that Scripture does not provide the definitive answer to this question, and that the way forward is (1) to discuss these issues with each other, to try to help each other toward a better understanding and more faithful lives, and (2) for each person to behave according to his or her own conscience as informed by Scripture. That's all any of us can do, anyway. On such issues, I am not willing to draw lines of fellowship.

Instead of looking for loopholes about how to get out of a marriage and seeking whom to blame when marriages turn sour, the church ought to be encouraging faithfulness.

Conclusion

This long discussion can be summarized in a few brief points:
- Stay true to your marriage vows. Be faithful.
- Singleness is a noble lifestyle. Don't quickly abandon it, especially if you're in a situation in which pursuing a marriage would be condemned as an act of "adultery" by our Lord.
- When you sin, repent.

7

How to Be Religious
Matthew 6:1-18

> For neither man nor angel can discern
> Hypocrisy, the only evil that walks
> Invisible, except to God alone.
> (*Paradise Lost* 3.682-84)

Oskar Schindler bought people.[1] He bribed Amon Göth and other Nazi officials so that he could select Jewish men, women, and children—more than a thousand of them—to work in his factory rather than go to the death camps. These purchases drained his fortune. Was it worth it?

Surely any Christian, or any person who has seen the film *Schindler's List*, would without hesitation affirm that Schindler gained much more than he lost. We know that there are all kinds of things worth more than money. Indeed, money is worth anything at all only if it allows us to get other things. (That's been

---

1. To remind yourself of how this goes in the movie, go to YouTube and search "This Is Life, Schindler's List."

a problem in places like Zimbabwe.)² At the very least, Schindler bought with his money the lasting gratitude of generations. Jesus represents such righteous actions as much more valuable even than that.

Heavenly Storerooms³

According to Jesus in Matthew's Gospel, there is a heavenly bank account—or, better, a 401k—into which people make deposits by doing deeds of righteousness. (I know this idea might make us uncomfortable. Stay with me, though. We'll talk about it.) In Matthew 6:1–18, Jesus says that people store up a reward in heaven by doing deeds of righteousness in secret. Immediately thereafter, Jesus tells his disciples not to store up treasure on earth but in the more secure accounts in heaven (vv. 19–20). Such an idea is found already in the Old Testament.

> Those who are gracious to the poor lend to the LORD,
> and the LORD will fully repay them. (Prov 19:17)

The idea also appears in some deuterocanonical books (the so-called Apocrypha). For example, in the book of Tobit, the character Tobit counsels his son Tobias to be good to poor people.

---

2. At Wikipedia, look up "Zimbabwean Dollar." I myself have a $50 billion bill from Zimbabwe, which will not buy me a stick of gum.

3. For an overview of this idea as it relates to our passage, see Nathan Eubank, "Storing Up Treasure with God in the Heavens: Celestial Investments in Matthew 6:1–21," *Catholic Biblical Quarterly* 76 (2014): 77–92. For much more, see Gary A. Anderson, *Sin: A History* (New Haven, CT: Yale University Press, 2009).

> Give aid, my child, according to what you have. If you have a lot, make a donation out of your riches. If you have only a little, don't be afraid to make a donation in proportion. In this way, you will store up a valuable treasure for a time of need. (Tobit 4:8–9)[4]

Or in the book of Ben Sira, we read this advice.

> Invest your treasure according to the commandments of the Most High,
> and it will profit you more than gold.
> Store up acts of charity in your treasuries,
> and it will deliver you from every distress. (Sir 29:11–12)

So, Jesus' audience would not have wondered at his speaking about treasures in heaven. They had heard about such storerooms stocked with good deeds.

Paul echoes the same concepts when writing to Timothy about how to instruct rich people.

> Tell them to do good, to be rich in good works, to be generous and willing to share, storing up treasure for themselves as a good foundation for the coming age, so that they may take hold of what is truly life. (1 Tim 6:18–19)

This is why Jesus told a parable (Luke 12:16–21) about a rich fool who had to build large barns to store all of his earthly treasure, and yet he was not "rich toward God" (v. 21). Just after telling this

---

4. Later, the angel Raphael instructs Tobit and Tobias: "Giving to the poor is better than storing up gold. Giving to the poor saves from death, and it washes away every sin" (Tobit 12:8–9). See also 4 Ezra 7:77.

parable, he tells people to "make money-bags for yourselves that won't grow old, an inexhaustible treasure in heaven" (v. 33). This can be accomplished, he says, by selling your possessions and giving to the poor.

Good deeds add up in the heavenly storeroom. They will prove more valuable than all of earth's gold.

Jesus has already told us in the Sermon that we can secure a reward in heaven by suffering persecution because of him (Matt 5:11–12), and he implies that we will gain a reward by loving our enemies (5:46; cf. Luke 6:35). If the Rich Young Ruler had given his fortune to the poor, he would have stored up treasure in heaven (Matt 19:21; Mark 10:21; Luke 18:22).

Like a 401k, we cannot really access this treasure now; it is for the future. But in the "renewal of all things" (Matt 19:28), "the Son of Man is going to come with his angels in the glory of his father, and then he will reward each according to what he has done" (16:27).[5]

But is this for real? Does Matthew—or Jesus—really expect us to believe that we are storing up treasure in heaven by our deeds here on earth? Doesn't that idea contradict the fundamental Christian notion that God saves us by grace, "not of works, lest any man should boast" (Eph 2:8–9)? I have two responses.

First, I have emphasized this notion of heavenly treasures so much because it is the notion that Jesus is working with in our passage. The way he phrases his instruction in Matt 6:1–18, it's about how to store up treasure in heaven. What he says here is

---

5. For other passages relying on this economic metaphor regarding salvation, see 2 Cor 5:10; Matt 20:1–16.

connected to this larger theme found in biblical and extra-biblical writings.

Second, sometimes the economic (or commercial) metaphor is a little different. The Lord's Prayer represents our sin as "debts" (Matt 6:12), which might make you think that your debts need to be less than your credits, or else there will be hell to pay (sorry, couldn't resist) at the judgment. But this way of reckoning our salvation is definitely too works-based to make room for grace. The language of "debts" is reminiscent of the Parable of the Unforgiving Servant (Matt 18:21–35), who was in debt up to his eyeballs, or, really, way beyond his eyeballs: he owed his master far more money than he could ever hope to repay. (Ten thousand talents [Matt 18:24] would be north of a billion dollars today.) This servant with the massive debt is obviously a representation of us, Jesus' disciples. With so much debt, there is no amount of righteous deeds that could possibly get us back in the black. Like that unforgiving servant, we must have God's grace, or we're lost.

This different way of looking at our heavenly account helps us to see that all this talk of credits in the heavenly treasury is just a metaphor for Jesus. He just wanted to help people understand what God thought about their good deeds. I don't think he really means that we're earning credits in heaven. But that is the metaphor he's using here, so we'll run with it.

Secret Righteousness

The main point of this whole section is that Jesus wants his disciples to be discreet—not ostentatious—about doing good works. Doing something righteous for the purpose of gaining some advantage ruins the value of the action.

We routinely operate with this same sort of logic. If your child receives a trophy for baseball, you'll probably be proud, and you might display the trophy in your home—unless it's a participation trophy. You'll happily attend a party when invited, unless the invitation was sent to you out of pity. The motivation for the good deed always matters; it matters to us and it matters to God.

We have come to accept ulterior motives in many circumstances in life. We know that when politicians show up at a charity event, they don't care about the charity as much as they care about votes.[6] When we receive a birthday card in the mail from our dentist or the auto repair shop, we don't put it in a keepsake box, nor do we call up the business to express our appreciation. But these things are not so bothersome to us, because we know the motives are not pure; self-interest is involved, and there's no secret about that.

Will the politician continue to support the charity after the election? Will the business send you a birthday card even if you move to a different town? Will someone do righteous deeds when no one is looking, when there's nothing to gain? The person who would do that exhibits the greater righteousness that Jesus requires of his disciples (Matt 5:20). The person who doesn't do that is a hypocrite, a word appearing for the first time here (6:2, 5, 16) and characteristic of Matthew's condemnation of people concerned only with the externals of religion.[7]

---

6. For ancient Roman examples, see the discussion of "civic euergetism" in John M. G. Barclay, *Paul and the Gift* (Grand Rapids: Eerdmans, 2015), 32–35.

7. The word 'hypocrite' appears 17x in the NT, 13 of which are in Matthew: 6:2, 5, 16; 7:5; 15:7; 22:18; 23:13, 15, 23, 25, 27, 29; 24:51. The abstract *hypocrisy* appears once, 23:28.

For those who are interested in a relationship with the Father who is in heaven, motivation matters. This whole Sermon is about the heart; that's what the greater righteousness is all about — obeying God from the heart, from the will, and not just externally with our actions. Good deeds done without the heart might earn a reward, but not with God. The politician who supports the charity (or holds a Bible) only when the cameras are rolling has already received his reward. He wanted a photo-op, and that's what he got. But God is looking for people who want to honor him and not themselves, who will do the right thing when nobody's looking because they know that God is looking.

In terms of the heavenly storeroom, your motivation determines which account receives your deposit. When you do something righteous, if you do it out of self-interest, then you are making a deposit into the earthly storeroom, which pays out in honor from people. If you do good deeds out of a desire to honor God and show love to his people, you are making a deposit in the heavenly storeroom, which pays out in honor from God. Jews at the time of Jesus commonly believed that good deeds produced treasure in heaven; Jesus modifies that idea with the crucial qualification that only those good deeds accomplished through pure motives produce treasure in heaven. Good deeds motivated by self-interest have already paid out.

Alms[8]

Giving to the poor is a righteous deed commended throughout Scripture. We have already seen that Proverbs 19:17 represents giving to the poor as equivalent to making a loan to God himself. That idea should remind us of the words of Jesus: "as you did it to one of the least of these my brothers, you did it to me" (Matt 25:40). God commanded the Israelites:

> When you reap the harvest of your land, you are not to reap all the way to the edge of your field or gather the gleanings of your harvest. Leave them for the poor and the resident alien; I am the LORD your God. (Lev 23:22; cf. 19:9–10; Deut 24:19)

Every third year, Israel was commanded to collect the tithe of their produce, unload it at the city gate, and leave it for the poor (Deut 14:28–29). Doing so would secure the blessing of God.

In Matthew 6:2–4, Jesus affirms this basic ethic but wants to make sure that his disciples practice greater righteousness than the Pharisees, who also encouraged giving alms. Jesus wants his disciples to give from a pure heart. The instruction to avoid letting your left hand know what your right hand is doing—since it's the right hand that will be reaching out to give money—is obviously hyperbole but it gets the point across. Give alms without any attention from others. Give in such a way that you receive no reward except from the One who is able to see even in secret. If

---

8. On the theme, see Gary A. Anderson, *Charity: The Place of the Poor in the Biblical Tradition* (New Haven, CT: Yale University Press, 2013); David J. Downs, *Alms: Charity, Reward, and Atonement in Early Christianity* (Waco, TX: Baylor University Press, 2016).

you've already gotten paid for your good deed, God is not going to pay you again.

There is, perhaps, a fine line between being rewarded by people (bad) and being a good example to people (good); in both cases, your good deeds need to be seen by others. Jesus commends good examples earlier in the Sermon (Matt 5:16). The difference is motivation: do you want people to praise you (bad—Matt 6:2) or do you want people to praise God (good—Matt 5:16). Dropping a check in the collection plate on Sunday in full view of anyone who wants to look is a good example, especially since no one knows the number on the check.

Prayer

Obviously, we should pray, and we don't always have to do it in our closet. The apostles provide a good example for us of prayer in Acts 4 (verses 24-31), and they were not in their closet. There are occasions for public prayer. And not all prayer needs to be short; Jesus prayed all night (Luke 6:12). And prayer sometimes can be repetitious; again, Jesus is the example (remember Gethsemane, Matt 26:44). But when you put all three things together—public prayer that is long and repetitive—then you've got problems, because that's the way the hypocrites do it. Then it seems like you're just showing off, and you're making earthly deposits.

Jesus tells us that our normal, everyday prayers need to be pretty short. He even provides an example of the type of prayer he has in mind, one that wouldn't take 60 seconds to say. (We'll talk more about this prayer in our next chapter.) There may be times for longer prayers, especially in times of intense need. But longer prayers can also provide an opportunity for us to show off our vocabulary or how pious we are, and the reward for that kind of prayer will come in the good opinion of people, not the good opinion of God.

One of the reasons that Jesus gives for not extending the length of our prayers is that there is no need to do so, "because your Father knows the things you need before you ask him" (v. 8). It is understandable that this idea seems to some people to undermine the entire enterprise of prayer: if God already knows, what's the point of telling him? Well, one response to that is that Jesus tells us to pray. And all of Scripture tells us to pray. "Pray without ceasing," says the apostle (1 Thess 5:17). Prayer is the fundamental defining characteristic of the religious person, demonstrating reliance on God and not on ourselves. James assures us that prayer works (5:16). That is to say, our prayers have some sort of influence on God. Certainly, they have an influence on us, reminding us every time we pray that our lives are in God's hands.

By saying that God knows our needs already, Jesus was not trying to make prayer seem useless. In this very passage he's telling us how to pray! Rather, what Jesus was trying to do is make the wording of our prayers seem not quite as important. We don't have to get all the words just right, say just the right things to God. If we mess up, if we don't say what we mean, or if we tell God we really need something and it turns out we really don't, God is not going to hold us accountable for these little slips. God already knows our needs, so there's no need to fret over saying the perfect prayer so that God will show his love to us. As Jesus says in Luke: "Don't be afraid, little flock, because your Father delights to give you the kingdom" (12:32).

Fasting

Uggh, fasting. The Bible doesn't talk a whole lot about fasting, and it's never commanded in the New Testament, so we can probably ignore it. Yeah, Jesus does sort of assume here that his disciples will fast, but he doesn't actually require it. Then again, he does say that when the bridegroom is taken away, his disciples will fast (Matt 9:15), but maybe that passage is too ambiguous, and it doesn't really encourage people to fast. Besides, some people have medical conditions such that fasting might compromise their health.

Excuses. The fact is Jesus does assume his disciples will fast, just like he assumes they will pray and give alms. And that probably was not such a big deal in previous times, but in America today food is so abundant, and we are so accustomed to eating our fill at all hours of the day that fasting just doesn't fit with our lifestyle.

That probably means American Christians *need* to fast more than any people in history.

More than any other people, we are the ones who need to learn that "man does not live by bread alone." Yes, some people have medical conditions, and they should talk to a doctor about possible implications of fasting. But the majority of us are just plain gluttons—we like to eat, and we don't want to stop. We hate the thought of fasting. That's precisely why we need to do it.

The church has not encouraged fasting, the church has encouraged eating. We have potluck meals with two long tables full of food and another long table full of deserts. Every time we get together outside of worship, there is food involved. That's not a bad thing because usually we're happy and we want to praise God for his gifts and enjoy his gifts at the same time. That's great. The church should do that.

But the church also has an obligation to encourage people to not live according to the flesh. And the practice of fasting could be very beneficial toward that end. Not only that, but we'd be imitating Jesus, who fasted, and standing in a long line of Christian spirituality, in which fasting has always been a vital component.

What is the point of fasting? The Bible never really says,[9] but we can imagine some benefits. Fasting helps us shift focus away from the flesh. It helps us not be satisfied at all times. It helps us look forward to satisfaction. Or to identify with those who have not the food we have. Bonhoeffer has the same idea: "A life which remains without any ascetic discipline, which indulges in all the desires of the flesh ... will find it difficult to enter the service of Christ. Satiated flesh is unwilling to pray and is unfit for self-sacrificing service."[10]

One time won't cut it. We might fast once and later say, "well that didn't work. I'm no more spiritual than I was." Just like we might go to one day of math class and complain that we still don't know calculus or take one karate class and complain that we're still not a black belt or take one dose of medicine and complain that we're still sick. Jesus seems to assume that his disciples will fast

---

9. Scot McKnight, *The Sermon on the Mount*, Story of God Bible Commentary (Grand Rapids: Zondervan, 2013), 194, argues that fasting is a response to a crisis, but the passages he cites (Lev 16; Ps 35; Isa 58) don't really support that view. He would have done better to cite Esther 4:16, but that passage cannot define the totality of fasting.

10. Bonhoeffer, Dietrich *Discipleship*, DBWE 4 (Minneapolis: Fortress, 2001),158.

repeatedly, that it will be a constant part of our spirituality, like prayer and giving.

One more important point for our cultural context: fasting is not about losing weight. That's not the point, and it shouldn't be the goal. In fact, if I may paraphrase Jesus, if you lose weight because of your fasting, you have received your reward. The point is to shift our focus away from the flesh. Fasting in order to lose weight is the exact opposite of shifting our focus away from the flesh. And young women who are tempted toward anorexia are decidedly not shifting their focus away from the flesh. These elements of our culture increase the complications of discussions of fasting.

Having said all that, don't look to me for an example. I'm not the type of hypocrite who fasts and draws attention to my fasting by talking about how great fasting is. I'm the type of hypocrite who doesn't practice what I preach.

All of that is not what Jesus is getting at in our passage. He assumes a habit of fasting; he encourages secret fasting. That's the point—don't tell people you're fasting, don't let on. That would be especially hard for us, since we're so unaccustomed to fasting. It's an unusual practice for us, so we'd be more tempted to talk about it, I think. "Oh, I'm so hungry. I'm trying out this fasting." Eating is such a part of our culture, we would stand out a bit if we don't join the others during our lunch hour, so it might require some extra planning on our part to fast without being noticed. But, let me say, we wouldn't refrain from praying on the chance that someone might see us do it, and we should probably think of fasting in the same way: just because someone might notice doesn't mean we shouldn't do it.

This teaching from Jesus once again stands in a tradition stretching back to the Old Testament prophets, who also condemned hypocritical fasts. In Isaiah, the problem wasn't so much that people received honor from men by their fasting, but that the people who were fasting were evil people, as if just by fasting they could win God to their side without any need to change their hearts and lives.

> Look, you do as you please on the day of your fast, and oppress all your workers. (Isa 58:3)

God did not care for such fasts. Just as elsewhere he would prefer obedience to sacrifice (cf. 1 Sam 15:22), so here he would prefer righteous living over fasting.

> Isn't this the fast I choose: to break the chains of wickedness, to untie the ropes of the yoke, to set the oppressed free, and to tear off every yoke? Is it not to share your bread with the hungry, to bring the poor and homeless into your house, to clothe the naked when you see him, and not to ignore your own flesh and blood? (Isa 58:6–7)[11]

Jesus is attacking a different problem. He certainly expects our deeds to be righteous rather than evil; he expects us to love our neighbor as ourselves (Matt 22:39). But he expects us to do so out of a desire to honor God and receive honor from God, rather than receiving honor from people.

---

11. There's a similar problem in Zechariah 7.

CONCLUSION

Good deeds done with the wrong motivation earn no credit with God. That's the way hypocrites act, and they earn credit only with people. The greater righteousness that Jesus requires in his disciples is not just about doing good deeds—the Pharisees do plenty of good deeds—but doing these good deeds with a pure heart out of a desire to honor God and not gain a good reputation among people. So do your righteousness in secret, "and your Father who sees in secret will reward you."

8

The Lord's Prayer

Upward falling, spirit soaring;
I touch the sky when my knees hit the ground.
—Hillsong United

Prayer can be hard. What are you supposed to say? I mean, Jesus himself said that God already knows your needs even before you ask him (Matt 6:8). Prayer is important to the Christian not least because it is an action of basic trust, a recognition that our lives are not ultimately ordered by ourselves but by the God who created us and sustains us. Prayer is an acknowledgment that God is in charge and we are not. And, as Pete Grieg points out in his book *How to Pray*, prayer is a natural language for humans, such that people who are not necessarily religious feel sometimes compelled to whisper into the dark, "please," or "thank you."[1] Still, it's not easy to think of things to say in prayer. Grieg himself says that he started thinking intensely about prayer when he realized how bad he was at it. It would be nice if we had a model to go by.

---

1. Pete Greig, *How to Pray: A Simple Guide for Normal People* (Carol Stream, IL: NavPress, 2019), ch. 1.

A model prayer is precisely what Jesus supplies his disciples in the middle of the Sermon on the Mount. There are other model prayers in Scripture—the book of Psalms is essentially a book of prayers, all serving as models for how we can approach God in prayer. And of course, Scripture—both Old Testament and New Testament—is full of prayers that can serve as models for us. But what sets apart the Lord's Prayer in this respect is that (a) it comes from Jesus our Lord and (b) he explicitly taught it as a model. As for the first point, the words of Martin Luther adequately state the matter:

> Since our Lord is the author of this prayer, it is without doubt the most sublime, the loftiest, and the most excellent. If he, the good and faithful Teacher, had known a better one, he would surely have taught us that too.[2]

Moreover, Jesus says that this prayer should serve as a model for his disciples. The Psalms and the prayer of Hannah (1 Sam 2:1-10) and that of Daniel (Dan 9:4-19) and of Mary (Luke 1:46-55) and of the apostles (Acts 4:24-30)—just to name a few—are only implicitly models for our own prayers. But Jesus actually says that he is providing the Lord's Prayer as a model for others: "Therefore, you should pray like this..." (Matt 6:9).

The Lord's Prayer (Matt 6:9-13) has been recited by Christians just about since the time Jesus taught it to them. Many people have seen in these few lines a summary of the teaching of Jesus, not just

---

2. Martin Luther, "Foreword," *An Exposition of the Lord's Prayer for Simple Laymen* (1519), trans. Martin H. Bertram in *Luther's Works*, ed. Jeroslav Pelikan and Helmut Lehmann, vol. 42: *Devotional Writings*, ed. Martin O. Dietrich (Philadelphia: Fortress, 1969), 21.

on prayer but on everything, or maybe at least a summary of the Sermon on the Mount. Jonathan Pennington has stressed that the Prayer is the epicenter of the Sermon, the center (6:7–15) of the center (6:1–21) of the center (5:17–7:12) of the Sermon.³

The Lord's Prayer works as a model prayer for Christians because it expresses profound theological insights in a compressed manner. Those characteristics have also made it the subject of numerous books.⁴ In this chapter we will cover briefly some of the important truths that Jesus teaches his disciples about prayer.

The Versions of the Prayer

The New Testament contains two different versions of the Lord's Prayer, one in the Sermon on the Mount in Matthew, the other in Luke 11:2–4. There's also another early version in the post-New Testament document called the *Didache*, written at the end of the first century.⁵ The *Didache* introduces the Lord's Prayer by explaining that people should "pray like this, just as the Lord

---

3. Pennington uses the term "epicenter" in *The Sermon on the Mount and Human Flourishing: A Theological Commentary* (Grand Rapids: Baker, 2017), 237. He uses the expression "center of the center of the center of the Sermon" at pp. 125, 131, 210, 210n2, 222.

4. A few recent books: Nijay Gupta, *The Lord's Prayer* (Macon, GA: Smyth & Helwys, 2017); David Clark, *On Earth as in Heaven: The Lord's Prayer from Jewish Prayer to Christian Ritual* (Minneapolis: Fortress, 2017); Wesley Hill, *The Lord's Prayer: A Guide to Praying to Our Father* (Bellingham, WA: Lexham, 2019); Pete Greig, *How to Pray: A Simple Guide for Normal People* (Carol Stream, IL: NavPress, 2019).

5. For information on the *Didache*, see Wikipedia. For the text, go to www.thedidache.com; the Lord's Prayer appears in ch. 8.

commanded in his Gospel" (8:2).[6] After giving the form of the prayer, the *Didache* then instructs: "Pray like this three times a day" (8:3).

Matthew's Version (ESV)	Luke's Version (ESV)	The Didache's Version
Our Father in heaven,	Father,	Our Father in heaven,
hallowed by your name	hallowed be your name	hallowed be your name,
Your kingdom come,	Your kingdom come,	your kingdom come,
your will be done, on earth as it is in heaven.		your will be done on earth as it is in heaven.
Give us this day our daily bread,	Give us each day our daily bread,	Give us today our daily bread,
and forgive us our debts, as we also have forgiven our debtors.	and forgive us our sins, for we ourselves forgive everyone who is indebted to us.	and forgive us our debt, as we also forgive our debtors;
And lead us not into temptation,	And lead us not into temptation	and do not lead us into temptation,

---

6. I follow the translation of the *Didache* in Michael W. Holmes, ed. and trans., *The Apostolic Fathers: Greek Texts and English Translations*, 3d ed. (Grand Rapids: Baker, 2007), 355.

but deliver us from evil.		but deliver us from the evil one.[7]
		for yours is the power and glory forever.

There are some variations between the versions in Matthew and Luke. Most striking is Luke's omission of the line about God's will being done on earth as in heaven.[8] The version in the *Didache* closely follows Matthew's version.

The Concluding Doxology

In neither of the versions in the New Testament do we find at the end of the prayer the doxology that is familiar from repeated recitations of the prayer and from the KJV—"for thine is the kingdom and the power and the glory, forever. Amen" (= KJV Matt 6:13). These words are not present in the earliest Greek manuscripts of Matthew's Gospel, and they are present in none of the manuscripts of Luke's Gospel. But this concluding doxology—or something close to it—is already found at the end of the first century in the version preserved in the *Didache*. Apparently, as people actually recited this prayer taught by Jesus, they found the

---

7. The Greek here is exactly the same as in Matt 6:13; it can be translated "evil" (= ESV Matt 6:13) or "the evil one" (= Holmes trans. *Didache* 8:2). See the discussion on this clause below.

8. This line is present in Luke's version in some Greek manuscripts, and so it is also found in some English translations, particularly the KJV. But scholars judge that those manuscripts that omit the line in Luke are superior and that the other manuscripts that include the line in Luke are adapted toward Matthew's version of the prayer.

ending "deliver us from evil" not quite appropriate for the end of a prayer, so they tacked on at the end the words now found in the KJV. Where'd they get the wording? It seems to be based on the prayer of David in 1 Chronicles 29:11. Though these words are not original to the prayer as taught by Jesus, they give us some insight into the functioning of the prayer in ancient worship settings.

The Brevity of the Prayer

Jesus presents this prayer as a model specifically because it is short and to the point. We can say that with full confidence because in the context of the Sermon on the Mount where he gives the Prayer he has just been criticizing the long-winded prayers of the hypocrites, who both want to show off to people and fail to understand that they don't have to inform God of every little thing—he already knows (Matt 6:5-8). Instead of praying like that, Jesus wants us to pray a simpler prayer, not for show, a prayer that demonstrates that we know that God understands our needs better than we do.

Think about the long appeals of the prophets of Baal on Mount Carmel (1 Kings 18:26-29). They spent all day trying to get Baal to pay attention, trying to manipulate their god (v. 28) into doing what they wanted, and they never received a reply. In contrast to their antics, Elijah's prayer is simple and effective (vv. 36-38). In the New Testament, Elijah becomes a model for prayer (James 5:17-18).

It's not necessarily about how long we pray. After all, Jesus' prayers weren't always short; he spent all night in prayer at least one time (Luke 6:12), and another time he repeated himself a few times (Matt 26:36-46). The issue that Jesus highlights is more about directing the prayer toward God and his glory and not our own glory and trusting that God understands what we need. Disciples of Jesus don't need to heap up words in prayer because we know that God loves us and will provide for us (Matt 7:11). We trust that he gets it.

An Analysis of the Prayer

Our Father in Heaven

The first word in the English form of the Prayer ("our") tells us something important about this prayer: it is framed as a communal prayer. This prayer speaks of *our* Father, *our* daily bread, *our* debts and *our* debtors. Jesus had just spoken about the need for private prayer, in a closet so that no one can see (v. 6), and he could have given a model prayer for such occasions— "my Father, give me today my daily bread." But the model prayer he provides assumes that his followers will be praying as a group.

Jesus teaches his disciples to address God as Father. This kind of language is not unique to Jesus. The Old Testament described Israel as the son of God (Exod 4:22–23; Hos 11:1; Isa 64:8), though admittedly, not very often.[9] The language could also be applied to the king of Israel, such as, for example, Solomon: "I have chosen him to be my son, and I will be his father" (1 Chron 28:6).[10] Jews at the time of the New Testament did sometimes address God as Father in their prayers.[11] There is even a Jewish prayer recited on

---

9. See also Deuteronomy 32:6; Isaiah 63:16; Jeremiah 31:9; Malachi 1:6; 2:10; cf. Jeremiah 3:19.

10. See also 2 Samuel 7:14; Psalm 2:7; 89:26–27.

11. For discussion of God as Father in ancient Jewish prayer, see Lutz Doering, "God as Father in Texts from Qumran," in *The Divine Father:*

Rosh Hashanah and Yom Kippur known as the *Avinu Malkeinu* ("our Father, our King").[12]

Jesus took this description of God—familiar but somewhat marginal in the Judaism of his day—and elevated it to perhaps the most important way of understanding who God is. This description of God as Father doesn't appear equally in all four Gospels: it's all over the place in John, but it barely comes up in Mark (only in 8:38; 11:25; 13:32; 14:36). Matthew has the theme prominently, but not so much as John. Sometimes in Matthew God is simply the Father (11:25–26; 24:36; 28:19), but usually he is either "your Father" (especially in the first half of the Gospel)[13] and "my Father" (especially in the second half of the Gospel).[14] The Sermon has God as "your Father" seventeen times. Jesus addressed God as Abba Father (Mark 14:36) and taught his disciples to do the same (cf. Rom 8:15; Gal 4:6).

Addressing God as Father suggests that there's no formal protocol for calling upon God, no real worry that we might call him by the wrong name. It's not like addressing British royalty.[15] Should I say, "your majesty" or "your royal highness" or just "your highness" or "your grace" or "your excellency"? Believe it or not,

---

Religious and Philosophical Concepts of Divine Parenthood in Antiquity, ed. Felix Albrecht and Reinhard Feldmeier (Leiden: Brill, 2014), 107–35.

12. There are Wikipedia entries on Rosh Hashanah, Yom Kippur, and *Avinu Malkeinu*.

13. These are the references to "your Father" that I found in Matthew: 5:16, 45, 48; 6:1, 4, 6, 8, 9, 14, 15, 18, 26, 32; 7:11; 10:20, 29; 23:9; cf. 13:43.

14. These are the references to "my Father" that I found in Matthew: 7:21; 10:32–33; 11:27; 12:50; 15:13; 16:17, 27; 18:10, 14, 19, 35; 20:23; 25:34; 26:29, 39, 42, 53.

15. See Wikipedia on "Forms of Address in the United Kingdom."

it matters when addressing human royalty.[16] Jesus teaches us to address God as "Father," a simple term of endearment, a term denoting the intimate relationship between us and our God, rather than a term of exaltation that sets God apart from us. (Of course, it is okay to use language of exaltation in prayer; note Acts 4:24.)

For some believers, addressing God as "Father" might be problematic because their own human fathers were so far from perfect that they recoil from the notion of an intimate relationship with their "father." But God is "our Father in heaven" (or, more literally, "in the heavens"). In Matthew, "heaven" is the place where God's will is carried out (as the Prayer itself attests, v. 10), the place where things are right. Our earthly fathers are not perfect examples of fatherhood precisely because they are *earthly* fathers; earth is the location where injustice rules, a place not now characterized by the will of God. Our Father in the heavens loves and cares for us perfectly.

HALLOWED BE YOUR NAME[17]

The Name of God is a crucially important concept in the Hebrew Bible, as in Judaism.[18] The Name was revealed to Moses at the burning bush (Exod 3:14) and the third of the Ten Commandments had to do with bearing well the Name (Exod

---

16. http://sandradodd.com/ideas/etiquette4.html

17. Advanced students interested in the Greek verbal tenses of the Lord's Prayer may benefit from the brief discussion in Benjamin L. Merkle, *Exegetical Gems from Biblical Greek: A Refreshing Guide to Grammar and Interpretation* (Grand Rapids: Baker, 2019), ch. 19.

18. On God's name, see Ed Gallagher, *The Book of Exodus: Explorations in Christian Theology*, Cypress Bible Study Series (Florence, AL: HCU Press, 2020), ch. 2.

20:7). Since God dwelt among the Israelites, Israel could in various ways defile God's Name.

> I myself will set my face against that man and will cut him off from among his people, because he has given one of his children to Molech, to make my sanctuary unclean and to profane my holy name. (Lev 20:3; cf. 18:21; 22:2, 32)

God's Name represents his own character, so that Israel would "trust in his holy name" (Psa 33:21) and "rejoice in his holy name" (1 Chron 16:10).

Because of the holiness of God's name, Jews have generally avoided saying it since ancient times.[19] They have tried in this way to preserve the sanctity of the Name.

But the moral failures of ancient Israel led to the defilement of God's Name, because his Name was placed on them. Isaiah, speaking in the voice of God, lamented that because of Israel's behavior, "my name is continually blasphemed all day long" (52:5), a complaint echoed by Paul (Rom 2:24). In the words of James Dunn, "The point is that God had committed his name to his chosen people ('the God of Israel'), so that their failure redounded to his discredit."[20] And so God himself would sanctify his Name.

---

19. This practice of avoiding pronouncing the Divine Name YHWH can be traced back even to the time of the biblical book of Chronicles; see Koog-Pyoung Hong, "The Euphemism for the Ineffable Name of God and Its Early Evidence in Chronicles," *Journal for the Study of the Old Testament* 37 (2013): 473–84.

20. J. D. G. Dunn, "Prayer," in *Dictionary of Jesus and the Gospels*, ed. Joel B. Green and Scot McKnight (Downers Grove, IL: IVP, 1992), 617–25, at 621.

And I will sanctify my great name, which is profaned among the nations, which you profaned in their midst; and the nations shall know that I am the LORD [= YHWH], when I am hallowed among you before their eyes. (Ezek 36:23)[21]

The prayer that Jesus encourages his followers to pray—hallowed be your name—is a petition that God will do what he said he would do in Ezekiel, to display the honor of his name, so that all people could see who God is and who his people are. "What Jesus has in mind is clear: he wants God to act to bring in the kingdom in order to display God's rule."[22]

THY KINGDOM COME

The Bible affirms that God has always been king. He is king over the whole earth.[23]

> The LORD reigns! Let the earth rejoice;
> let the many coasts and islands be glad. (Ps 97:1)

> With trumpets and the blast of the ram's horn
> shout triumphantly in the presence of the LORD, our King.
> (Ps 98:6)

---

21. For further discussion of this passage in relation to the Lord's Prayer, see D. M. Crump, "Prayer," in *Dictionary of Jesus and the Gospels*, 2d ed., ed. Joel B. Green (Downers Grove, IL: IVP, 2013), 684–92, at 687, who believes that "Jesus almost certainly had in mind" this passage from Ezekiel, as well as Ezekiel 38:16, 23; 39:7, 25–27.

22. Scot McKnight, *The Sermon on the Mount*, Story of God Bible Commentary (Grand Rapids: Zondervan, 2013), 177.

23. See also Exodus 15:18; Psalm 10:16; Psalm 45; 74:10–12.

> The LORD reigns! Let the peoples tremble.
> He is enthroned between the cherubim. (Ps 99:1)

But the Old Testament also anticipates that he will establish his kingdom in such a way that all people will recognize it. The most well-known verse for us is probably Daniel 2:44.[24]

> In the days of those kings, the God of the heavens will set up a kingdom that will never be destroyed, and this kingdom will not be left to another people. It will crush all these kingdoms and bring them to an end but will itself endure forever.

Jesus came announcing that this moment had arrived: "Repent, because the kingdom of heaven has come near" (Matt 4:17; cf. the message of John the Baptist, 3:2). The end of the Gospel of Matthew shows that Jesus has become king, he has established God's kingdom—"All authority has been given to me in heaven and on earth" (28:18). We who are the followers of Christ are a part of that kingdom now, since we have accepted Christ's rule over us. That's why Paul can tell the Colossians, "He has rescued us from the domain of darkness and transferred us into the kingdom of his beloved Son" (Col 1:13).

These are the concepts that I have heard frequently in churches of Christ since my youth. The emphasis has been that God has established his kingdom, that the church is that kingdom, and so there is nothing more to anticipate in that regard. As far as I can tell, churches of Christ have traditionally taught these things in order to oppose the doctrine of premillennialism, which posits

---

24. On ancient Jewish hope for the kingdom, see Clark, *On Earth as in Heaven*, 46n25.

that Jesus has not yet established his kingdom, but that at the end of time he will return and reign for a thousand years from Jerusalem, and that reign will be the kingdom that the Bible promises. I agree that this idea of premillennialism is off base, and I feel no need to offer arguments against it here. In the churches of which I have been a part, we have rightly emphasized the close relationship between the church and the kingdom: it is not right to say that Jesus will, in the future, establish his kingdom, because he has already established his kingdom, and the church is that kingdom.[25] Again, Paul implies in Colossians 1:13 that the kingdom has already been established.

This idea—which I fully endorse—has led some of us also to say that we should not now pray "thy kingdom come," since the kingdom has already come. But I'm not so sure. To my mind, the New Testament is clear that Jesus has already established his kingdom. We are not looking forward to the inauguration of the kingdom, because Jesus accomplished that through his ministry and his death and his resurrection. His ascension to heaven marked his ascension to the throne; he now reigns as king over his people. But that does not mean that we do not anticipate anything further with regard to the kingdom. Just because the kingdom has been inaugurated doesn't mean that it has fully come. Not everyone accepts the reign of Christ, and we look forward to the day when every knee shall bow to him and confess his rule.

---

25. This way of stating the matter has been traditional within churches of Christ in my experience. I myself would insist on a little more nuance. I would not be willing to equate the church with God's kingdom; rather, the church is the present, earthly manifestation of the kingdom of God. The church is the people over whom God reigns as king.

Jesus told some parables that illustrate the way I'm understanding the nature of the kingdom. I'm thinking specifically about the Parable of the Minas in Luke 19:12–27 (which is a little different from the Parable of the Talents in Matt 25:14–30). Notice that the reason Luke tells the Parable of the Minas is because some people "thought the kingdom of God was going to appear right away" (Luke 19:11). The parable he tells shows that the coming of the kingdom could be described as gradual rather than sudden. In the parable, a nobleman leaves a place in order "to receive for himself a kingdom and then to return" (v. 12), and so he leaves his servants in charge and doles out to them each a mina. Then he comes back as king and judge, and he assesses how his servants have behaved, how they have used their minas. Well, Jesus is obviously the nobleman who becomes king, and we are obviously the servants who receive the minas. This parable suggests an understanding of the kingdom of God such that, even though it is inaugurated, it will only be fully realized when Jesus returns.

Think also about 1 Corinthians 15:24–28:

> Then comes the end, when he delivers the kingdom to God the Father after destroying every rule and every authority and power. For he must reign until he has put all his enemies under his feet. The last enemy to be destroyed is death. For "God has put all things in subjection under his feet" [Psa 8:6]. But when it says, "all things are put in subjection," it is plain that he is excepted who put all things in subjection under him. When all things are subjected to him, then the Son himself will also be subjected to him who put all things in subjection under him, that God may be all in all.

You could think of this passage also as written against those who think "the kingdom of God was going to appear right away." In this passage, Paul describes Christ as already king, as already reigning over God's kingdom, but he still has work to do, he still has enemies to defeat, even now. "He must reign until he has put all his enemies under his feet. The last enemy to be destroyed is death." Let's compare this statement to the prophecy in Daniel 2:44, which says that the kingdom of God will put an end to all other kingdoms. Obviously, that has not happened yet. Paul seems to be saying, though, that it is happening even now, that what seemed in Daniel 2:44 to be a single action—the kingdom of God would come suddenly and destroy all other kingdoms—is actually spread out between the first and second advents of the Lord. The kingdom has been inaugurated, and we long for it to be consummated, for all enemies to be put down and "all things to be subjected to him."

New Testament scholars use the term "already/not yet" to describe the tension that we see in Scripture: the kingdom has already come, the kingdom has not yet fully come.[26] We live between the ages, when God has started fulfilling his promises, and we look forward to when he brings all things to completion.

In that sense, I believe we can still pray "thy kingdom come" because even though we ourselves are a part of God's kingdom, the earth is not yet full of his glory, not everyone has accepted Christ's rule, and we still live in the midst of people who are under the control of the "god of this age" (2 Cor 4:4), the "prince of the power of the air" (Eph 2:2). By praying "thy kingdom come," we can

---

26. https://ca.thegospelcoalition.org/columns/cowboyology/already-not-yet/.

petition God to finally destroy the works of Satan and bring his kingdom fully.[27]

Bonhoeffer puts it this way:

> In Jesus Christ the disciples have experienced the inbreaking of God's kingdom on earth. This is where Satan is overcome, the power of the world, sin, and death are broken. God's kingdom still is found in suffering and in struggle. The small community of those called forth will participate in such suffering and struggle. They stand under the rule of God in new righteousness, but also in enduring persecution. May God grant that the kingdom of Jesus Christ on earth grow in his community. May God soon put an end to the kingdoms of this world and bring about God's own reign with power and glory.[28]

Essentially, we are asking God to reign over us and over this earth. We might prefer to ask for God's guidance or wisdom, but Jesus instructs us to ask for his kingdom. "Rule over us as your subjects; execute your will on this earth!"

Thy Will Be Done on Earth as It Is in Heaven

Commentators often take this clause with the previous one on the kingdom, and for good reason. The kingdom of God and the will of God are closely related—where God reigns, his will is done. God's reign in heaven is complete and all-encompassing. We might think of a time when there was rebellion in heaven, but that

---

27. On how we can pray this petition of the Lord's Prayer, see Gupta, *The Lord's Prayer*, 77. For a description of what God's rule over his people looks like, see Clark, *On Earth as in Heaven*, 48.

28. Bonhoeffer, *Discipleship*, DBWE 4 (Minneapolis: Fortress, 2001), 156.

is not the case now. John the Revelator depicts this scene in heaven:

> Immediately I was in the Spirit, and there was a throne in heaven, and someone was seated on it. The one seated there had the appearance of jasper and carnelian stone. ... Four living creatures covered with eyes in front and in back were around the throne on each side...they never stop saying "Holy, holy, holy, Lord God, the Almighty, who was, who is, and who is to come." Whenever the living creatures give glory, honor, and thanks to the one seated on the throne, the one who lives forever and ever, the twenty-four elders fall down before the one seated on the throne and worship the one who lives forever and ever. They cast their crowns before the throne and say, "Our Lord and God, you are worthy to receive glory and honor and power, because you have created all things, and by your will they exist and were created." (Revelation 4)

That is a picture of the will of God being fully accomplished, of the rule of God filling everything. Jesus tells us to pray that God's will be accomplished on earth just as it is in heaven, that God's reign will fill the earth just as it fills heaven. Moreover, it is possible that the phrase "on earth as in heaven" doesn't apply to the third petition only—thy will be done—but to all of the preceding petitions: hallowed be thy name, on earth as it is in heaven; thy kingdom come, on earth as it is in heaven; thy will be done, on earth as it is in heaven.[29]

---

29. See Pennington, *The Sermon on the Mount and Human Flourishing*, 223n33.

Give Us This Day Our Daily Bread

Here the prayer turns from praising God to focusing on human needs, and first is our basic need for sustenance.

The term "daily" is the usual translation for the Greek word *epiousios* (ἐπιούσιος), but we actually don't really know what this term means.[30] The third-century Christian writer Origen commented:

> First we must note that the term *epiousios* (supersubstantial) is not used by the Greeks: neither does it occur with the scholars, nor does it have a place in the language of the people. It seems to have been invented by the Evangelists. (*On Prayer* 27.7)[31]

According to modern lexicography, it appears that Origen was right.[32] This word doesn't appear before the New Testament, and it appears in the New Testament only in the Lord's Prayer (Matt 6:11; Luke 11:3). So, while it is hard to say for sure what this word meant for Matthew—since we have no other examples of its use—the traditional translation "daily" is probably not that far off. Most

---

30. There is a Wikipedia entry for "Epiousios." For the various possibilities for translation, see also Gupta, *The Lord's Prayer*, 95–97; Brant Pitre, *Jesus and the Last Supper* (Grand Rapids: Eerdmans, 2015), 171–78.

31. I am using the translation in Origen, *Prayer; Exhortation to Martyrdom*, trans. John J. O'Meara, ACW 19 (New York: Newman, 1954), 96. Another translation is available online (https://www.ccel.org ccel/ origen/prayer.xviii.html), where the relevant paragraph comes in about the middle of the page, and the chapters are numbered differently (it's ch. 17).

32. BDAG 376 (for the full reference, see note 2 in Chapter Two above).

of the proposals for what *epiousios* means come to something close to "daily," so we'll stick with that translation for the purposes of this discussion.

This petition for daily bread makes us think of multiple contexts. First, there is the context of Jesus and his disciples, for whom daily bread was no guarantee. Itinerant teachers who preach the renunciation of the world tend not to know where their next meal is coming from. We see in the Gospels Jesus relying on the hospitality of people, such as Mary and Martha (Luke 10:38–42) or Matthew (Matt 9:9–10) or Zacchaeus (Luke 19:5) or even some Pharisees (Luke 7:36; 11:37; 14:1). Daily bread would have been a concern for the people to whom Jesus taught.

Second, there is the context of Scripture, where daily bread makes us think first of all of the wilderness and the miraculous supply of manna.[33] Jesus instructs us to ask for *daily* bread, and the supply of manna was daily, which not only prevented hunger but also prevented hoarding. Indeed, they could not store it up, because Moses commanded, "No one is to let any of it remain until morning" (Exod 16:19). Each new day they had to rely on God for their daily bread, which was entirely the point.

> He humbled you by letting you go hungry; then he gave you manna to eat, which you and your fathers had not known, so that you might learn that man does not live on bread alone but on every word that comes from the mouth of the LORD. (Deut 8:3)

---

33. For this interpretation, within an overall interpretation of the Lord's Prayer as calling on God for a "new exodus" as promised in the prophets and as announced by Jesus, see Pitre, *Jesus and the Last Supper*, 159–93.

In the words of Walter Moberly, "the heavenly bread is resistant to one of the most basic of human urges: to save up and to hoard."[34] So we could relate this petition for "daily bread"—as opposed to asking God for a year's worth of bread, or complete financial security, or some such—to our spiritual need to be content with what God gives us, and to resist the constant urge to accumulate. Certainly, our culture—but I guess all human culture is the same in this respect—teaches us to accumulate as much as possible. "He who dies with the most toys wins." To which Jesus would respond, "wins what?" Whatever such a person would win, it is not the kingdom of heaven (Matt 5:3). The story of the contented fisherman (google it) provides a good illustration of the problem we face in modern America with the constant desire for more. And, of course, Jesus is about to get there in the Sermon, also: "don't worry about tomorrow, because tomorrow will worry about itself. Each day has enough trouble of its own" (Matt 6:34).

Jesus instructs us to ask for bread, not for a banquet, not for steak. People today often want to avoid bread because they're on a low-carb diet or they're trying to stay away from gluten. But in ancient Mediterranean culture, bread was the basic part of every meal. The meals that Jesus provided revolved around bread (e.g., Matt 14:17; 15:34; Luke 24:30). These were not luxuriant meals, like what Marie Antoinette was used to, who, when she heard that the people of France had no bread, reportedly advised them, "Let them eat cake" (though, apparently, she did not actually say this).[35]

---

34. R. W. L. Moberly, *Old Testament Theology: Reading the Hebrew Bible as Christian Scripture* (Grand Rapids: Baker, 2013), 82. Moberly's entire ch. 3 is worth reading in this connection.

35. See the Wikipedia entry on "Let Them Eat Cake."

The disciples of Jesus are content with the simple sustenance that God provides day by day. This is a prayer of trust and not of greed.

This request for bread also makes us think of Jesus himself, the bread of life. "This is the bread that comes down from heaven so that anyone may eat of it and not die" (John 6:50). Each new day, we seek God's providential care, trusting his guidance and not our own, and we long to be filled spiritually with the life-giving bread that is Jesus.

Forgive Us Our Debts as We Forgive Our Debtors

Of course, we need to ask God to forgive us. Bonhoeffer explains why:

> The disciples' daily sorrow is the recognition of their guilt. They, who could live without sin in community with Jesus, sin daily in all sorts of ways: they lack faith, are lethargic at prayer, lack bodily discipline, and give in to self-indulgence, envy hatred, and ambition. So they must pray daily for God's forgiveness. But God will only hear their prayer when they forgive each other's guilt in a loving and willing way. Together, they bring their guilt before God and pray together for grace. May God forgive not only me my sins, but us our sins.[36]

The way Jesus presents this petition emphasizes the reciprocal nature of forgiveness: we ask God to forgive us as we forgive others.[37] Jesus ups the ante right after the model prayer, reiterating in

---

36. Dietrich Bonhoeffer, *Discipleship*, 157.
37. On this point, see the discussion in Gupta, *The Lord's Prayer*, 118–21.

Matthew 6:14–15 that "if you don't forgive others, your Father will not forgive your offenses."[38] Later in Matthew, Jesus tells the Parable of the Unforgiving Servant (18:23–35), which illustrates the point he's making. In that parable, the servant initially enjoys the forgiveness of his debt, but his subsequent stinginess toward his fellow servant leads to the re-institution of his own debt. This shows that our forgiving others does not earn the forgiveness of God, but the two are closely related. "While the forgiveness of God is unmerited (our forgiving of others does not *earn* God's forgiveness), still Christians are obligated to live properly in and from the forgiveness we so graciously receive from God."[39] Or, as Peter Kreeft says, "it is impossible for someone with a closed fist to receive a gift."[40]

Paul instructs his churches:

> bearing with one another and forgiving one another if anyone has a grievance against another. Just as the Lord has forgiven you, so you are also to forgive. (Col 3:13)

Lead Us Not into Temptation but Deliver Us from Evil

The word "temptation" can also be translated "testing" or "trial." And while God might not lead us into temptation (James 1:13–15), Scripture fully attests that he puts his servants to test. It was God,

---

38. A similar thought is expressed in the deuterocanonical book of Ben Sira 28:1–7. See also similar thoughts in other ancient Jewish documents: the Mishnah *(Yoma* 8.9) and the Talmud *(b. Shabbat* 15b; *Rosh Hashanah* 17a).

39. Gupta, *The Lord's Prayer*, 120.

40. Peter J. Kreeft, *Catholic Christianity* (San Francisco: Ignatius, 2001), 399.

after all, who tested Abraham's faith (Gen 22:1), and it was the Spirit of God that led Jesus into the wilderness to be tempted by Satan (Mark 1:12–13). So, God does this kind of thing, testing his servants, and, of course, he does it for our good. But Jesus teaches us here to ask God to spare us from these tests. "They ask God not to tempt their weak faith and to protect them in the hour of temptation."[41] So we might do better to translate this petition as "lead us not into trial."

The last word of the Prayer could be translated "evil," as is traditional, or "the evil one." Other passages use the term "the evil one" as a description of Satan, including other passages in Matthew (13:19, 38; cf. John 17:5; Eph 6:16; 2 Thess 3:3). Here Jesus teaches us to ask God to grant us victory over Satan, against whom is our battle (Eph 6:10–12). Satan prowls around looking to devour people (1 Peter 5:8), but we know that God has already made us more than conquerors through him who loved us (Rom 8:37). Jesus' own fight was against Satan, and he won the victory (Heb 2:14–15; Col 2:15; 1 John 3:8).

Should We Recite This Prayer?

Many Christians throughout the centuries have recited the Lord's Prayer word-for-word. Earlier we saw that the early Christian document the *Didache* instructed its readers to recite the Lord's Prayer three times a day. When I played high school football in Kentucky in the mid-90s, we ended every practice and began every game with a recitation of the Lord's Prayer. I remember one time someone suggested that we say a different prayer, that one of the

---

41. Bonhoeffer, *Discipleship*, 157.

team members actually lead an extemporaneous prayer, and the coach replied, "Nah, just say the normal one." The coach never said prayer with us; he seemed to just want us to get it over with so we could move on to the next thing.

Every aspect of Jesus' teaching on prayer is against the *mindless recitation* of words that do not arise from our heart. The whole problem with religion, as Jesus sees it, is that it is too concerned with externals, of getting the forms just right, and not concerned enough with making people good, of shaping people's hearts. I have no doubt that when I used to recite the Lord's Prayer after a football practice, without thinking in any way about the words, that God was not honored by such an action.

> [R]epeating the Lord's Prayer is a meaningless exercise unless one encounters it as a guide for how to pray, what to pray, and in what spirit to pray, so that one's life is changed accordingly.[42]

On the other hand, reciting words does not necessarily mean that they do not arise from our hearts. Usually our wedding vows have been planned out word-by-word, perhaps weeks or months or (if we use the traditional vows) centuries beforehand, but surely as we say these planned-out words, they are coming from our hearts. The songs that we sing in a worship service are not written on the spot, but surely, we believe we can sing these words form our hearts, even though we didn't write the words and we might not know who did. We should consider the point of reciting a formula, such as the Pledge of Allegiance, or the words we say before

---

42. D. E. Garland, "The Lord's Prayer in the Gospel of Matthew," *Review and Expositor* 89 (1992): 215–28, at 215.

performing a baptism, or how we swear in people in a court of law, or at the inauguration of a president. Of course, we could do all of these activities mindlessly, but normally they are not done mindlessly. We recite these specific words, such as the Pledge of Allegiance, because they are well written, and they accurately portray what we want to declare. They are not spontaneous compositions, but that doesn't make them any less an expression from our hearts.

So, is it possible to recite a written prayer and do it from the heart? Sure it is.

This would probably have been the culture in which Jesus grew up—reciting traditional prayers. Apparently Jews in the first century would recite daily certain set prayers, such as the Amidah and the Shema.[43] The very beginning of the Mishnah is all about how and when to recite the Shema.[44] Daniel (Dan 6:10) and the apostles (Acts 3:1) prayed at set times during the day, though we don't know what exactly they prayed (cf. also Psa 55:17).

"Prayer was and is both a spontaneous act and a recitative act."[45] We need to pray spontaneously sometimes, but thinking beforehand about what we should pray is also a good thing. And using the Lord's Prayer as a model for writing our own prayers is probably what Jesus intended by it. And then again, reciting the Lord's Prayer verbatim is a legitimate act of worship, as long as it comes from the heart.

---

43. Wikipedia has entries on both of these prayers.
44. See Mishnah tractate *Berakhot* 1.1–2, at https://www.sefaria.org/Mishnah_Berakhot.1?lang=bi.
45. McKnight, *The Sermon on the Mount*, 162.

9

HANDLING POSSESSIONS
MATTHEW 6:19-34

> Do not say to yourself, "My power and the might
> of my own hand have gotten me this wealth."
> (Deut 8:17)

This past Saturday I felt good about what I accomplished. It was a day of getting things done. The overhead light in the spare bedroom has been unworkable for months. The hall bathroom tub has been draining slowly for a while. The chicken coop out back needed some hinges and a lock put on the window. A table I had recently made needed to be sanded. And one of our little fans had just stopped working. So early in the day—not too early, since it was a Saturday—I went to Walmart and bought a part for that bedroom light, and some hinges and a lock for the chicken coop, and some sandpaper, and a fan. I was glad Walmart had everything I needed, and I didn't have to go across town to Lowes. Over the next few hours, I crossed everything off my to-do list. It felt good.

I spent the entire day acquiring stuff and fixing the stuff I already had.

A typical American now makes the kind of money that would

have seemed extravagant a generation ago. But what we do with that money doesn't seem so extravagant. Maybe we've lost our sense of perspective. A smart phone is now deemed a necessity. So, instead of a $15 landline phone, we require a $1000 mobile computer. Plus, all the accessories. Putting it like that makes it sound absurd, like something only movie stars should do, but in our world it's hard to think that a smartphone isn't necessary. And a car, of course, or a few of them, and an enormous wardrobe, and a few TV's, and—of course—if you're going to get a TV now, you might as well get a smart TV. As our income has increased, the things that just seem necessary for our very existence have become fancier. And as that stuff wears out, with hardly a thought we replace it with an even fancier model.

Americans have a lot of stuff, and we spend a lot of our time taking care of our stuff. Almost like we're serving Mammon. When you step back and think about it, you might wonder whether God has given us all this stuff, or whether an enemy has been planting thorns (Matt 13:22).

Jesus had a lot to say about money, more than you might expect for a guy who had "no place to lay his head" (Matt 8:20). And not much of his teaching focused on how useful money is, or how it makes life better. He focused more on how money is a trap of Satan, that you'd better divest yourself of (Matt 19:21).

Now, I happen to be writing this book on a $1000 Macbook. I haven't given away all my possessions, and I'm not going to advocate that in this chapter. I think Jesus' words can be understood in a different way. But I do recognize how self-serving my interpretation is. And I'm not entirely comfortable with it.

Between writing the previous paragraph and writing this sentence, I have spent 45 minutes on an online call with a Filipino.

We were making some plans for offering training to church workers and trying to settle things about my next visit to the Philippines. Maybe Jesus would say that a $1000 Macbook can come in handy sometimes.

Treasure that Lasts

The first half of Matthew 6 is all about rewards for righteousness: you only get one reward, either from God or from people. Verse 19 continues the thought but gives it a little twist. Now, instead of speaking against receiving praise from people, Jesus speaks against accumulating wealth. Jesus wants us to be more concerned about heavenly treasure, just as he earlier wanted us to pursue the heavenly reward.

What he says against earthly treasure makes a ton of sense, and our own lives prove the wisdom of his words. My family has experienced a break in—when we arrived home, our front door was lying flat in our foyer, and we could see the footprint in the middle of it where the perpetrator had kicked it in. I can imagine his disappointment when he discovered how little treasure we had to steal. Mostly he got away with some of my wife's jewelry, among which were a few sentimental pieces but nothing of much monetary value. People often don't keep their real valuables—certainly not the bulk of their money—at their house but in a bank or in investments, so perhaps in our society Jesus would talk about the uncertain treasure in the stock market.

Rust has affected some of our possessions, especially when the kids leave their toys out in the yard. We don't really worry about moths too much. But we certainly have a clothing budget to replace the jeans with holes in them, or the worn-out shoes—so many worn out shoes! —or the shirts that are now too small. Of course, I myself am done growing (well, never mind) and so I'm still wearing some of the same clothes I've had for twenty years (suits, mostly), but that doesn't mean I've stopped accumulating new clothes. Jesus is certainly correct that anything we treasure up here on earth is going to wear out—it's not going to last. Like I said before, I spent my whole Saturday fixing my stuff that had broken.

The problem that Jesus is identifying isn't so much about wealth (said the rich man to reassure himself!) but about what we trust in. His words stand as a challenge to all that we've been taught to do with our money. Save, invest, accumulate, build wealth. This is just good sense, wise use of money. Certainly, saving and investing is a wiser course of action than some alternatives. The lottery winner who declares bankruptcy a few years later is a cliché in our society. We have little sympathy for the professional athlete in financial trouble. We know that the reason these people have no money is not because they gave it to the poor or invested in inner-city schools or some other noble purpose, but they spent too much on cars and houses and vacations and junk. They should have saved. They should have invested. They should have laid up some treasure on earth.

But they should not think that such earthly treasure is the cure-all for the human condition. This is our problem. We have been told that we need to achieve financial independence, financial security, that money will secure our future, that—if you give it sufficient time—the stock market always goes up.

Jesus identifies two problems with this sort of thinking:

    (1) It doesn't always work.
    (2) It never works.

The first problem is the one we've been talking about. Things happen. People betray you. Jobs disappear. Investments collapse. There are still thieves, and moths, and rust. And floods. I live in Florence, Alabama, where in February 2019 there was so much rain that the Tennessee River crested to its second highest point (29 feet) since 1897.[1] Flood level is 18 feet. Places were flooded that are not near the river. After the rain finally stopped, the *Times Daily*, our local newspaper, surveyed the damage. In a story that ran on the front page, the paper reported on a lady who had just finished remodeling her home. She went to bed Saturday night at 12:30am after hanging curtains and was evacuated from her home a few hours later. She said she did not have flood insurance because she doesn't live in a flood zone.[2] Yep, that happens.

This does not mean we should not have any wealth, but it does mean that we should recognize how tenuous our wealth is, how volatile it is, how dependent it is on so many forces going just our way, how easily it can all evaporate. And, anyway, trusting in wealth or in the market to provide security sounds a lot like idolatry. Don't trust in wealth, trust in God.

The second problem, it never works, also goes under the name, "You can't take it with you." All our financial security has nothing whatsoever to do with heavenly security. And therefore, our financial security really just provides a false sense of security. This is the constant human problem—reliance on ourselves rather than reliance on God—applied to money. Treasure on earth will necessarily not last long enough, because it won't last into the next

---

1. See "River Drains after Nearly 11 Feet above Flood Stage," *Times Daily*, Tuesday, February 26, 2019, p. A10.
2. See "Relentless Flooding Chases Residents from Homes," *Times Daily*, Sunday, February 24, 2019.

life. The moths and rust will win, after all. Seeking security in stuff on earth is a Ponzi scheme.

Here's the way Paul puts it:

> Instruct those who are rich in the present age not to be arrogant or to set their hope on the uncertainty of wealth, but on God, who richly provides us with all things to enjoy. Instruct them to do what is good, to be rich in good works, to be generous and willing to share, storing up treasure for themselves as a good foundation for the coming age, so that they may take hold of what is truly life. (1 Tim 6:17–19)

Jesus doesn't say in our section how we can accumulate heavenly treasure, but he has already addressed that in the earlier passage, when he spoke about the reward that our heavenly Father would give us for righteousness not noticed by others. With regard to money, the relevant point would be the first example Jesus used in regard to the heavenly reward (6:2–4), about giving alms. Use your money on behalf of others. That's how you store up heavenly treasure. Paul says the same thing in the passage quoted just above.

This passage teaches that we need to loosen our grip on things in this life. We need to hold our possessions lightly, realizing both that they could vanish at any moment and they cannot—ever—supply us the security we're really longing for. And if we loosen our grip on our possessions, we can grip tighter to God.

The Good and Bad Eye

In verses 19–21, Jesus talked about money. In verse 24, he will talk about money. And in verses 25–34, Jesus will talk about worry in such a way that his concerns there are clearly rooted in what he had just been saying about money. So, we are in a "money" context in verses 22–23, where he talks about the eye, and we should probably try to relate his statements here to money. It's not really too hard to think about someone's eye being "bad" when it comes to money; the bad eye would be the greedy eye, the lustful eye, the ungenerous eye, the eye that wants to acquire and store up and hoard, the eye attracted to shiny things.

Note the warning in Deuteronomy 15:9, which concerns the Sabbatical year (the seventh year) when all debts are remitted.

> Take care lest there be an unworthy thought in your heart and you say, "The seventh year, the year of release is near," and your eye look grudgingly on your poor brother, and you give him nothing, and he cry to the LORD against you, and you be guilty of sin.
>
> Is it not lawful for me to do what I will with mine own? Is thine eye evil, because I am good?

The good eye, then, is the opposite—the eye that is generous, not greedy. The eye that sees the poor in need and doesn't mind reducing its own comfort for the sake of the comfort of others, that is the good eye.

As for the idea that the eye is a lamp, Jesus' words here seem to relate to ancient views on the process of seeing, how the eye works, whether the eye takes in light (the so-called intromission view) or projects light onto objects (the extramission view). In the words of Pennington: "either way the point is that the eye is a metaphorical window between the inside and the outside of a person."³ The eye reveals the heart.

Mammon

In *Paradise Lost*, Mammon is one of the fallen angels who joined with Satan in battle against God. He is

> the least erected spirit that fell
> From heaven, for even in heaven his looks and thoughts
> Were always downward bent, admiring more
> The riches of heaven's pavement, trodden gold,
> Than aught divine or holy else enjoyed
> In vision beatific.⁴

The personification of Mammon as a god or evil angel goes back in Christianity a long way, at least to the fourth century.⁵ But it goes back no further, so we can be sure that Jesus did not mean to personify Mammon as a god, but greed is so closely identified with idolatry (cf. Eph 5:5; Col 3:5) that Mammon can become a god to us.

Mammon is a Greek word (μαμωνᾶς) that comes from Aramaic (מָמוֹן) that basically means "wealth" or "property." The word

---

3. Jonathan T. Pennington, *The Sermon on the Mount and Human Flourishing: A Theological Commentary* (Grand Rapids: Baker, 2017), 240–41.

4. John Milton, *Paradise Lost* (1674), 1.679–84. Mammon makes a speech at 2.226–83, advising against renewed war with heaven.

5. See the Wikipedia entry on "Mammon" under the heading "Personifications."

appears infrequently in the New Testament: only here and in Luke 16:9, 11. You cannot serve God and Mammon, "wealth," "property," "stuff." You have to choose. A fundamental notion of the Christian (and Jewish) religion is monotheism and the command to act like monotheists. "Thou shalt have no other gods before me" (Exod 20:3). Serving our stuff, spending our time thinking about our stuff, caring for our stuff, honoring our stuff, and acquiring more stuff, sounds like idolatry.

In Bonhoeffer's words:

> Either you love God or you love the goods of the world. It does not matter at all whether you intend to do it or whether you know what you are doing. Of course, you will not intend to do so, and you will probably not know what you are doing. It is much more likely that you do not *intend* what you do; you just *intend* to serve both masters. You intend to love God and goods, so you will always view it as an untruth that you hate God. You love God, you think. But by loving God and also the goods of the world, our love for God is actually hate; our eye no longer views things simply, and our heart is no longer in communion with Jesus.[6]

In other words, hatred for God does not mean that we *say* that we hate him, or even that we *feel like* we hate him. The ancient Israelites who bowed down to the idol of Baal would have argued that such an action was not an expression of hatred toward the LORD. But the prophets argued differently.

---

6. Dietrich Bonhoeffer, *Discipleship*, DBWE 4 (Minneapolis: Fortress, 2001), 164.

Don't Worry

The last ten verses of Matthew 6 give the familiar warnings against anxiety. Paul echoes our Lord when he advises the Philippians: "Don't worry about anything, but in everything, through prayer and petition with thanksgiving, present your requests to God" (Phil 4:6). We sing about this theme:

> I care not today what the morrow may bring,
> If shadow or sunshine or rain.
> The Lord, I know, ruleth o'er everything,
> And all of my worry is vain.[7]

But whether we live it or not is a different story. The fact is, a focus on stuff necessarily creates worry, for just the reasons that Jesus has already mentioned. The moth and the rust and the thief cause us anxiety as we try to preserve our stuff against the inevitable decay. Around the time of Jesus, Rabbi Hillel acknowledged, "the more possessions, the more care."[8] In that sense, our instinct to accumulate in order to create security for ourselves will have the opposite effect if we hold too tightly to our stuff; it will make us insecure with anxiety. As Bonhoeffer observed, "Earthly goods deceive the human heart into believing that they give it security and freedom from worry. But in truth, they are what cause anxiety."[9]

---

7. James Wells, "Living by Faith," 1918.
8. Mishnah Avot 2.7, in Herbert Danby, *The Mishnah,* 448. Hillel's statement almost sounds like it could have inspired a hit song by Christopher Wallace from back in my high school days.
9. Bonhoeffer, *Discipleship,* 165.

Jesus instructs us to trust that God will provide for us, just as he provides for birds and flowers. Of course, Jesus doesn't say here everything that could be said about money.[10] He doesn't say here that you should not be lazy, that you should work hard and provide for your family, as the Proverbs do routinely, and as Paul does (2 Thess 3:10; 1 Tim 5:8). Neither is he talking to people that are going through a famine and are under threat of starvation. We can imagine that his basic message would be the same, but he would say it somewhat differently. And neither is he talking to people that make so much money that they have an expectation of retiring at some point in their 60s, by which time they will have accumulated so much wealth that they can live for decades longer without earning additional income. Again, we can imagine that his words would be somewhat different with the same basic message.

That message is: don't trust in wealth. Don't serve Mammon. And if you don't trust in wealth for your security, you won't worry so much about wealth. You can acknowledge that the wealth might well evaporate, due to whatever—a bear market, some investment fraud, a war, or the same thing that came back to bite the Rich Fool (Luke 12:16–21), the same thing that comes to bite us all: our own death. In that situation, no matter how much we have stored up on earth as surety against the moth or rust, we will be in bad shape unless we are also "rich toward God" (Luke 12:21).

Trust God instead of wealth. Our Father in heaven will supply our needs. (But we need to remember that God thinks people *need* hunger sometimes; Deut 8:3.) Of course, God often supplies our needs not through some miraculous means (like giving manna

---

10. See Scot McKnight, *The Sermon on the Mount*, Story of God Bible Commentary (Grand Rapids: Fortress, 2013), 221–22, for one negative way that the Sermon could be read.

from heaven) but through our own hard work. There is a tension here, just like we saw a tension earlier between doing righteous deeds in front of people so that they would glorify God (Matt 5:16) or so that they would glorify us (Matt 6:1). Here, when it comes to money, the tension revolves around who or what we trust: do we trust ourselves and our own ability to provide for ourselves, or do we trust our heavenly Father? Who gets the credit?

Jesus speaks about our relationship to God as children with a Father who supplies our needs. I know I would hate it if my kids worried about whether we would be able to eat or afford housing or clothes. (And I know some kids do have legitimate worries about those things, and I hate that for those kids.) It is a common story that when foster kids get into a home, they will hoard food in their rooms because they have been trained to doubt whether they will always have access to food. They don't trust their foster parents, and it takes time, sometimes years, for them to learn that hoarding is unnecessary.

Instead of pursuing wealth, we should pursue the kingdom of God (Matt 6:33). What we want to tell the foster kids is that if you want plenty of access to food, then the first thing to do is to get in the right house, with parents who are going to provide for you. (I know; easier said than done.) Jesus tells us that the first thing we need to do if we want security is: get in the right house; get the right Father. When God rules your house, God provides for your needs.

Seek God's rule—God's kingdom—like an athlete pursues a goal. Like Rudy Ruettiger pursued the chance to play football for Notre Dame. In practical terms, such seeking looks like praying, reading Scripture, talking with spiritual people about how to live more like Jesus, and truly thinking about what things in our lives need to change. Chances are, something Jesus has said about money should make us think about our relationship with money and how it might be misleading us.

LIVING OUT JESUS' TEACHING

There's a lot to say, but I've already said some of it. McKnight begins his reflections on what to do with this passage by asking the question, "How do we, the affluent, follow Jesus, the poor man?"[11]

The church in America faces many challenges, but one challenge we don't talk enough about is, "What do we do with all this money?" Decades ago, Ron Sider wrote a book called *Rich Christians in an Age of Hunger*.[12] The very title of that book makes me feel dirty. I've been to places where hunger is a pressing concern; I've met people for whom living paycheck to paycheck seems beyond reach. And I recognize what separates me from them is largely an accident of birth. I don't mean that I weep over my wealth, but it does force me to evaluate what is the point of it all. Luke 12:48 echoes in my mind: "From everyone who has been given much, much will be required; and from the one who has been entrusted with much, even more will be expected."

So, what do we do?

1) At the very least, we need to think continually about ourselves as rich and what that fact means for our relationship with God. This issue is especially pressing because the Bible—

---

11. McKnight, *The Sermon on the Mount*, 209.
12. Ronald J. Sider, *Rich Christians in an Age of Hunger: A Biblical Study* (London: Hodder & Stoughton, 1977), now in a sixth edition with a new subtitle, *Moving from Affluence to Generosity* (Nashville: W Publishing Group, 2015).

certainly the New Testament—doesn't say a lot of positive things about rich people. We need to confront that reality, own up to it, and allow it to shape the way we approach money.

2) We ought to use our money to bless others. The Parable of the Talents (Matt 25:14–30) presents a picture of God who becomes angry with a servant who received a ton of money (a talent of gold = roughly a million dollars) and did nothing with it. He praises the servants who took the money they received and "used" it. The parable does not detail how God wants his servants to use the money he gives them, but given the nature of Jesus' life, and the content of the Sermon on the Mount (Matt 6:2–4), it's not that hard to guess what God wants us to do.

3) We need constantly to remind people that our value is not defined by our paycheck. Some people have the idea that any promotion offered should be accepted, no matter the consequences on one's family or one's participation in the work of God. The church must discourage this way of thinking. I'm not saying that promotions should automatically be refused, but a very prominent place in the decision-making ought to be given to the questions: how will this affect my ability to serve God? How will this affect my ability to encourage others? Is this promotion liable to encourage me to serve Mammon?

4) We need to simplify our lives.[13] You can think of Marie Kondo here, except that I'm not sure her method—keeping only the stuff that sparks joy—lines up with Jesus' theology. I think Jesus would say that your joy ought to be sparked by the kingdom of God, not by your stuff. But anyway, getting rid of stuff,

---

13. McKnight, *The Sermon on the Mount*, 210: "Jesus summons us to simplify our lifestyle to focus on the kingdom" (italics removed).

downsizing, simplifying, will help us conform to Jesus, I believe. Not because Jesus wants us to have a tidy home, but because Jesus wants us to be less concerned with stuff, and so the less stuff we have, the more likely we are to live out Jesus' message. It's like fasting—I think one major reason we ought to renew fasting is because in our gluttonous society taking a break from food will help us squash the lust of the flesh. Likewise, in our society of hoarders, getting rid of stuff will help to free us from the tyranny of Mammon.

> Goods are given to us to be used, but not to be stored away. …But if they store it up as lasting treasure, they will spoil both the gift and themselves. The heart clings to collected treasure. Stored-up possessions get between me and God. Where my treasure is, there is my trust, my security, my comfort, my God. Treasure means idolatry.[14]

5) We need to recognize that for the most part our wealth has not come to us because we are good people. That type of idea (that wealth comes to the righteous) might make a little bit of sense if you think only about (certain parts of) America. One reason some Americans—I said *some*—are poor is because they are lazy and/or stupid. We have money because we are industrious and smart. But even if this sort of blunt analysis worked for America—the land of opportunity—it does not work the world over. Now, yes, we have money because we have worked for it and we have been smart with our money, but a much more powerful factor than either of those two things is that we have had the opportunity to accumulate wealth, and that same opportunity is not found in equal measure

---

14. Bonhoeffer, *Discipleship*, 162–63.

throughout the world. Opportunity, like wealth, is not distributed equally. I have often said that if I had been born in Haiti, my career would consist of selling bags of water on the side of the street.

Opportunity is a privilege. We live a privileged life. Our privileged lifestyle means that some people—a lot of people—can make a good living by doing nothing other than talking about sports. Not playing sports. Not running a sports franchise. But talking about sports. That's something you couldn't have done a century ago, or in many parts of the world. I feel like I can make a positive impact on this world through my preaching, teaching, and writing, but I recognize that all of my value in this area is completely dependent on my ability to know things, and I can only know things if I have access to a pretty well-stocked library, and a computer, and a comfortable office, and time to sit and think—all a product of immense privilege, the type of privilege Jesus never enjoyed, the type of privilege that I would not be able to enjoy if I lived in most other times, and in most other places. My entire career is utterly dependent on the happenstance of my birth—I was born at the right time in the right place. It's not merely—or even mostly—that I'm smart and a hard-worker. God put me in this time and location, and he expects me to make the most of it.

What I'm Not Saying

I am not prepared to say that accumulating wealth is inherently evil. Doing righteousness in front of people is not inherently evil: it depends on what our motives are (again, Matt 5:16 vs. 6:1). There is a tension to all these things. We must live with balance, and constantly calibrate our lives toward Jesus.

I don't think Jesus is telling us that it's wrong to have a savings account, or a Roth IRA or 401k. He *would* tell us that it's wrong—it's sinful—to use all this accumulated wealth on our own comfort and enjoyment. I don't see any other way to make sense out of the Parable of the Rich Man and Lazarus (Luke 16:19–31). When there are Lazaruses outside your gate, you really ought to be inviting them in for dinner. And with telecommunications and jet airplanes, there are Lazaruses all over the world that are just outside our gate. Woe to us if we hear the same message from Abraham as that rich man did: "Son, remember that during your life you received your good things, just as Lazarus received bad things, but now he is comforted here, while you are in agony" (v. 25).

One of my sons has muscular dystrophy. As I went on a mission trip to a less prosperous country a couple weeks ago, I reflected on what it would be like to raise a child with muscular dystrophy there. Every time we take our son to the doctor here, it's hard to fathom the thousands of dollars that go into those visits, paying the dozen or so medical professionals we see during the visit at the nice, modern hospital. The opportunity to meet with these highly trained professionals is a product of my own privileged position as a child of America. The average person in a less prosperous country might have no similar opportunity to meet with medical professionals. A parent of a child with muscular dystrophy might never even receive a diagnosis; they might just watch their child's muscle function slowly deteriorate. I am a rich American, and so my sick child can get care that sick kids in other parts of the world cannot even imagine exists. And I am not willing to give that up, not when the opportunity is right in front of me, and the need is so real. (And, of course, I would be able to offer my child even better medical care if I lived in Baltimore or Houston.)

So, I will take advantage of our American privilege to help my kids. And I do save for retirement. And I will buy items that make life easier. And I will constantly pray to God, asking for wisdom in how to use my money, and asking that he accept my imperfect obedience and strengthen me to do better.

Jesus wants us to recognize that no matter who we are or where we live or how much money we have, all of it comes from our Father in heaven. And we should use it all to his glory. We need to redeem our lives, jobs, families, dedicating all to God. We cut ourselves off from service to Mammon, we refuse to worry about our stuff, and we use the opportunities God presents to demonstrate our love for God and our love for others.

10

Judge Not
Matthew 7:1-12

> So whatever you wish that others would do to you, do also to them, for this is the Law and the Prophets. (Matt 7:12)

The world wants you to be judgmental. We need to know what you think about everything. That's the reason Twitter exists. That's the reason basically all social media exists. In the Dark Ages about fifteen years ago, it was very difficult to inform everyone in the world about your thoughts on stuff you know hardly anything about. Thank goodness for the internet! Now you can pontificate endlessly. Not an expert in economic policy? Or foreign relations? Or the fashion industry? Or professional football? No matter—the world has a right to know what you think about Brexit, and about that dress somebody wore to the Oscars, and about why the refs didn't call pass interference. Don't wait to learn the entire context of what you're commenting on (remember the Covington Catholic incident?), you need to get your view out there now. Please keep your opinion as shallow as possible—no room for nuance when you're working with 280 characters—and if you can make your post funny enough or harsh enough, maybe you'll make it into one of those "Twitter Reacts" stories on the *Huffington Post*.

Our supremely tolerant society is more judgmental than ever.

But we're not just talking about social media here. For a while now, TV news has been less about reporting the events of the day and much more about passing judgment (= offering a hot take) on the events of the day. Since we're supposed to have an opinion on everything, there are plenty of talking heads prepared to tell us what our opinion should be. They want to usher us into the right version of moral outrage, maybe get us to sign a petition to get somebody fired, maybe even get us to picket somebody, or join a march. It doesn't take much to engender good-ole moral outrage today. Of course, if you commit some major public transgression, there will be some appropriate outrage. But even if you just say something stupid, or what some people think is stupid, you should probably be stripped of your American citizenship and have your mouth duct-taped shut. (Ask the ~~Dixie~~ Chicks, or Roseanne Barr.)

And, of course, if anybody disagrees with your hot take, you need to tell them, "Jesus said not to judge." But be sure to say it in the most condescending way, to make it clear that you have completely missed the point of what Jesus said. (Am I being too judgmental?)

How to Judge

> Judge not, that ye be not judged. (Matt 7:1)
> Judge not according to the appearance, but judge righteous judgment. (John 7:24)

We can understand that Jesus did not literally forbid all manner of judging on our part in his famous judgment against judging in the Sermon on the Mount. First of all, that would be impossible—we cannot live life without making judgments. We have to evaluate good and bad actions in order to decide how we need to behave. That's what this entire Sermon is about, telling us how to make such judgments. Just before this statement against judging, Jesus told his audience to avoid being like the hypocrites (6:2, 5, 16)—sounds sort of judgmental. Right after this statement against judging, Jesus is going to compare certain people to dogs and swine (7:6)—sounds sort of judgmental. And then there are those statements like John 7:24 (quoted above) where Jesus actually encourages his listeners to make a certain type of judgment (a righteous one, not a wicked one). For all these reasons, we might lump Matt 7:1 in with certain other statements in the Sermon that we should not take completely literally, like the one about poking out our eyes (5:29–30) or about keeping a secret from our hand (6:3). Jesus can sometimes exaggerate for rhetorical effect (we call that "hyperbole"), just like any good speaker.

I don't mean to say that Jesus doesn't have something important to say, something we need to hear, when he warns us against judging. But we do need to think about what he means. What sort of judging is Jesus forbidding in his followers?

The answer is not that hard to decipher, and the second half of the verse helps us to see what is going on. "Judge not, that ye be not judged."

At a basic level, this proverbial wisdom works on a purely human level. No need to invoke judgment from God. If you make judgments about human behavior, people will roast you if they catch you involved in that behavior. That's why people love it when famous preachers get caught in sin—a taste of their own medicine.

We can call this concept "karma," which basically means "what goes around comes around." There is a doctrine of Karma in eastern religions, such as Buddhism and Hinduism, where it is closely tied to reincarnation. But we can also talk about a looser idea of karma (small "k") that means people often get what's coming to them. This sort of karma, this balance in the universe, is something that humans crave. This desire could be positive and hopeful: we root for the underdog who works hard. We love to see the quarterback picked in the sixth round of the NFL draft prove all the doubters wrong by leading his team to a Super Bowl victory. More often, our desire for karma is negative; when that same sixth-round quarterback ends up winning six Super Bowls, a lot of people just want to see him fail. The rich pretty-boy who seems to get everything he wants, especially when he seems like a jerk, is ripe for some negative karma. That's one reason so many people hate Christian Laettner (especially people from Kentucky—and CBS won't let us forget why).[1]

There are a lot of movies based around the premise of somebody getting what's coming to them. *The Karate Kid* pops into my mind; I love to see Daniel LaRusso kick Johnny Lawrence in the face. Or when Bob Ewell winds up dead at the end of *To Kill a Mockingbird*, we feel less pity than relief or satisfaction. Karma.

We could see Jesus as affirming this idea of karma in Matt 7:1. If you're going to be somebody who offers judgments on other people, you should be prepared to be judged any time you slip up.

---

1. If you must see it, go to YouTube and search "Christian Laettner the Shot." But also take a look at "Christian Laettner Stomp."

That's just the way life works. This is the type of thing we could read in the book of Proverbs.

That's a good lesson, but that's not necessarily what Jesus is getting at. Listen to the words of Jesus again:

> Do not judge, so that you won't be judged. For you will be judged by the same standard with which you judge others, and you will be measured by the same measure you use. (vv. 1–2)

These words could mean that people will judge you in the way that you judge others, but that's really only partially true. People often won't judge you the way you judge others. Sometimes they will, but sometimes you will be able to hide your own peccadillos from people. The #metoo movement has highlighted sexual abuse that has largely been hidden or ignored for decades. (Who are we kidding? Centuries, millennia.) I can think of examples of well-known Christian leaders (inside and outside the churches of Christ) whose sexual sins—though perhaps suspected, and even reported, during their lifetimes—became widely known only after their deaths.[2] People always judge imperfectly because they cannot possibly evaluate a situation according to all the relevant details. Only God can do that. And we trust that he will. These people who were not judged correctly during their lifetimes will not escape the judgment of God.

So, let's re-read Jesus' words. If you judge others, God will judge you. The standard you use to judge others will be the standard God uses to judge you.

---

2. Shall we name names? For an example, go to Wikipedia and look up John Howard Yoder.

Taken in this way, there is a two-fold warning here: (1) do not engage in harsh condemnation of others; (2) don't be a hypocrite.

If you engage in harsh condemnation of others, you are setting a pretty high bar for yourself, and God is going to judge you according to that same high bar.[3] You might well think better of yourself than God does. And you need to be sure to practice what you preach, or at least make sure that you don't come across as if you have everything figured out when you're condemning the behavior of others. (This is the sort of hypocrisy that we usually think about with that term, rather than the kind of hypocrisy Jesus condemns earlier, in which people do good deeds for the wrong reasons; cf. Matt 6:1.)

We have already observed that these instructions do not absolutely forbid all manner of judgment making. Jesus—our perfect example—made all kinds of judgments during his ministry. "Woe to you scribes and Pharisees, hypocrites!" (Matt 23:13–32). In this very passage in the Sermon, he tells us that we need to be able "to take the splinter out of your brother's eye" (7:5); it's just that we need to get the plank out of our own eye first. The guy that has been married five times might have something helpful to say about marriage, but really, I'd rather listen to the guy that's been married only once for fifty years. Cautionary tales can be helpful, but even more helpful is listening to those who've had success doing what we want to do. If you're a successful gardener and you want to come over to my house and criticize my garden, I'll listen to what you have to say. But if you've never planted a garden, why don't you just keep your mouth shut?

---

3. On the idea of the same measure in judgment, see Nathan Eubank, "Storing Up Treasure with God in the Heavens: Celestial Investments in Matthew 6:1–21," *Catholic Biblical Quarterly* 76 (2014): 85–86.

These verses (vv. 3-4) are really encouraging self-awareness. Understand the position you're in. Critically reflect on who you are. Do not think that you are qualified to offer an opinion on every topic, or that we want to know your opinion on every topic. To be self-aware means that you recognize your own faults. You recognize that you have faults and you know what those faults are. No, rather, you know what some of those faults are, but no doubt you have others that have not come to your attention. And be prepared for some of those faults to be thrown back in your face when you try to discuss someone's splinter with them. I'm reminded of the PSA about drugs from when I was a kid: "I learned it by watching you!"

The guy with the splinter in his eye doesn't just want the guy with the plank in his eye to leave him alone; he wants someone to help him get the splinter out of his eye. He needs someone who can see clearly. He needs someone with righteous judgment, not someone who's just going to make fun of him for having a splinter in his eye.

Some people would accuse churches of Christ of needing to hear this message from Jesus perhaps more than most. Some people think that we have a reputation for offering harsh condemnations. What should we do? We should uphold doctrine, we should warn against bad behavior, we should condemn departures from the faith, and we should always speak the truth in love, recognizing that we must imitate Jesus not only in the content of our message but in the attitude with which we present it. We know that we all stand condemned, for all have sinned and fall short of the glory of God (Rom 3:23). We rejoice that there is no condemnation for those who are in Christ Jesus (8:1), because there is nothing that can separate us from the love of Christ (8:35).

We rejoice in the extent to which God went to redeem us from judgment, so that we—the recipients of mercy—could become dispensers of mercy. We seek to embody the words of James 2:12–13:

> Speak and act as those who are to be judged by the law of freedom. For judgment is without mercy to the one who has not shown mercy. Mercy triumphs over judgment.

We cultivate a posture toward the world, and toward other religious groups, not of condemnation but of compassion, thereby imitating our Lord, who wept over Jerusalem, the city that kills the prophets (Matt 23:37).

As in many areas, C. S. Lewis gets it.

> Some of us who seem quite nice people may, in fact, have made so little use of a good heredity and a good upbringing that we are really worse than those whom we regard as fiends. Can we be quite certain how we should have behaved if we had been saddled with the psychological outfit, and then with the bad upbringing, and then with the power, say, of Himmler? That is why Christians are told not to judge. We see only the results which a man's choices make out of his raw material. But God does not judge him on the raw material at all, but on what he has done with it. Most of the man's psychological make-up is probably due to his body: when his body dies that will fall off him, and the real central man, the thing that chose, that made the best or the worst out of his material, will stand naked. All sorts of nice things which we thought our own, but which were really due to a good digestion, will fall off some of us: all sorts of nasty things which were due to complexes or bad health will fall off others. We shall then, for the first time,

see every one as he really was. There will be surprises.[4]

Pearls before Swine

I don't know if the saying in v. 6 is connected to its context or not. Scot McKnight has a whole (brief) chapter dedicated to this one verse, because he thinks it doesn't really have a context.[5] These sayings in the first half of Matthew 7 have some parallels in Luke (none in Mark), but the parallels are scattered around, suggesting maybe that the context is not all that important.

	Matthew	Luke
Don't judge	7:1–2	(6:37)
Log & splinter	7:3–5	6:41–42
Pearls before swine	7:6	--
Ask & receive	7:7–8	11:9–10
Heavenly Father responds to requests	7:9–11	11:11–13
Golden Rule	7:12	6:31

As you can see, Luke doesn't have a parallel to the "pearls before

---

4. C. S. Lewis, *Mere Christianity* (New York: Macmillan, 1952), 71–72, in book 3, ch. 4, "Morality and Psychoanalysis."
5. Scot McKnight, *The Sermon on the Mount*, Story of God Bible Commentary (Grand Rapids: Zondervan 2013), 236–40.

swine" saying. So, to interpret this verse, it doesn't do any good to look at the parallel in Luke (there's not one), and the context in Matthew probably doesn't really help either.

You've probably heard the same interpretation of this verse that I have, and I think that interpretation is correct[6]—with one caveat: this is a proverbial saying, which means that it fits into all kinds of situations. It's sort of like our proverb "the early bird gets the worm." That proverb doesn't really have a whole lot to do with birds and worms—although, yes, it does work on that literal level. But usually we're not talking about birds when we say it, we're talking about people. You need to be ready to rush into Walmart on Black Friday, because the early bird gets the worm, meaning you get the good deal on electronics if you beat other people there. You need to get to Cracker Barrel for Sunday lunch before the other churches let out, because the early bird gets the worm, meaning you're going to be waiting in the gift shop for a table if you don't get there soon enough. We could keep going.

This saying by Jesus—don't give what is holy to dogs, and don't throw your pearls before swine—is like that. It could fit into all sorts of contexts, with the basic meaning, "don't give something good to people who won't appreciate it." I remember one time in my younger days, when I had just gotten a Bible software program that could do impressive original language functions, I was showing an elder at a church, and he sort of sheepishly told me I was casting my pearls before swine, meaning he was sure this

---

6. For the usual interpretation—about not preaching the gospel to those who refuse to listen—see Jonathan T. Pennington, *The Sermon on the Mount and Human Flourishing: A Theological Commentary* (Grand Rapids: Baker, 2017), 261–62. But the *Didache* 9:5 interprets the saying in regard to withholding the Lord's Supper from the unbaptized.

program was impressive, but he didn't understand it enough to be sufficiently impressed by it. We've all been in situations like that. I can't count how many movies I've been to that were supposed to be just fantastic, profound, and all that, and I just didn't care for it, didn't get it. I guess I was a swine. I feel like that with a lot of "artsy" things—paintings, yes, but even more, poetry. Sometimes even novels—I couldn't get through *Moby Dick*, and *A Tale of Two Cities* is boring me to tears. I'm sure they're wonderful works of fiction; I'm just a swine.

But I'm sure Jesus has something more specific in mind—the gospel, or the kingdom of heaven, is a pearl (Matt 13:45–46); Jesus warns us against offering it to swine. What could that possibly mean? Who does Jesus think does not deserve the kingdom of heaven?

Jesus told a parable about a guy sowing seeds (Matt 13:3–9), and some of those seeds fell on the road, "where the birds came and devoured them." Jesus is telling us in Matthew 7:6 not to go back to that road and keep dropping seeds there. We'd just be feeding the birds. Go do something more useful. Jesus also said, "If anyone does not welcome you or listen to your words, shake the dust off your feet when you leave that house or town" (Matt 10:14).

I heard a missionary one-time stress that one soul is worth just as much as another, which is why he concentrates his missionary efforts in places that demonstrate receptivity to the gospel. He doesn't go preach the good news in places where people tend to be resistant, he goes to places where people are receptive, because he feels like he can do a lot more good, bring many more souls to God, in those places rather than in some more difficult field. It's not that he doesn't care about the people in those harder fields, but experience has taught him that some people are willing to listen, and others are not, so why beat your head against the wall trying to get some pig to wear a pearl necklace? If one soul is worth just as much as another, then you don't get bonus points for converting the "hard-to-reach" people. This same line of thinking entered my mind in November 2018 when news broke that an American missionary had been killed by the island inhabitants he was trying to convert, island inhabitants who had made it clear for decades (or centuries) that they had no interest in outsiders approaching their island. You might do a lot of good in spreading the gospel, but you probably need to go to a place where they don't shoot arrows at you as soon as you show your face. Don't cast your pearls before swine.

Ask, Seek, Knock

Jesus has already expounded on prayer in this Sermon (6:5–15). Here, we re-approach the topic by a different course.

The main point this time is that God is good, and we need to trust that fact in our prayers. God is like a father who willingly and joyfully gives to his children what they ask for. So, we should not be afraid of asking God for things. He wants to give us our desires. (I know there are issues. We'll get to them. For now, let's just go with what Jesus wants to tell us.)

God is not like the Monkey's Paw. Have you read that story, "The Monkey's Paw," written in 1902 by W. W. Jacobs? It's a great story, very creepy. The Monkey's Paw is a magic charm that grants wishes, but the wishes are always fulfilled in bad ways, like when an elderly couple wishes for $200 (or actually £200—they're British) and the next day a messenger comes from the factory where their son works to inform them that their son has been killed in an accident, but here's £200 as compensation. God is not the Monkey's Paw. When you ask for a fish, he won't give you a snake, and he won't give you a fish laced with arsenic. He doesn't want to hurt you. He loves you and wants to give you everything you need.

So, if you'll just ask, God will grant your request. This is not the only time Jesus says something like this. There's the direct parallel in Luke 11:9-13, but then there are also verses like Mark 14:24 ("everything you pray and ask for—believe that you have received it and it will be yours") and John 14:14 ("If you ask me anything in my name, I will do it") and 15:16 ("whatever you ask the Father in my name, he will give you"). The letter of James acknowledges that sometimes it doesn't work out this way, sometimes prayers are not answered, and James offers a couple possible reasons: maybe the guy doing the praying doesn't really believe (James 1:5-8) or maybe he has evil motives (4:3). But James insists that prayer does work: "The effectual fervent prayer of a righteous man availeth much" (5:16).

Anytime we think about these passages that seem to indicate that God will always give us what we ask for in prayer, we need to remember that Jesus asked three times for "this cup to pass from me" (Matt 26:39), and he knew very well he was going to have to drink the cup (Matt 20:22-23), and indeed the cup did not pass from him. Paul prayed three times for his thorn in the flesh to be taken away, and the reply came back, "My grace is sufficient for you" (2 Cor 12:8-9).

Once again, it seems like Jesus is saying things in the Sermon that we cannot take absolutely literally, or perhaps we should say that we can't press his meaning too far. The fact is, not everything we pray for are we going to get, and Jesus and Paul are exhibits A and B for that. And you know what? If we think about Jesus' analogy to fathers and children, I would want to offer a little nuance there. I say no to my kids all the time. My son Marvin likes to ask every morning when he gets up whether he can watch a movie. He hasn't figured out yet that we watch TV in the morning only on one day a week, Saturday; or he hasn't figured out which day is Saturday, so he just asks every day.[7] Most days I say, "No, this isn't Saturday, it's a school day." So, when he asks for a movie, I give him schoolwork. But I don't do that because I'm cruel, I do it because I love him.

Or some of my other kids will ask to start a TV show when it's almost bedtime, or they'll ask to go to Chick-Fil-A when we have other plans, or they'll ask me to play a game when I have to go to work … and I have no trouble turning down all of these requests from my children. And none of my denials arise from any contempt for my children, or because I just don't care.

There are also many, many times, when my kids ask me for something, and I respond positively. If they ask about an hour before bedtime to watch a show, I usually say, "sure." If they ask me to help them with something, I will often help. When they ask me to play something with them, I do, and we have fun.

Jesus talks about a kid asking for bread and a fish. I'm not sure why a kid would want a fish except to eat it, and surely that's what he's going to do with the bread. The examples Jesus uses are not about having fun—they're about the basic necessities of life. In such a situation, when the kid is hungry, the father is not going to be harmful, by giving a stone or snake to eat. (Presumably ancient

---

7. Since I first wrote these words in Spring 2019, Marvin has stopped asking about TV every morning. :)

Jews did not indulge in "snake surprise.") There are sometimes that the kid will ask for a steak, and the father will give a piece of bread, and there are other times that the kid will ask for a piece of bread, and the father will give a steak.

This passage in the Sermon, then, doesn't teach that you're going to get everything you ask for. It seems to say that, I admit, but it can't mean that, both because that line of thought does not fit reality and because it doesn't fit with Jesus' own experience, as we have seen.

What this passage really emphasizes, then, is the goodness of God. That's the point (v. 11). Jesus is like a good earthly father, except even better. I completely identify with McKnight when he says that he doesn't really understand why God seems often not to answer our prayers, but his own response is to "focus on who God is, and I continue to lay my petitions before that God in faith, trust, and hope."[8] I trust that even when God doesn't give me what I ask for, God loves me and has both the power and the desire to make things work out in a way better than my requests (Rom 8:28).

> Now to him who is able to do immeasurably more than all we ask or imagine, according to his power that is at work within us, to him be glory in the church and in Christ Jesus throughout all generations, for ever and ever! Amen (Eph 3:20–21).

The Golden Rule

This verse forms a nice conclusion to a passage that began with the warning, "Judge not lest ye be judged." The Golden Rule states the

---

8. McKnight, *The Sermon on the Mount*, 246.

exact opposite: judge people the way you would want to be judged by people.

I'm sure you already know that this maxim is not original with Jesus. All kinds of societies, maybe every society, have had a version of the Golden Rule (as Wikipedia's "Golden Rule" article documents). It is reported about Aristotle that he was asked "how we should behave to friends," and his answer was, "as we should wish them to behave to us."[9] There are a few versions of the Golden Rule in Judaism (see, e.g., Tobit 4:15), including one associated with Rabbi Hillel, the most famous rabbi from the time of Jesus' childhood.[10] Pennington notes that the final appeal to drivers on the State of Kentucky Department of Motor Vehicles' driving course is "treat other drivers as you would want to be treated."[11]

This teaching isn't new or revolutionary, and, according to C.S. Lewis, that was the point.

> The first thing to get clear about Christian morality between man and man is that in this department Christ did not come to preach any brand-new morality. The Golden Rule of the New Testament (Do as you would be done by) is a summing up of what everyone, at bottom, had always known to be right. Really great moral teachers never do introduce new moralities: it is quacks and cranks who do that. As Dr. Johnson said,

---

9. As reported in the third-century AD Greek writer Diogenes Laertius, *Lives of Eminent Philosophers* 5.21, trans. R. D. Hicks, Loeb Classical Library (Cambridge, MA: Harvard University Press, 1925), 465. A yet more ancient version of this saying from Greece is attributed to Maeandrius, briefly tyrant of Samos, in Herodotus, *Histories* 3.142.

10. The story appears in the Babylonian Talmud, *Shabbat* 31a.

11. Pennington, *The Sermon on the Mount and Human Flourishing*, 266.

"People need to be reminded more often than they need to be instructed." The real job of every moral teacher is to keep bringing us back, time after time, to the old simple principles which we are all so anxious not to see; like bringing a horse back and back to the fence it has refused to jump or bringing a child back and back to the bit in its lesson that it wants to shirk.[12]

But the ubiquity of this moral precept does not make it easy to fulfill. We much prefer holding people to different, inconsistent standards; we like to overlook or minimize our own faults while expressing shock and dismay at the faults of others. This sort of thing is especially hard to avoid in a fight with—for example—one's spouse. In such a situation, we take great offense whenever our spouse even slightly misrepresents our actions or motives, and we also take great offense whenever our spouse is annoyed by our gross exaggerations of our spouse's behavior. "You know what I meant!"

But according to the Golden Rule, "The entire will of God is about learning to love others, or to treat others, the way we treat ourselves!"[13] All the Law and the Prophets boil down to this point, just as later Jesus will say that the summation of everything is to love God and love others (Matt 22:34–40). Miss this point, and you miss everything. Fail here, and you show that you just don't know what it means to follow Jesus.

---

12. Lewis, *Mere Christianity*, 64. This is the opening paragraph of Book 3, Chapter 3, "Social Morality."
13. McKnight, *The Sermon on the Mount*, 252.

Conclusion

The way we usually think is: "I'm going to treat you the way you treat me." Scripture has already revealed to us what faulty thinking that is (Prov 24:29). Jesus wants us to think: "I'm going to treat you the way I wish you would treat me." That's an enormous difference. It's a difference that amounts to what Christianity is all about. Avoid the hot take; don't harshly condemn people and stop thinking that you need to offer a judgment on everything. When people fail, think about how you would like to be treated in their situation. And then do it. (Easier said than done.) We can be thankful to Jesus. He just cut out three quarters of the time we devote to social media.

11

THE WAY OF LIFE
MATTHEW 7:13-23

Yes, there are two paths you can go by, but in the long run, there's still time to change the road you're on.

Or so Robert Plant claims, and, of course, he's right. There are two paths that you can go by, and, if you're reading this, there is still time to change the road you're on.

Jesus talks about the two paths here at the end of the Sermon on the Mount (Matt 7:13–14). Actually, the whole Sermon is about the two paths. There is the way of Greater Righteousness (5:20), and there is the way of hypocrisy. There's the path of obeying God from the heart and the path of obeying God only externally. The one path leads to reward from God, the other path leads to reward from people. One path promises heavenly treasure, the other path promises earthly treasure.

One path leads to life; the other path leads to destruction.

The Biblical Context

Jesus sounds here like an Old Testament prophet (he often sounds like an Old Testament prophet); the prophets routinely called people away from the path leading to destruction toward the path leading to God. Samuel told the Israelites that he would show them "the good and straight path" (1 Sam 12:23).

The greatest of the prophets presented these words to Israel just before his death:

> See, today, I have set before you life and prosperity, death and adversity. For I am commanding you today to love the LORD your God, to walk in his ways, and to keep his commands, statutes, and ordinances, so that you may live and multiply, and the LORD your God may bless you in the land you are entering to possess. ... I call heaven and earth as witnesses against you today that I have set before you life and death, blessing and curse. Choose life so that you and your descendants may live, love the LORD your God, obey him, and remain faithful to him. For he is your life, and he will prolong your days as you live in the land the LORD swore to give to your fathers Abraham, Isaac, and Jacob. (Deut 30:15–20)

Moses' successor Joshua encouraged the Israelites similarly as his own death approached: "Choose this day whom you will serve... but as for me and my house, we will serve the LORD" (Josh 24:15). The entire book of Proverbs is based on the notion of a path of wisdom leading to life, and a path of folly leading to death. The book of Psalms begins by presenting the two paths, "for the LORD watches over the way of the righteous, but the way of the wicked leads to ruin" (Psa 1:6).

Entering through the Narrow Gate

While these Old Testament passages have a great deal in common with Jesus in the Sermon on the Mount, Jesus does say something that these other passages don't: the way leading to life is narrow and difficult, while the way leading to destruction is wide and easy.

© Tim Graves, Dog Mountain, Washington

© Eric Muhr, Tamanawas Falls, Oregon

© Azzedine Rouichi, Bülach, Switzerland

The difficulty of the life-giving path was not something that Moses mentioned, or Joshua. In fact, the Old Testament associates the way of life with prosperity so closely that a reader might get the impression that the way of life is the easier path. But a little more thought will probably dispel that notion. The Old Testament frequently encourages readers to follow the way of life, which seems to imply that there is something very attractive about the way to death. Some Old Testament passages come closer than others to highlighting this aspect of the two paths: in Proverbs 1, the gang members make their lifestyle look very attractive to a young man at first (Prov 1:8–19), and later Lady Folly attracts the unsuspecting boy (9:13–18), just as the "strange woman" does (7:6–23).

Jesus says it more bluntly than others: the way of life is narrow and hard; few people find it. Most people go by the wide and easy path that leads to destruction. The easy path is the way of the hypocrites with their skin-deep righteousness. The difficult and unpopular path is that of the transformed life with the heart fully committed to God.

Jesus invites us to follow him on the path toward life. "Life" in the Gospels is another way of talking about the kingdom of God/heaven. In fact, the Gospel of John hardly ever mentions the kingdom of God (only John 3:3, 5), but it talks a lot about life (5:24–29), which amounts to largely the same thing. The Synoptic Gospels (Matthew, Mark, and Luke) talk about the kingdom of God quite a bit, but they also make it clear that the same concept can be labeled "life" (cf. Matt 18:3–4, 8–9) or "eternal life" (19:16; cf. vv. 23–24) or being "saved" (19:25). The path toward life is the path toward God's reign.

There are a couple other aspects of this saying that deserve some reflection.

Are Only a Few People Going To Be Saved?
One-time Jesus was asked this exact question (Luke 13:23). Jesus's reply: "Strive to enter through the narrow door. For many, I tell you, will seek to enter and will not be able" (v. 24). In other words, Jesus answered this question by quoting himself, the words he spoke in the Sermon on the Mount about the narrow gate, when he had said that "few find it."

So, yes, only a few will be saved. "The disciples are few and will always be only a few. This word of Jesus cuts off any false hope of their effectiveness. Disciples should never invest their trust in numbers."[1]

This idea is consistent with some other things Jesus says, particularly the Parable of the Sower (Matt 13:1–23). As that story is told, think about how much seed is scattered and how many fruitful plants result. The parable doesn't necessarily correspond perfectly to actual farming (hopefully farming would be a little more successful), but the way Jesus tells the story makes it sound like there's quite a bit of wasted seed. A lot of people either ignore the proclamation of the gospel, or initially receive it gladly but eventually fall away. Either way, there is no fruit.

But, a couple of points offer nuance about what Jesus says in the Sermon. First, "few" is a relative term. The number of the saved is represented differently in Revelation 7. In that chapter, John the Revelator reports that he heard about 144,000 "servants of our God" with the seal of God on their foreheads (vv. 3–8), but, of course, the number 144,000 is just symbolic (= 12,000 from each of the 12 tribes of Israel). When John turns to look at these servants

---

1. Dietrich Bonhoeffer, *Discipleship*, DBWE 4 (Minneapolis: Fortress, 2001), 175–76.

of God, he saw "a vast multitude from every nation, tribe, people, and language, which no one could number" (v. 9). This chapter cautions us from attaching a number to the saved.

Second, "few" is not the point of Jesus' statement. He's not trying to tell us how many will be saved, he's trying to tell us that you need to pay attention, put forth some effort, make sure you're on the right path. Don't just follow the crowd, because the crowd is headed for destruction. Don't just do what seems easy, because that way leads to destruction. Don't just do what the hypocrites do, because that way leads to destruction. Rather, the hard way of Jesus is the way that leads to life. How many people actually follow Jesus is not the relevant point. The relevant point is that following Jesus is not a cakewalk, and it's not the popular choice.

Is the Way of Jesus Hard Or Easy?

A few chapters, hence, Matthew will present these words of Jesus: "my yoke is easy and my burden is light" (11:30). So, which is it? Is it easy or hard to follow Jesus?

Let's take a moment to notice that—as far as I remember— basically everything in the Gospels (except for Matt 11:30) shows Jesus describing discipleship as difficult; nothing easy about it. Remember this one?

> If anyone wants to follow after me, let him deny himself, take up his cross, and follow me. For whoever wants to save his life will lose it, but whoever loses his life because of me will find it. (Matt 16:24–25)

Or this one?

> Behold, I am sending you out like sheep among wolves. ... You will be hated by everyone because of my name. (10:16–25)

And later in the same chapter:

> And whoever does not take his cross and follow me is not worthy of me. Whoever finds his life will lose it, and whoever loses his life for my sake will find it. (10:38–39)

Early in the Sermon on the Mount, Jesus had called "fortunate" the one who is "persecuted for the sake of righteousness, for theirs is the kingdom of heaven" (5:10). We remember what he said to the Rich Young Ruler about giving away his stuff (19:21), or to James and John about drinking the cup (of suffering; 20:20–23), which then led to a little speech about how followers of Jesus should imitate their master in terms of service and sacrifice (20:25–28).

The way of Jesus is hard, because he calls us to imitate *him*. The whole Sermon has emphasized the hard way of greater righteousness. As Bonhoeffer put it, "To give witness to and to confess the truth of Jesus, but to love the enemy of this truth, who is his enemy and our enemy, with the unconditional love of Jesus Christ—that is a narrow road."[2]

So, what does Jesus mean that his yoke is easy? I appreciate the words of Thomas Long, who points out that to those who are weary and heavy-laden, "What Jesus offers ... is not a hammock, but a yoke."[3] Long goes on to explain that the yoke of Jesus "is the way of God, and it is profoundly satisfying to the human soul."

---

2. Bonhoeffer, *Discipleship*, 176.
3. Thomas G. Long, *Matthew*, Westminster Bible Commentary (Louisville: WJK, 1997), 132.

What I get out of that is that the yoke of Jesus is the path of life, and the alternative path leads to destruction. Jesus might lead us through a narrow gate and on a rough path, but life is easier than destruction. Any path—no matter how rough—leading to a beach is going to be easier to our soul than any path—no matter how wide and smooth—leading to Siberia. Our knowledge of the destination affects fundamentally the easiness of the path—all the more so since Jesus walks the path ahead of us. This is all very similar to what we find in Proverbs, where the path of wisdom is always easier and more joyful than the path of folly, no matter how much more attractive folly might seem.

Bonhoeffer describes it this way:

> Bearing the cross does not bring misery and despair. Rather, it provides refreshment and peace for our souls; it is our greatest joy. Here we are no longer laden with self-made laws and burdens, but with the yoke of him who knows us and who himself goes with us under the same yoke. Under his yoke we are assured of his nearness and communion. It is he himself whom disciples find when they take up their cross.[4]

But a few pages earlier in the same chapter, Bonhoeffer writes probably his most-quoted words:

> [The cross] is laid on every Christian. The first Christ-suffering that everyone has to experience is the call which summons us away from our attachments to this world. It is the death of the old self in the encounter with Jesus Christ. Those who enter into discipleship enter into Jesus' death. They turn

---

4. Bonhoeffer, *Discipleship*, 91.

their living into dying; such has been the case from the very beginning. The cross is not the terrible end of a pious, happy life. Instead, it stands at the beginning of community with Jesus Christ. Whenever Christ calls us, his call leads us to death.[5]

The last bit in the older English translation by R. H. Fuller is justly famous: "When Christ calls a man, he bids him come and die."[6]

There is a tension here (as in many aspects of the Christian life) between joy and suffering, life and death. We see Paul living out this tension, as he exclaims on the one hand that he himself has been crucified with Christ (Gal 2:20), while, on the other hand, the second thing that comes to his mind when he thinks about the fruit of the Spirit is joy (Gal 5:22).

Good and Bad Trees

Jesus imagines that the community of disciples will be targeted by false prophets, "who come to you in sheep's clothing but inwardly are ravaging wolves" (v. 15). Later in the Gospel, he will warn about "false messiahs and false prophets [who] will perform great signs and wonders to lead astray, if possible, even the elect" (24:24).

Moses had warned about false prophets also. According to Deuteronomy, the way to spot a false prophet is if his prediction

---

5. Bonhoeffer, *Discipleship*, 87.
6. This older English translation has been reprinted many times. I own this edition: Dietrich Bonhoeffer, *The Cost of Discipleship* (New York: Touchstone, 2018), 89. Bonhoeffer's original German runs: "Jeder Ruf Christi führt in den Tod."

doesn't come true (Deut 18:22) or if he tells the people to worship other gods, even if he is able to perform signs and wonders (13:1–5).

According to Jesus, you can spot a false prophet by his fruit. What kind of fruit are we talking about here? Since Jesus isn't at all specific about the fruit, I guess we can say that the fruit is any kind of outcome from the prophet's ministry. Maybe, like the prophets in Deuteronomy 13, someone will try to get you to compromise the standards of Jesus, to stray off the narrow path and get on the wide path. Or, maybe the prophet's own life will not line up with the standards of Jesus. That is, maybe he'll say all the right things—he'll tell you to give alms secretly (6:2–4)—but he'll talk about the big donations he makes to charity, claiming that he can thereby set a good example for others. Maybe he'll tell you to watch out for lust (5:27–30), but he himself has reached such an exalted level of spirituality that the same rules do not apply to him.

Of course, none of our lives line up with the standards of Jesus, not all the way. So, it may occur to us that we ourselves are the false prophets about whom Jesus warns. I don't think that needs to be our concern. The way Jesus presents them ("ravaging wolves"), they know exactly what they're doing. Those who are trying to follow Jesus from the heart, though they be not perfect, cannot be considered ravaging wolves seeking to take advantage of the gullible disciples. The ravaging wolves aren't really trying to follow the way of Jesus.

Surprising Judgment

The idea that some people may be false prophets, appearing as holy men but not leading holy lives, leads naturally to a consideration of the surprising judgment in store for some. At least, Jesus speaks as if the people being judged will be surprised (similar at Matt 25:31–46). Maybe this is just for rhetorical effect. Pennington suggests that they are not really surprised at their fate; they were just trying to justify themselves (7:22).[7]

But it may be surprising to us to read about people who are able to "prophesy in your name, drive out demons in your name, and do many miracles in your name" but who do not know Jesus. How could they do all these powerful works—obviously granted by the Spirit of God—without having a real relationship with Jesus?

It's actually not that uncommon in the Bible. Take Samson as an example (Judg 13–16). He was empowered by God's Spirit to do all kinds of things, and he mostly abused that power to glorify himself. He was certainly not a model of piety, an example of the moral life. I'm not saying that we won't see Samson in heaven, but I am saying that the stories told about him are at least as often examples of what not to do as they are examples of what to do.

Or, think about the Corinthian church. They were able to do amazing things by God's Spirit, things like speaking in tongues and prophesying (1 Cor 12, 14). But Paul does not tell the Corinthian Christians that their empowerment to perform such works proves that they are living in harmony with God's will. Actually, just the opposite. Paul brings up the spiritual gifts enjoyed by the Corinthians in order to criticize them for how they are abusing those gifts, using those gifts for their own glory.

C. S. Lewis describes this type of person:

---

7. Jonathan T. Pennington, *The Sermon on the Mount and Human Flourishing: A Theological Commentary*, (Grand Rapids: Baker, 2017), 279.

> How is it that people who are quite obviously eaten up with Pride can say they believe in God and appear to themselves very religious? I am afraid it means they are worshipping an imaginary God. They theoretically admit themselves to be nothing in the presence of this phantom God, but are really all the time imagining how He approves of them and thinks them far better than ordinary people: that is, they pay a pennyworth of imaginary humility to Him and get out of it a pound's worth of Pride towards their fellow-men. I suppose it was of those people Christ was thinking when He said that some would preach about Him and cast out devils in His name, only to be told at the end of the world that He had never known them. And any of us may at any moment be in this death-trap. Luckily, we have a test. Whenever we find that our religious life is making us feel that we are good—above all, that we are better than someone else—I think we may be sure that we are being acted on, not by God, but by the devil.[8]

There are other examples of people being able to perform apparently supernatural works or being able to prophesy, without actually having a close relationship with Jesus: the Egyptian magicians (Exod 7:11, 22; 8:7; cf. 8:19); Balaam (Num 23–24); the false prophets (mentioned above) about whom Jesus warned (Matt 24:24); Caiaphas (John 1:51); the Man of Lawlessness (2 Thess 2:9–10); the Earth Beast who performs wonders in order to get the world to worship the Sea Beast (Rev 13:11–15). Of course, not all of these people are performing their works by God's Spirit, but some of them are. Luke actually tells a story about some Jewish

---

8. C. S. Lewis, *Mere Christianity* (New York: Macmillan, 1952), 96, in book 3, ch. 8, "The Great Sin."

exorcists who drive out demons—or try to—in the name of Jesus (Acts 19:23-26), just as the people in Matthew 7:22 claim. We remember that Cornelius, even before he was baptized, enjoyed some spiritual gifts (Acts 10:44-48).

We need to note carefully that these amazing works are not the fruit that reveals the true follower of Jesus. When the people in Matthew 7:22 recite such accomplishments, Jesus is completely unimpressed. "Not everyone who says to me, 'Lord, Lord,' will enter the kingdom of heaven, but only the one who does the will of my Father in heaven" (7:21). Jesus is talking about the teachings of the Sermon; those are the things that characterize "the will of my Father in heaven." Jesus has not been telling people in the Sermon that they need to learn to speak in tongues, or they need to drive out demons, or prophesy. He's been telling them that they need to obey God from the heart. People who do that—regardless of the amazing spiritual gifts that they display—will enter the kingdom of heaven. But to the people who do not follow Jesus' teaching in the Sermon, "I will announce to them, 'I never knew you. Depart from me, you lawbreakers'" (7:23).

Conclusion

The Sermon on the Mount presents to us two different paths. The Bible as a whole presents to us two different paths. There is the way of following God not only with our hearts and minds, but with our actions, and there is the way of destruction. "I have set before you life and death, blessing and curse" (Deut 30:19). "Choose you this day whom ye will serve," which path you'll take. There's still time to change the road you're on.

12

A Solid Foundation
Matthew 7:24-27

When the tempest passes, the wicked are no more, but the righteous are established forever. (Prov 10:25)

About 50 miles west of Florence, Italy, there sits on the coast of the Mediterranean Sea what I would consider a fairly large city of about 100,000 people, the city of Pisa, whose history stretches back hundreds of years before Christ. Here lives the Roman Catholic Archbishop of Pisa—currently Giovanni Paolo Benotto—in a Cathedral constructed over the half-century between 1063 and 1118. Work on a bell tower for the cathedral began in 1173 and progressed in stages over the next two centuries. But already in 1178, when the builders reached the second floor of the tower, they noticed that it had begun to lean because of an inadequate foundation set in unstable soil. The builders tried to compensate somewhat by making the rooms taller on one side of the tower. The addition of the seventh floor in 1319 finally allowed for the installation of the bell-chamber in 1372. Today, the Leaning Tower of Pisa is nearly 186 feet tall on one side, and just over 183 feet tall on the other.

Nearly 900 years after construction began on the Pisa Cathedral, a tower was unveiled at the 1962 World's Fair in Seattle. The Space Needle stands 605 ft. tall, more than 3 times the height of Pisa's Tower, no matter which side you measure. Its foundation is somewhat more stable than that of the Pisa Tower, consisting of 6000 tons of concrete poured by 467 trucks into a hole measuring 30 feet deep by 120 feet across. It can withstand earthquakes measuring up to a magnitude of 9.[1]

The image of a building's foundation provides a good illustration for the importance of Jesus' words. We can probably think of several examples of good or bad foundations. My favorite coffee mug is one with a really wide base because it's harder to tip over onto my computer. We can probably also think of plenty of examples of people that have either a great foundation in their lives—they know how to get along in life—or a poor foundation. When small-time criminals appear before judges for sentencing, the judge often wants to know whether this criminal has a network of people in place (family members, friends) who can help the person stay on the strait and narrow. Many, many people lack this basic kind of foundation. There's an enormous industry geared toward helping people establish a foundation in their life, whether we're talking about Dr. Phil or Joel Osteen or Matt Foley.

The way of life that Jesus has presented in the Sermon on the Mount is a hard way, a strait and narrow way. But it also provides the only foundation to protect against a great crash bringing everything to ruin.

---

1. Go to YouTube and look at the brief video, "Space Needle Fun Facts."

The Coming Storm

Let's start at the end. The houses of both the wise man and the foolish man face a violent storm, but only one of the houses survives. The house built on sand "fell, and great was the fall of it" (Matt 7:27). It's easy to see the destruction of this house within the world of the parable—it's something similar to our saying about castles made of sand.

But what is the real-life application? What kind of "fall" is Jesus thinking about? We could give this a very immediate application: people who don't build their lives on the teachings of Jesus will suffer in this world. Their lives will fall apart. After all, we often talk about "the storms of life," by which we mean stressful times of life, like the loss of a job, or marriage trouble, or national crises, or pandemics. In these times we need to be secure in the foundation of Jesus to help us stand firm through the storm. The person who is not anchored in Jesus (to change the metaphor a little bit) will not weather the storm as securely as the man whose house is built on rock.

That might be what Jesus means, but I doubt it. After all, in this Sermon Jesus has told us that his way is hard and the other way is easy (7:13–14), that followers of Jesus can expect persecution (5:10–12), whereas people who reject his teaching will seek out (and receive!) praise from men (6:1–18). What makes it worthwhile for the follower of Jesus is the reward he or she has laid up in heaven. Following Jesus is not about making your life easier, making your life better so that you can weather the storms of life. Jesus is interested in getting you ready for the kingdom of heaven. Remember the words of John the Baptist:

> Who warned you to flee from the coming wrath? Therefore produce fruit in keeping with repentance. ... The one who is coming after me is more powerful than I am. ... His winnowing shovel is in his hand, and he will clear his threshing floor and gather his wheat into the barn. But the chaff he will burn with unquenchable fire. (Matt 3:7–12)

The message of the New Testament is that "the wrath of God is coming on the sons of disobedience" (Eph 5:6). Paul made it a part of his initial preaching to talk to people about "the coming wrath" (1 Thess 1:10). That's where he is aiming in his sermon on Mars Hill; he wants those Athenian pagans to know that God "has set a day when he is going to judge the world in righteousness" (Acts 17:31). Only those who "have now been declared righteous by the blood" of Christ "will be saved through him from wrath" (Rom 5:9).

A day of judgment is coming (cf. 2 Cor 5:10; Matt 25:31–46), but those who dedicate their lives to Jesus' teaching will survive the storm. When the house of the foolish man goes splat, that's not something that happens in this life. In the present age, the foolish man is often honored and secure, like the rich fool of Luke 12:16–21 or the rich man of Luke 16:19–31. But the storm is coming, the wrath of God is coming, and neither riches nor reputation will provide any protection, but only the blood of Jesus, only following in his way. That way provides a sure foundation, but the house built on sand will not survive God's wrath.

Doing

The wise man and the foolish man both hear Jesus' words. The difference is that only one of them actually lives according to Jesus' teaching. For us to have a solid foundation for our lives, the point is to do what Jesus says, not simply to familiarize ourselves with what he says. Reading the Bible is a foolish pastime unless we commit ourselves to living out what we read. According to Jesus, a person who reads the Bible and does not put its teachings into practice is a fool. The foundation is only helpful once you pour the concrete, not when you read up about how to mix concrete.

Jesus' brother put it this way:

> But be doers of the word and not hearers only, deceiving yourselves. Because if anyone is a hearer of the word and not a doer, he is like someone looking at his own face in a mirror. For he looks at himself, goes away, and immediately forgets what kind of person he was. But the one who looks intently into the perfect law of freedom and perseveres in it, and is not a forgetful hearer but a doer who works—this person will be blessed in what he does. (James 1:22–25)

This is in part a maturity issue: coming to understand that the things Jesus said should really affect every facet of our lives. The lifestyle Jesus lays out in the Sermon is difficult, and we tend to resist parts of it. Usually you have to tell your kids certain things a thousand times before they actually do it, whether we're talking about cleaning their room or cleaning behind their ears or sharing with their siblings. Mostly they fail to practice what you preach because they haven't grown enough to understand which way is the better way. But eventually they get there (hopefully).

This is in part a trust issue: sometimes it's hard to trust that the hard way of Jesus is really going to turn out better than the easier way of vengeance, or lust, or showing off, or self-reliance. Football coaches deal with this lack of trust all the time. It's not that the player would actually say, "I don't trust you, Coach," but in the moment of the game, the player must fight his own bad instincts and do what the coach has told him to do.

I played on the offensive line for our high school team, and some of my most vivid memories of playing are the mistakes I made because I didn't trust the coach. In one of the final games of my career, we called a certain pass play that required me to block the man in front of me—or, if there was no one directly in front of me, to pull out and block the guy coming off the edge. The problem was that the whole game there had been a guy directly in front of me, so I got used to just blocking him, and we really hadn't practiced very much throughout the week the situation in which I had to pull and block the guy off the edge, because we knew this team usually lined up with a guy directly across from me. Well, on this play—you know what happened. I got to the line, and there was no one across from me. I started thinking, "Oh, great! What am I supposed to do now? I think I'm supposed to pull, but maybe I should hang out here for a second just to make sure nobody comes through my gap." And that's what I did; I did not do what the coach had told me to do, because I was worried it wouldn't work out the way he had said. What if the guy doesn't come off the edge? What if someone tries to come through my gap? Fortunately, our quarterback threw a touchdown pass on that play, and he released the ball right before the guy off the edge took him down. As our team reviewed the game film the following week, the coach replayed that particular play over and over so that the team could relive this glorious touchdown pass that had won the game for us, but the tape also clearly showed me pausing too long in my spot and then flailing hopelessly trying to block the guy off the edge. While everyone rejoiced, I hung my head in shame. There's a reason football coaches constantly preach execution. They want their teams not just to listen but to do, to execute.

Jesus told a parable:

> "What do you think? A man had two sons. And he went to the first and said, 'Son, go and work in the vineyard today.' And he answered, 'I will not,' but afterward he changed his mind and went. And he went to the other son and said the same. And he answered, 'I go, sir,' but did not go. Which of the two did the will of his father?"
>
> They said, "The first."
>
> Jesus said to them, "Truly, I say to you, the tax collectors and the prostitutes go into the kingdom of God before you. For John came to you in the way of righteousness, and you did not believe him, but the tax collectors and the prostitutes believed him. And even when you saw it, you did not afterward change your minds and believe him." (Matt 21:28–32)

It's not what you say, it's what you do. The tax collectors and prostitutes are going to enter the kingdom of God because they actually changed their lives at the preaching of John the Baptist. When John preached repentance (Matt 3:2), the tax collectors and prostitutes are the one who repented. The so-called righteous people turned out to have only skin-deep righteousness. They were hypocrites, talking about love of God but refusing to obey God's Son.

Actions speak louder than words. The foundation of our lives is laid by actions, by actually doing what Jesus says.

Hearing

There are many people who did not hear and have not heard Jesus' words. Before you can do, you must hear. We in churches of Christ have traditionally emphasized "hearing" as an essential element in the process of salvation, the first step in receiving God's grace, and that emphasis agrees with Scripture: "So faith comes from hearing, and hearing through the word of Christ." (Rom 10:17). The Old Testament stresses the importance of hearing. The Greatest Command—recited twice daily by Jews in the time of Jesus (as also today)—begins: "Hear O Israel..." (Deut 6:4; cf. Mark 12:29).

This concluding section of the Sermon on the Mount is directed at people who have heard the entire Sermon, so Jesus' "invitation" at the end of his Sermon is for people to do what he has just said. But it is not out of step with what Jesus says here to stress that this parable about the wise and foolish builders also suggests the importance—the necessity—of hearing.

For Jesus' original audience, that meant listening to him. For us, it means studying Scripture. I think Joel Green correctly diagnosed the church's great problem as biblical illiteracy and theological amnesia.[2] Christians all around us are turning away from Scripture because the Bible is boring and theology is too hard and you don't

---

2. Joel B. Green, *Practicing Theological Interpretation: Engaging Biblical Texts for Faith and Formation* (Grand Rapids: Baker, 2011), 75.

really have to know all that stuff to be like Jesus, you just have to love people where they are, and didn't Jesus reserve his harshest condemnation for the Bible experts, anyway?! Well, I guess all of those points are true in a certain sense, but it's going to be hard to imitate Jesus if we refuse to listen to his words, and those words are found now in Scripture. As people around us turn away from (so-called) boring and irrelevant theological discussions, we should give increased attention to the words of Scripture, to meditating on those words, to discussing those words with other believers.

Note the familiar affirmation of Paul:

> All scripture is given by inspiration of God, and is profitable for doctrine, for reproof, for correction, for instruction in righteousness: That the man of God may be perfect, thoroughly furnished unto all good works. (2 Tim 3:16–17)

God has given us Scripture to form us into the people he wants us to be. Scripture trains us, corrects us, reproves us, instructs us, perfects us. If Scripture is boring and irrelevant, then so is God. So is Jesus.

On the contrary, far from being irrelevant…

> …the word of God is living and active, sharper than any two-edged sword, piercing to the division of soul and of spirit, of joints and of marrow, and discerning the thoughts and intentions of the heart. (Heb 4:12)

I think "piercing" is a spot-on description of the Sermon on the Mount, for instance, but not just the Sermon. You read much of

Scripture, and really pay attention to what it says, and it will pierce you.

That's not to say that it's easy. There is much of the Bible that is just downright difficult to understand. Oh, the book of Ezekiel, for instance, or many parts of Isaiah. A lot of people would cite Revelation as a particularly difficult book. Honestly, I get lost in Romans; it's hard for me to keep tracking along with Paul in that letter, since he seems to be going in a lot of different directions. And then some of the things that Jesus said just puzzle me to no end. I'm not sure what point he was trying to make with the Parable of the Unrighteous Steward (Luke 16:1–8). People in Jesus' own day struggled with the meaning of some of his sayings: "This is a hard saying; who can understand it?" (John 6:60). Jesus actually said that the reason he spoke in parables sometimes was to conceal his meaning from people, to make his meaning harder to comprehend. "That is why I speak to them in parables, because looking they do not see, and hearing they do not listen or understand" (Matt 13:13). I think what he meant by that is that he's trying to make people work for it; the people who really want to understand, the people who are really spiritually attuned, the people who are seeking first the kingdom of God, will meditate on his words and discover their meaning. But he's not going to cast his pearls before swine (cf. Matt 7:6–7).

Just because it's hard doesn't mean it's irrelevant. The basics are easy. If all we're trying to do is learn how to receive God's grace, then Scripture lays that out for us pretty clearly, and we have traditionally boiled Scriptural teaching on that subject down to the even easier five-step plan: hear, believe, repent, confess, be baptized. But that's kindergarten Christianity; I don't mean to say it's wrong, any more than what we learn in kindergarten about colors and shapes is wrong. But it is basic, and there is more to learn (Heb 5:11–6:3). Algebra and calculus build upon simpler math that we learn when we are young; not many of us need algebra and calculus for our careers, but just because they're hard doesn't mean they're irrelevant. Advanced mathematics is clearly relevant to the world we live in, although not every single person needs to know about it.

I suppose it's the same with the Bible. The only people who need to worry about what Scripture means are the people who care about learning the will of God.

Practical Tips for Bible Study

These tips are completely personal to me. What I mean by that is that these are not "the right tips" that are superior to any other set of Bible reading tips. These are just the ones that have occurred to me. On the other hand, I do think that following these tips is (1) pretty do-able for most folks (i.e., these do not require a PhD in theology) and (2) rewarding—they actually work; you will learn more about the Bible by doing these things.

(1) Have the main points of Scripture firmly planted in your mind. When I read a long, complicated book—I mean a modern, non-fiction book—I will almost always read a summary or a review of that book first so that I can keep track of where we're going. The same sort of thing would benefit your reading of Scripture. Jesus presents a summary of Scripture with his choices for the two greatest commands: love God, love others, "for on these two commandments hang all the Law and the Prophets" (Matt 22:37–40). He gives a similar summary in the Sermon on the Mount (Matt 7:12, the Golden Rule). So, this clues us in that

Scripture, at its root, is supposed to encourage love of God and love of neighbor.[3]

It also helps to have the main storyline of the Bible in your head. That storyline can be summed up in this way: Creation, Sin, Abraham, Moses, exodus, Law, Promised Land, David, Exile, Jesus, Church.[4] You might want to add other points, but even if you just keep the basics to these eleven points, and if you're able to fit each book of Scripture somewhere around these points, you'll certainly be smarter than the average bear. One very helpful resource for locating each book within the overall biblical storyline is the Bible Project.[5]

(2) Concentrate on a single book at a time. Choose a book you want to know more about and dedicate yourself to reading that book several times in a row. I'm not completely opposed to the idea of reading through the entire Bible in a year, but I think generally that approach is not very helpful, because you cover so much ground that it's hard to keep anything in your head. I think you'd do better to commit yourself to reading the book of Genesis twelve times in a year, or read through the Gospels twelve times in a year, or read through a book four times in a month, and go through twelve biblical books that way over the course of a year.

(3) Take notes. I use Google Docs for this purpose. I name the document "Notes on Genesis" or "Notes on Matthew." The

---

3. Some folks will notice that I'm echoing Augustine here.
4. Many books seek to lead readers through this story. I have found especially helpful Christopher J. H. Wright, *Knowing Jesus through the Old Testament* (Downers Grove, IL: IVP, 1992; 2nd ed. 2014). Another good one is Craig G. Bartholomew and Michael W. Goheen, *The Drama of Scripture* (Grand Rapids: Baker, 2004).
5. The Bible Project videos are available on YouTube.

document is mostly organized chapter by chapter; that is, I have a heading "ch. 4" (underlined) and then I list all my notes on that chapter, and then "ch. 5" (underlined) and my notes from that chapter. My notes consist of whatever jumps out to me as important, or interesting, something I'd like to remember. I also routinely write in my Bible and underline, always in blue ink so that it stands out more. And I always use a straightedge for underlining, because I want my Bible to look tidy.

I try to think of questions to ask as I read through the book, basic questions, like "what are the major themes of this book?" sometimes more complex questions. One time when I was reading through Genesis, I wanted to keep track of the geography, where Abraham was, or where Joseph was. So, for each chapter, my notes begin with a recording of the geography. I also freely used Google Maps to help me identify where these places were, to give me a better sense of the distance between locations. Reading through Matthew, I wanted to mark down all the Old Testament quotations, and then I wanted to compare that with the other Gospels; which Old Testament quotations are shared by the other Gospels, which ones are unique to Matthew? I've got charts on all the Gospels for these things. It took me several months, but I was in no rush. (See next point.) One time reading through the second half of Isaiah (chs. 40–66), I just wanted to figure out who was speaking in each chapter—is God speaking? is the prophet speaking? are the people speaking? It can get quite confusing, but usually the language provides sufficient clues that you can figure it out.

Look for different things each time you read through the book. Read through it the first time just to get familiar with the book, and to look for interesting things. Then read the book again looking for whatever key words or themes occurred to you on that initial read. I've read through the Minor Prophets looking for the theme of judgment, and then salvation, and then the fate of the nations, and then the Messiah, and then the Spirit, etc. I've read through Mark looking for demons, or repentance, or teaching on the family, or what the future holds, or what Jesus wanted people to do, or how Jesus thought about the Mosaic Law. Stop reading that book when you get tired of it, or you can't think of any other theme to look for or question to ask.

The basic question for each book is always: "What does God want to communicate to his people through this book of Scripture?"

(4) Take your time. There's no rush to get this done. You're not trying to squeeze something in by the end of the year. You're in this for the long haul. In five years, you want to know more about the Bible than you do today. In twenty years, you want to know even more. But it's not like you're trying to learn everything about the Bible by the time you die. No one's ever going to know everything about the Bible. Take as long with a particular book as you want to take. Your basic goal is to learn, to meditate on the words of Scripture, to allow God to use his word to shape your life, to form your imagination, for the Spirit to transform you. That's a never-ending process—but just for that reason it's a process that should not be delayed. Get on it now and take your time.

(5) Keep reading. Don't get discouraged when it gets hard. The Bible is hard. The Ethiopian eunuch found Isaiah 53 hard, so he asked Philip for help (Acts 8:31–35). So, it's not just we who find this stuff difficult. Remember: no pain, no gain. The difficulties of Scripture are intended by God to mold us, like a wrestler advancing in his craft by facing an equal or better challenger. If

you're decent at Ping Pong, it does you no good at all to play against someone who doesn't know how to keep the ball on the table, or how to hold a paddle. But the challenge of playing against someone a little bit better than you improves your game. So, don't get discouraged by the challenge of Scripture, but rejoice that God uses this difficult Scripture to shape us, if we persevere, if we meditate on these words.

I often think about the advice my brother-in-law gave me when I was painting my kitchen dark red. I had already put three coats on, and it looked terrible, very streaky. He said, "Just keep going." So, I added a fourth coat of paint, and it looked a little less terrible, and a fifth coat made it look sort of okay, and a sixth coat was finally the last. When you hit up against a tough bit of Scripture, just keep going—just keep reading it. Read Revelation over and over, or Isaiah, or Ezekiel. There will be some things for which you'll never be satisfied with your understanding, but you will grow in your understanding for almost every bit of Scripture if you'll just keep on reading it.

(6) Memorize Scripture. Pick out some good verses from the book you're currently reading and commit them to memory. I think that'll be easier if you use the KJV for memorization. I'm not recommending the KJV for reading, because it can be tough to understand. But for memorization, the wording is so distinctive (= strange) that it sticks in the mind more easily. One of my teachers used to say that memorizing the NIV was like memorizing the newspaper, and the same applies to all modern translations. The wording is too normal. But that's just a suggestion. Memorize Scripture in whatever version you prefer.

Memorization helps the message of Scripture take root in our lives. As we work on memorizing a verse, we say that verse over and over to ourselves, and that sort of meditation helps us understand the verse better. I remember when I was committing to memory John Donne's poem "Death Be Not Proud," there were parts of it I didn't really understand until I said it to myself for the hundredth time, and then not only did I have it stuck in my head, but I also finally understood the meaning. That's what memorization can do for you: it helps you understand what you're memorizing. But having Scripture stuck in your head also helps to shape your character. You will start to think like God, because you have God's thoughts in your mind.

Long ago, Socrates complained that writing—just using a pencil and paper—will be bad for educated folk because they'll stop remembering things.

> For this invention [= writing] will produce forgetfulness in the minds of those who learn to use it, because they will not practice their memory. Their trust in writing, produced by external characters which are no part of the people themselves, will discourage the use of their own memory within them.[6]

Oh, what would Socrates say if he knew about the smartphone?

Don't keep your brain in your pocket. Commit Scripture to memory.

The Authority of Jesus

One thing that's amazing about these last few verses of the Sermon on the Mount is how Jesus-centered it all is. Jesus does not say that

---

6. Socrates' thoughts are presented in Plato's dialogue called *Phaedrus* 275a.

the wise man builds his house on the words of Torah but on "my words." He's talking about the words in the Sermon on the Mount. If you'll just do what Jesus says here, Jesus guarantees you a solid foundation. No wonder "the crowds marveled at his teaching, because he was teaching them like one who had authority, and not like their scribes" (Matt 7:28–29).

Appendix

Questions for Reflection

Chapter 1: The Kingdom of Heaven

As we begin a study of the Sermon on the Mount (Matthew 5–7), read through the entire Gospel of Matthew. A main theme of this Gospel is "the kingdom of heaven," a phrase unique to Matthew (the other Gospels have "kingdom of God"). What does this Gospel say about the kingdom of heaven?

Which verses on the kingdom of heaven are the most helpful or surprising?

According to this Gospel, what is the role that Jesus plays in the kingdom of heaven?

What do Jesus' disciples think they are getting themselves into by following him?

How does the Sermon on the Mount relate to the overall mission of Jesus?

How would you answer someone who wonders whether the Sermon on the Mount is irrelevant to Christians because it is not a part of the new covenant?

Chapter 2: The Good Life, According to Jesus

The series of nine blessings that Jesus speaks to open the Sermon on the Mount present a view of the blessed life or the "good life" opposite to the way we usually think about the good life. What does Jesus mean when he says that these particular characteristics are "blessed"?

We find a similar block of Jesus' teaching at Luke 6:20–26. What similarities and differences do you notice between the Beatitudes in Matthew and this passage in Luke?

Which beatitude do you find most difficult? Why?

Do you want to "inherit the earth"?

Which beatitude do you think is most sorely in need today? Do you think the answer to this question would have been different in Jesus' day?

Chapter 3: Salt and Light

What about salt makes it a good metaphor to describe followers of Jesus? Do you think other biblical references to salt might come into play here, such as Leviticus 2:13 or Ezekiel 16:4?

APPENDIX: QUESTIONS FOR REFLECTION / 241

When Jesus talks about un-salty salt (Matt 5:13), what are the implications for followers of Jesus?

Jesus calls his disciples "the light of the world." Do you think this description has a connection to the use of the word "light" in Matthew 4:16 (which is a quotation of Isa 9:1–2)?

God talks about a "light to the nations" in Isaiah 51:4, and he has already used this phrase, "a light to the nations," in Isaiah 49:1–6 in reference to "my servant, Israel" (v. 3). How might these concepts be connected to what Jesus says in the Sermon on the Mount?

How does Jesus define "light" in Matthew 5:16? What implications does this verse have for your life?

Chapter 4: Fulfilling the Law and the Prophets

What do you think the difference is between abolishing the Law and the Prophets and fulfilling them?

Did people think that Jesus was trying to abolish the Law and the Prophets? What might lead them to think that?

What is Jesus getting at in Matthew 5:18–19? Does he mean to say that his disciples need to keep the laws commanded at Sinai? How does the rest of the chapter, Matthew 5, help to explain what Jesus means about fulfilling the Law?

How is it possible that the scribes and Pharisees are not righteous enough (Matt 5:20)? How can someone be more righteous than them?

Chapter 5: Personal Relationships

This section of the Sermon on the Mount illustrates the "greater righteousness" (Matt 5:20) that Jesus' disciples were supposed to display. Jesus explains six test cases. What do you think is the main principle for these test cases?

The first test case is murder (Matt 5:21–26). What does Jesus teach about murder? How do the examples offered by Jesus in this passage illustrate his teaching?

The second test case is adultery (Matt 5:27–30). How does Jesus' teaching on adultery relate to the Tenth Commandment (Exod 20:17)? Where does Jesus lay the responsibility for avoiding sin in this case, on the man or the woman?

What problems do you see with abiding by Jesus' teaching in the fifth test case (Matt 5:38–42)? How do you think Jesus would respond to these issues?

What does Jesus mean when he says that his followers ought to be "perfect" (Matt 5:48)?

Chapter 6: Marriage and Divorce

In Matthew 5:31, Jesus is recalling Deuteronomy 24:1 (as the Pharisees will in Matt 19:7). What does the law in Deuteronomy

24:1–4 command? What is the main point of this command?

In Matthew 5:32, what is the main point Jesus wants people to understand about marriage and divorce?

Compare Matthew 5:31–32 to Matthew 19:1–9. What does the passage in Matthew 19 add to our understanding of marriage? What do the Pharisees misunderstand about marriage?

In Matthew 19:10–12, why are the disciples so surprised at Jesus' teaching? What does Jesus' response to them mean?

Paul talks about marriage in 1 Corinthians 7. What does he teach in verses 10–16? Does he add or alter anything about the teaching of Jesus?

Chapter 7: How to Be Religious

In Matthew 6:1–18, what motivation for righteous deeds does Jesus condemn? Can you think of biblical examples of people doing the right things for the wrong reasons? Can you think of examples from our own culture?

Jesus gives three examples of right actions with sinful motivation. First up is almsgiving, or charity. Did Jesus expect his audience to give to the needy? What examples can you name of people giving money to gain attention, or—the opposite—of people practicing Jesus' teaching?

Second, prayer. (We'll talk about the Lord's Prayer next chapter.)

What problems do people have with prayer? How can our prayers be more like what Jesus wants them to be?

Third, fasting. Does Jesus think his followers will fast? How does Mark 2:18–22 fit into this discussion? Do you think that the church has missed anything about fasting?

Consider again Matthew 5:16. How do we balance this text with Matthew 6:1?

Chapter 8: The Lord's Prayer

Is this prayer that Jesus gives his followers a private prayer or a communal prayer? How is it related to Jesus' earlier instructions on prayer (Matthew 6:5–8)?

Do you think that the petition "Thy kingdom come" is relevant for Christians today, something that Christians today ought to pray? Are we somehow still waiting on God's kingdom? What do we mean by "kingdom" in this context?

Jesus tells his followers to ask God for their "daily bread" (v. 11). Does this remind you of a story in the Old Testament? (Hint: Exod 16) Does this petition strike an American audience differently from an ancient Jewish audience?

In what sense is God's forgiveness dependent on our forgiveness? See Matthew 6:12, 14–15.

Chapter 9: Handling Possessions

What is the main point Jesus is making in Matthew 6:19–34? What do you think these instructions would have meant for his original audience hearing this message?

How do verses 19–21 relate to what Jesus had said earlier about doing righteousness in front of people (6:1–18)?

What do you think Jesus is getting at with his comment on good and bad eyes at 6:22–23?

How do you think the call not to worry about material concerns (6:25–34) would have sounded to his original audience, and how is that different from how it might sound to us?

Jesus tells us that if we will seek first God's kingdom, God will supply our material needs. What does it mean to "seek" God's kingdom? What does Jesus want us to do?

Chapter 10: Judge Not

Do you think there are any limitations on Jesus' prohibition of judging? In other words, are there occasions in which "judging" is appropriate? Can you think of times that Jesus "judged"?

Jesus says that those who judge will be judged (Matt 7:1) … will be judged by whom?

What does the saying about dogs and swine mean (Matt 7:6), and how does it fit into its context?

"Everyone who asks receives" (Matt 7:8). Is that true? What about Matthew 26:39?

Compare the Golden Rule (Matt 7:12) to the Greatest Commands (Matt 22:37–40). Are they saying different things or the same thing? Do you think these ideas connect to Matthew 5:17?

Chapter 11: The Way of Life

What does Jesus mean that the way to life is narrow and difficult? Does that mean that not many people are going to be saved?

What do you think is the "bad fruit" that the false prophets will produce? (Matt 7:15–20)

Can you think of situations where it is hard to tell a tree by its fruit, or a person's heart by their actions? What do you think about Jesus' statement here and what he had said earlier about hypocrites in 6:1–18?

How do you think the paragraph about the trees and fruit (vv. 15–20) is related to the paragraph about some people not entering the kingdom of heaven (vv. 21–23)?

According to Jesus in Matthew 7:21–23, what is the "entrance requirement" for the kingdom of heaven? Upon what basis do some people get rejected by the Lord? How do you relate this entrance requirement to other things that the New Testament says, such as Ephesians 2:8–9?

Chapter 12: A Solid Foundation

What is the difference between the wise and foolish man in Jesus' parable? What is the characteristic of the wise man as opposed to the foolish man?

What words does the wise man put into practice? What "words of mine" (7:24) is Jesus talking about?

What happens to the house of the wise man (7:25)? How does this description connect to our lives?

What fate does Jesus have in mind for the foolish man (7:27)? What does the crashing of his house correspond to in real life?

What about this final teaching from Jesus in the Sermon on the Mount might make the crowds marvel (7:28)?

Glossary

AMIDAH. The Amidah is an important prayer in Jewish tradition, recited thrice daily.

APOCRYPHA. In biblical studies, this term often refers to the books present in the Bible of Roman Catholics or Greek Orthodox that are not present in the Bible of Protestants. These books include Tobit, Judith, books of Maccabees (there are four total), Wisdom of Solomon, and Sirach (a.k.a. Ecclesiasticus, a.k.a. Wisdom of Ben Sira). Another term for the apocrypha is the deuterocanonical books.

BARUCH. The book of Baruch is one of the apocrypha or deuterocanonical books, absent from the Jewish Bible and the Protestant Bible but present in the Roman Catholic Bible and other Bibles. The book is named for Jeremiah's scribe. It is a brief book (five chapters) that mourns the sins of the people.

Ben Sira. The Jewish scribe named Jesus Ben Sira lived in the early second century BC and wrote a book of wisdom about 180 BC. This book is also known as Sirach and Ecclesiasticus. It is one of the apocrypha or deuterocanonical books.

CODEX SINAITICUS. Codex Sinaiticus is a fourth-century copy of the Greek Bible.

DAMASCUS DOCUMENT. The Damascus Document is one of the Dead Sea Scrolls.

Dead Sea Scrolls. These scrolls were discovered in the 1940s and 1950s in caves near a settlement called Qumran, on the northwest shore of the Dead Sea, about 20 miles east of Jerusalem.

Deuterocanonical. The term "deuterocanonical" was coined in 1566 by Sixtus of Siena to refer to the books that Protestants often call "apocrypha." The term means that these books were considered canonical later than the other books (*deutero*: in a second phase).

Didache. The Didache is an early Christian document, perhaps from the late first century or early second century, that consists of a church manual, a how-to for being a Christian.

Essenes. The Essenes were an ancient Jewish sect mentioned by Josephus and others and commonly now associated with the Dead Sea Scrolls.

4 Ezra. This apocalyptic work written in the name of Ezra was probably composed about the year AD 100.

Get. The word *get* (pl. *gittin*) is Hebrew for "divorce certificate."

Hillel. Hillel was one of the famous rabbis from just before the time of Jesus.

Maccabees. There are four books of Maccabees, two of which are included in the Roman Catholic Bible and therefore are considered deuterocanonical. These books are named for the family of warrior priests led by Judah the Maccabee, who fought to wrest control of Jerusalem and the surrounding area from the power of the Seleu-cid king Antiochus IV Epiphanes and his royal successors in the mid-second century BC.

Marcion. From the town of Sinope on the southern coast of the Black Sea, Marcion moved to Rome in about AD 140 and quickly became known as a Christian heretic. Marcion denied that the God of the Old Testament was the same as the Father of Jesus; he argued that Christians should worship only the God newly revealed by Jesus, and he accepted as Scripture only certain books in the modern New Testament (ten letters of Paul and an abridged version of Luke's Gospel).

MISHNAH. This rabbinic document is usually dated to around AD 200, though it contains some traditions going back long before that time, some perhaps from the time of Jesus or before. It is arranged as a group of sixty-three tractates. To find something in the Mishnah, you first have to open it to the right tractate, just like when you want to find something in the Bible you first have to open to the right book. Each tractate is divided into chapters and small paragraphs (called mishnahs, but you can also think of each paragraph as like a verse).

PENTATEUCH. See Torah.

QUMRAN COMMUNITY. This is the community responsible for the Dead Sea Scrolls.

RABBINIC WORKS. The Rabbis became the predominant leaders within Judaism following the destruction of the temple by the Romans in AD 70. The early Rabbis wrote in Hebrew, and later Rabbis wrote mostly in Aramaic. The literature they left behind includes preeminently the Mishnah and the Talmud, along with many other works, including the Targums and various Midrashim (commentaries on Scripture). These works date from around the year AD 200 to around the sixth or seventh century.

ROSH HASHANAH. Literally "head of the year," this is the Jewish New Year, in the autumn, as spelled out in Leviticus 23:23–32.

SEPTUAGINT. The Septuagint is the Greek translation of the Old Testament. The word "Septuagint" comes from the Latin *septuaginta*, "seventy," and refers to the legend of the translation of the Old Testament into Greek by seventy(-two) Jewish sages.

Shammai. Shammai was one of the famous rabbis from just before the time of Jesus.

Shema. The *Shema* is a Jewish prayer recited by observant Jews twice each day. The text of the prayer comes from three Bible passages (Deut 6:4–9; 11:13–21; Num 15:37–41), the first of which begins with the word *shema* ("hear").

Shepherd of Hermas. *The Shepherd of Hermas* is an ancient Christian composition from the second century. Today it is included in the collection known as the Apostolic Fathers.

Sirach. The book Sirach has two other names: the Wisdom of Ben Sira and Ecclesiasticus. It is a collection of wise sayings, similar to Proverbs. It was written in Hebrew in about 180 BC by a sage named Jesus Ben Sira. The full Hebrew text has not survived to the modern period, but Ben Sira's grandson translated the book into Greek in the late second century BC, and this Greek translation has survived. The book of Sirach is included in the Roman Catholic biblical canon.

Synoptic Gospels. The gospels of Matthew, Mark, and Luke are referred to as the synoptic Gospels because they include many of the same stories, often in a similar sequence and in similar or sometimes identical wording.

Talmud. The Talmud is the chief work of rabbinic literature. It is a commentary on the Mishnah. Whereas the Mishnah is written in Hebrew, the commentary is written in Aramaic. There are actually two Talmuds, one from Jerusalem, completed perhaps in the early fifth century AD, and one from Babylon, completed perhaps around the sixth century AD. Whenever someone simply mentions "the Talmud," they are invariably referring to the Babylonian Talmud, which is much larger than the Jerusalem Talmud and traditionally much more authoritative. The Talmud is referenced according to the tractate name (like the Mishnah) and the page number and page side (e.g., 18a = page 18, side a) of the "Vilna Shas," i.e., the edition of the Talmud printed in Vilna, Lithuania in the 1870s and 1880s and still commonly reprinted.

TOBIT. The book of Tobit is one of the deuterocanonical books in the Roman Catholic Bible. It tells the story of Tobit and his son Tobias, their sufferings despite their faith in God, and their eventual return to prosperity.

TORAH. This Hebrew term meaning "instruction" or, sometimes, "law," is the traditional Jewish designation for the first five books of the Bible, the Torah of Moses (i.e., the Pentateuch).

YOM KIPPUR. This is the Hebrew term translated "Day of Atonement," a day of fasting, rest, reflection, and atonement, observed in the autumn. See Lev 16; 23:26–32.

Bibliography

Aramaic, Hebrew and Greek documentary texts from Nahal Hever and other sites: with an appendix containing alleged Qumran texts (The Seiyal Collection II). Discoveries in the Judaean Desert 27. Oxford, England, Clarendon Press, 1997.

Anderson, Gary A. *Charity: The Place of the Poor in the Biblical Tradition.* New Haven, CT: Yale University Press, 2013.

———. *Sin: A History.* New Haven, CT: Yale University Press, 2009.

Babylonian Talmud, tractate Bekhorot 8b.

Bacon, Benjamin W. "The Five Books of Matthew Against the Jews," *The Expositor* 25 (1918): 56–66.

Barclay, John M. G. *Paul and the Gift.* Grand Rapids: Eerdmans, 2015.

Barnett, Victoria J. "Bonhoeffer and the Conspiracy." Pages 65–76 in *The Oxford Handbook of Dietrich Bonhoeffer.* Edited by Philip G. Ziegler and Michael Mawson. Oxford: Oxford University Press, 2019.

Bartholomew, Craig G. and Michael W. Goheen. *The Drama of Scripture.* Grand Rapids: Baker, 2004.

Boles, H. Leo. *The New Testament Teaching on War.* Nashville: Gospel Advocate, 1923.
Bonhoeffer, Dietrich. *The Cost of Discipleship.* New York: Touchstone, 2018.
———. *Discipleship.* DBWE 4. Minneapolis: Fortress, 2001.
Campbell, Alexander. "An Address on War" (1848). Pages 122-23 in *Christian Peace and Nonviolence: A Documentary History.* Edited by Michael G. Long. Maryknoll, NY: Orbis, 2011.
———. *Familiar Lectures on the Pentateuch* (1867).
———. "Sermon on the Law." *The Millennial Harbinger* (1846).
Casey, Michael W. "From Religious Outsiders to Insiders: The Rise and Fall of Pacifism in the Churches of Christ." *Journal of Church and State* 44 (2002): 455–75.
Charlesworth, James H., ed., *Temple Scroll and Related Documents.* PTSDSSP 7. Tübingen: Mohr Siebeck; Louisville: WJK, 2011.
Clark, David. *On Earth as in Heaven: The Lord's Prayer from Jewish Prayer to Christian Ritual.* Minneapolis: Fortress, 2017.
Cnaan, Ram A. *The Other Philadelphia Story: How Local Congregations Support Quality of Life in Urban America.* Philadelphia: University of Pennsylvania Press, 2006.
Collins, John J. "Marriage, Divorce, and Family in Second Temple Judaism." Pages 104–62 in *Families in Ancient Israel.* Edited by Leo G. Perdue et al. Louisville: WJK, 1997.
———. *What Are Biblical Values? What the Bible Says on Key Ethical Issues.* New Haven, CT: Yale University Press, 2019.
Community Rule (1QS 1.10–11).
Crews, Kyle, ed., *Pacifism and Politics in the Churches of Christ: The Collected Essays of Michael W. Casey.* Eugene, OR: Pickwick.

Crossley, James G. *The New Testament and Jewish Law: A Guide for the Perplexed*. London: T&T Clark, 2010.

Crump, D. M. "Prayer." Pages 684–92 in *Dictionary of Jesus and the Gospels*. 2d ed. Edited by Joel B. Green. Downers Grove, IL: IVP, 2013), 684–92.

Danby, Herbert. *The Mishnah*. Oxford: Oxford University Press, 1933.

Danker, Frederick W., Walter Bauer, William F. Arndt, and F. Wilbur Gingrich, *A Greek-English Lexicon of the New Testament and Other Early Christian Literature*, 3d ed. Chicago: University of Chicago Press, 2000.

Davies, W. D. and Dale C. Allison, *Matthew 1–7*, ICC. London: T&T Clark, 1988.

deSilva, David A. *The Jewish Teachers of Jesus, James, and Jude: What Earliest Christianity Learned from the Apocrypha and Pseudepigrapha*. Oxford: Oxford University Press, 2012.

Diogenes Laertius. *Lives of Eminent Philosophers* 5.21. Translated by R. D. Hicks, Loeb Classical Library. Cambridge, MA: Harvard University Press, 1925.

Doering, Lutz. "God as Father in Texts from Qumran." Pages 107–35 in *The Divine Father: Religious and Philosophical Concepts of Divine Parenthood in Antiquity*. Edited by Felix Albrecht and Reinhard Feldmeier. Leiden: Brill, 2014.

Downs, David J. *Alms: Charity, Reward, and Atonement in Early Christianity*. Waco, TX: Baylor University Press, 2016.

Dunn, J. D. G. "Law," Pages 505–15 in *Dictionary of Jesus and the Gospels*, 2d ed., Edited by Joel B. Green. Downers Grove, IL: IVP, 2013.

———. "Prayer," Pages 617–25 in *Dictionary of Jesus and the Gospels*. Edited by Joel B. Green and Scot McKnight. Downers Grove, IL: IVP, 1992.

Edwards, Earl D. "What about Matthew 19:9?" *The Spiritual Sword* 41.3 (April 2010): 26–29.

The Ekklesia of Christ. Berean Study Series. Florence, AL: HCU Press, 2015.

Eubank, Nathan. "Storing Up Treasure with God in the Heavens: Celestial Investments in Matthew 6:1–21." *Catholic Biblical Quarterly* 76 (2014): 77–92.

Ferguson, Everett. *Early Christians Speak: Faith and Life in the First Three Centuries*, Rev. ed. Abilene, TX: ACU Press, 1987.

———. *Early Christians Speak: Faith and Life in the First Three Centuries*. vol. 2. Abilene, TX: ACU Press, 2002.

Gallagher, Ed. *The Book of Exodus: Explorations in Christian Theology*. Cypress Bible Study Series. Florence, AL: HCU Press, 2020.

Garland, D. E. "The Lord's Prayer in the Gospel of Matthew." *Review and Expositor* 89 (1992): 215–28.

Green, Joel B. *Practicing Theological Interpretation: Engaging Biblical Texts for Faith and Formation*. Grand Rapids: Baker, 2011.

Greig, Pete. *How to Pray: A Simple Guide for Normal People*. Carol Stream, IL: NavPress, 2019.

Gupta, Nijay. *The Lord's Prayer*. Macon, GA: Smyth & Helwys, 2017.

Hays, Richard B. "A Letter from Christ." Pages 122–53 in *Echoes of Scripture in the Letters of Paul*. New Haven: Yale University Press, 1989.

———. *The Moral Vision of the New Testament: Community,*

Cross, New Creation; A Contemporary Introduction to New Testament Ethics. New York: HarperCollins, 1996.

Heine, Ronald E. *Reading the Old Testament with the Ancient Church: Exploring the Formation of Early Christian Thought.* Grand Rapids: Baker, 2007.

Heth, Williams A. "Jesus on Divorce: How My Mind Has Changed." *The Southern Baptist Journal of Theology* 6 (2002): 4–29.

Hill, Wesley. *The Lord's Prayer: A Guide to Praying to Our Father.* Bellingham, WA: Lexham, 2019.

Hitchcock, Christina S. *The Significance of Singleness: A Theological Vision for the Future of the Church.* Grand Rapids: Baker, 2018.

Holmes, Michael W. ed. and trans., *The Apostolic Fathers: Greek Texts and English Translations.* 3d ed. Grand Rapids: Baker, 2007.

Hong, Koog-Pyoung. "The Euphemism for the Ineffable Name of God and Its Early Evidence in Chronicles." *Journal for the Study of the Old Testament* 37 (2013): 473–84.

Hylen, Susan E. *Women in the New Testament World.* Essentials of Biblical Studies. Oxford: Oxford University Press, 2019.

Instone-Brewer, David. "Divorce." Pages 212–16 in *Dictionary of Jesus and the Gospels.* 2d ed., Edited by Joel B. Green. Downers Grove, IL: IVP, 2013.

———. *Divorce and Remarriage in the Bible: The Social and Literary Context.* Grand Rapids: Eerdmans, 2002.

———. "1 Corinthians 7 in the Light of the Graeco-Roman Marriage and Divorce Papyri." *Tyndale Bulletin* 52 (2001): 101–16.

———. "1 Corinthians 7 in the Light of the Jewish Greek and Aramaic Marriage and Divorce Papyri." *Tyndale Bulletin* 52 (2001): 225–43.

Josephus. Translated by Henry St. J. Thackeray et al. 10 vols. Loeb Classical Library. Cambridge: Harvard University Press, 1926–1965.

Kelly, Geffrey B. *Reading Bonhoeffer: A Guide to His Spiritual Classics and Selected Writings on Peace.* Eugene, OR: Cascade, 2008.

Kreeft, Peter J. *Catholic Christianity.* San Francisco: Ignatius, 2001.

Kurlansky, Mark. *Salt: A World History.* New York: Penguin, 2002.

Le Donne, Anthony. *The Wife of Jesus: Ancient Texts and Modern Scandals.* London: Oneworld, 2013.

Lewis, C. S. *The Horse and the His Boy.* The Chronicles of Narnia. New York: HarperCollins, 1954.

———. *Mere Christianity.* New York: Macmillan, 1952.

Lipscomb, David. *Civil Government.* Nashville, 1887.

Long, Thomas G. *Matthew.* Westminster Bible Commentary. Louisville: WJK, 1997.

Lunger, Harold L. *The Political Ethics of Alexander Campbell.* St Louis: Bethany, 1954.

Luther, Martin. "Foreword," *An Exposition of the Lord's Prayer for Simple Laymen* (1519). Translated by Martin H. Bertram in *Luther's Works.* Edited by Jeroslav Pelikan and Helmut Lehmann, vol. 42: *Devotional Writings.* Edited by Martin O. Dietrich. Philadelphia: Fortress, 1969.

Luz, Ulrich. *Matthew 1–7: A Commentary,* Hermeneia. Minneapolis: Fortress, 2007.

Marsh, Charles. *Strange Glory: A Life of Dietrich Bonhoeffer.* New York: Knopf, 2014.

Matthews, John W. *Bonhoeffer: A Brief Overview of the Life and Writings of Dietrich Bonhoeffer.* Minneapolis: Lutheran University Press, 2011.

McGinn, Thomas A. J. *Prostitution, Sexuality, and Law in Ancient Rome.* Oxford: Oxford University Press, 1998.

McKnight, Scot. *Kingdom Conspiracy: Returning to the Radical Mission of the Local Church.* Grand Rapids: Baker, 2014.

———. *The Sermon on the Mount.* Story of God Bible Commentary. Grand Rapids: Zondervan, 2013.

Merkle, Benjamin L. *Exegetical Gems from Biblical Greek: A Refreshing Guide to Grammar and Interpretation.* Grand Rapids: Baker, 2019.

Milton, John. *Paradise Lost* (1674), 1.679–84.

Moberly, R. W. L. *Old Testament Theology: Reading the Hebrew Bible as Christian Scripture.* Grand Rapids: Baker, 2013.

Origen. *Prayer; Exhortation to Martyrdom.* Translated by John J. O'Meara. ACW 19. New York: Newman, 1954.

Pennington, Jonathan T. *Heaven and Earth in the Gospel of Matthew.* Leiden: Brill, 2007.

———. *The Sermon on the Mount and Human Flourishing: A Theological Commentary.* Grand Rapids: Baker, 2017.

Philo, *Every Good Man Is Free.* 84.

Pitre, Brant. *Jesus and the Last Supper.* Grand Rapids: Eerdmans, 2015.

Plato. Translated by Harold North Fowler. 2 vols. Loeb Classical Library. Cambridge: Harvard University Press, 1914-1982.

Provan, Iain. *The Reformation and the Right Reading of Scripture.* Waco, TX: Baylor University Press, 2017.

Quarles, Charles. *Sermon on the Mount: Restoring Christ's Message to the Modern Church.* NAC Studies in Bible & Theology. Nashville: B&H, 2011.

"Relentless Flooding Chases Residents from Homes." *Times Daily.* Sunday, February 24, 2019.

"River Drains after Nearly 11 Feet above Flood Stage." *Times Daily.* Tuesday, February 26, 2019, p. A10.

Shelly, Rubel. *Divorce and Remarriage: A Redemptive Theology.* Abilene, TX: Leafwood, 2007.

Sider, Ronald J. *Rich Christians in an Age of Hunger: A Biblical Study.* London: Hodder & Stoughton, 1977.

———. *Rich Christians in an Age of Hunger: Moving from Affluence to Generosity.* 6th ed. Nashville: W Publishing Group, 2015.

Stanglin, Keith D. *The Letter and Spirit of Biblical Interpretation: From the Early Church to Modern Practice.* Grand Rapids: Baker, 2018.

Strauss, Mark L., ed., *Remarriage after Divorce in Today's Church: 3 Views.* Grand Rapids: Zondervan, 2006.

Weaver, Dorothy Jean. "Transforming Nonresistance: From *Lex Talionis* to 'Do Not Resist the Evil One'." Pages 32–71 in *The Love of Enemy and Nonretaliation in the New Testament*, Edited by Willard M. Swartley. Louisville: WJK, 1992.

Weber, Jeremy Weber. "No Cheeks Left to Turn," *Christianity Today* (Oct 19, 2018),

Wells, James. "Living by Faith." 1918.

Wenham, Gordon J. and William E. Heth, *Jesus and Divorce: The Problem with the Evangelical Consensus.* Carlisle, UK: Paternoster, 1984.

Wise, Michael, Martin Abegg Jr., and Edward Cook, trans., *The Dead Sea Scrolls: A New Translation.* San Francisco: HarperSanFrancisco, 1996.

Wright, Christopher J. H. *Knowing Jesus through the Old Testament.* 2nd ed. Downers Grove, IL: IVP, 2014.

Wright, N. T. *Paul and the Faithfulness of God.* Minneapolis: Fortress, 2013.

———. *Simply Jesus.* New York: HarperCollins, 2011.

Yoder, John Howard. *The Politics of Jesus: Vicit Agnus Noster.* 2d ed. Grand Rapids: Eerdmans, 1994.

Ziegler, Philip G. and Michael Mawson, eds. *The Oxford Handbook of Dietrich Bonhoeffer.* Oxford: Oxford University Press, 2019.

Subject Index

Abraham (patriarch), 3, 9, 17, 19, 31, 34, 167, 187, 208, 232–233
alms, xiv, 136, 139, 176, 216, 243
American Civil War, 87
American Restoration Movement, 52
see also Stone-Campbell Movement
Amidah, 169, 249
Amos (biblical prophet), xx, 68–69
Aristotle, 204
Baptism, 53, 55, 169
Barr, Roseanne, 190
Beatitude(s), xii, xvii, xvi, 26, 28–36, 81, 101, 240
Ben Sira, 73, 89–90, 131, 166, 245, 249
Benotto, Giovanni Paolo, 221
Bethlehem, 55
Boles, H. Leo, 87

Bonhoeffer, Dietrich, ix, xvii–xviii, xix, 31, 43, 47, 62–63, 70, 74–75, 77–78, 81–83, 85, 90–93, 119, 140, 160, 165, 167, 179–180, 185, 211, 213–215
Calvin, John, 70
Campbell, Alexander, 52–53, 70, 87
Chicks, the (country band), 190
Churches of Christ, 23, 52, 87, 103, 121, 156–157, 193, 195, 228
commandments, 59–62, 65, 67, 131, 231
Cornelius (biblical figure), 88, 219
Didache, 147–149, 167, 198, 250
divorce, xiv, 59, 73, 77, 93–122, 125–126, 242–243, 250
Donne, John, 236
Egypt, 55, 58, 218

Erasmus, 105
Ewell, Bob, 85
Ezekiel (biblical prophet), 16, 155, 230, 235, 240
Family Ties, 93–94
fasting, xiv, 5, 139–142, 185, 244
Finch, Atticus, 85
Foley, Matt, 222
Gandhi, 85
Golden Rule, xv, 197, 203–205, 231
Ghraib, Abu, 61
grace, xviii, 99–100, 132–133, 152, 165, 201, 228, 230
The Greatest Story Ever Told (1965), xvi
Bryan Harsin, 66
Heaven, xi, xiii–xv, 3–4, 6–13, 22–24, 30–31, 33–36, 38, 46, 58, 60, 62, 65, 70, 100, 130–133, 135, 148–149, 151, 153, 156–157, 160–161, 164–165, 173, 175–176, 178, 181–182, 188, 197, 199, 207–208, 210, 213, 217, 219, 223, 239
Herod, 55, 77
Hillel, 111–112, 116–117, 180, 204, 250
Hitler, Adolf, xviii, 81–82

Holy Spirit, 19, 60
hypocrites, 12, 137, 143, 150, 191, 194, 210, 212, 228
Israel, 5, 15–17, 21, 28, 31–32, 34–35, 47, 57–58, 61, 114, 136, 151, 154, 298, 211, 228, 241
Israelite(s), 35, 136, 154, 179, 208
Jeremiah (biblical prophet), 55, 68, 151, 249
Jerusalem, 24, 32, 157, 196, 250, 252
Jesus of Nazareth (1977), xvi
Jews, 4, 15, 22, 35, 47, 52, 57, 90, 116, 135, 151, 154, 169, 203, 228, 252
John the Baptist, xi, 10, 53, 55, 88, 107, 116, 156, 223, 227
Josephus, 77, 112, 250
Judaism, 23, 113, 115–116, 118, 152–153, 204, 251
Judgment, 30, 68, 75, 88, 101, 133, 189–196, 206, 216–217, 224, 234
The Karate Kid, 192
Keanton, Alex P., 93
King, Martin Luther, Jr., 85
King of Kings (1961), xvi
kingdom, xi, 3–4, 6–17, 22–24, 30–31, 33–36, 38, 56–57, 60, 62, 75, 138, 148–

149, 155–161, 164, 182, 184, 199, 210, 213, 219, 223, 227, 230, 239, 244
Kondo, Marie, 184
Laettner, Christian, 192
LaRusso, Daniel, 192
Law, xiii, 21, 27, 51–54, 57–63, 68, 71, 76–79, 81, 90, 108–110, 115–119, 169, 177, 189, 196, 205, 214, 225, 231–232, 234, 241–242, 249
Lawrence, Johnny, 192
Leaning Tower of Piza, 221
Lex talionis, 78–81
Lipscomb, David, 70, 87
Lord's Prayer, xiv, xvi, 8, 133, 146–147, 153, 155, 160, 162–163, 165–169, 244
Lord's Supper, 56, 162–163, 198
Luther, Martin, 70, 146
Mammon, 172, 178–179, 181, 184–185, 188
Marcion, 51–53, 250
marriage, 93, 95–101, 103–109, 113, 115, 117–128, 194, 223, 242–243
McGraw, Phil, 222
Messiah, 16–19, 21–22, 51, 53, 57, 215, 234

Money, x, 114, 129–130, 132–133, 136, 171–177, 181–185, 188, 243
"The Monkey's Paw", 200–201
Moses (biblical leader), 5–6, 21, 35, 54, 57, 77, 118, 125, 153, 163, 208–209, 215, 232, 249
Muslim, 61
pacifism, 36, 86–87
parables, 5–6, 158, 230
Paradise Lost, 129, 178
Paul (Apostle), 39, 45, 51, 53, 59, 62, 90–91, 96, 98–99, 115, 118, 120–122, 126–127, 131, 154, 156–157, 159, 166, 176, 180–181, 201, 215, 217, 224, 229–230, 243, 251
Pentateuch, 53–54, 251
Pharisees, 6, 9, 12, 53, 61–63, 72, 116–117, 136, 143, 163, 194, 242–243
Philo, 77
poor, 9, 16, 21, 25, 27, 29–33, 43–44, 130–132, 136, 142, 174, 177, 183, 185, 222
prayer, xiv, xvi, 8, 22, 86, 93, 133, 137–138, 141, 145–151, 153–155, 160, 162–163, 165–169, 180, 200–201, 203, 243–249, 252

remarriage, 102, 106, 119, 121, 126
righteousness, 6, 9, 13, 16, 25, 30–33, 55, 61–63, 67, 72, 90, 92, 130, 133–136, 143, 160, 173, 176, 186, 207, 210, 213, 224, 227, 229, 242
Ruettiger, Rudy, 182
Saban, Nick, 66
Sabbath, 53, 59
salt, xiii, 39–48, 240–241
salvation, 60, 132–133, 228, 234
Shammai, 111–112, 116–117, 252
Seinfeld, 29, 94
singleness, 97–100, 127–128
Socrates, 83, 236
Space Needle, 222
Stone-Campbell Movement 52
see also American Restoration Movement
Swaggart, Jimmy, 61
Synoptic Gospels, 40, 42, 105, 210, 252
Ten Commandments, 58, 73, 153
To Kill a Mockingbird, 85, 192

Torah, 5, 51, 53–54, 60–61, 67–69, 71–72, 79, 92, 237, 251, 253
Wallace, Christopher, 180
Walsh, Joe, 25
World War I, 87

Index of Ancient Literature

Athenagoras (2nd cent.)
Plea for the Christians,
ch. 33, 104

Babylonian Talmud
Bekhorot 8b	46
b. Shabbat 15b	166
Shabbat 31a	204
Rosh Hashanah 17a	166

Baruch
1:11	90

CD (Damascus Document)
4.21	118

Community Rule
1QS 1.10–11	90

Didache
8:2	149
9:5	198

Discoveries in the Judeaen Desert (DJD) 27 (1997)
67, 114

4 Ezra
7:77	131

Herodotus,
Histories 3.142	204

2 Maccabees
6–7	85

Mandate
4.1.6 [29.6]	104
4.4.2 [32.4]	104

Mishnah
Arakhin 5.6	114
Avot 2.7	181
Berakhot 1.1–2	169
Gittin 9.3	114
Ketuboth	
5.5–8	111
7.2–10	111

    Yoma 8.9   166

Plato
    Phaedrus 275a   236

Sirach
12:4–7   89–90
28:1–7   166
29:11–12   131
34:25–26   73

Temple Scroll
11Q19 57.16–19   113

Tobit
4:8–9   131
4:15   204
8:4–9   118
12:8–9   131

Scripture Index

Old Testament

Genesis
1	122
1:3	44
1:27	118
2	117, 122
2:18	98, 99
2:24	117
2:24n	118
12:7	34
12:7n	31
14:3	41
19:26	42
22:1	156
27:27	27
28:13	34
39:3	48

Exodus
3:14	153
4:22–23	151
7:11	218
7:22	218
8:7	218
8:19	218
15:18n	155
16	244
16:19	163
20:3	179
20:7	153–154
20:13c	72
20:14c	73
20:17	242
21:10–11	115, 126
21:10–11n	112
21:22	80
21:22–25	79
21:24	78
21:24c	73
29:45	35
30:35	41
33:11	35
33:20	35

Leviticus
2:13	41, 42, 240
5:4–6	77
11	59
16	249
16n	140
18:16	116
18:21	154
19:2	71
19:9–10	136
19:12c	73
19:18	90
19:18c	73
20:3	154
20:21	116
22:2	154
22:32	154
23:22	136
23:23–32	247
23:26–32	249
24:17–20	79–80
24:20	78
24:20c	73
26	28

Numbers
12:6–8	35
15:37–41	248
18:19	42
23–24	218
30:2c	73
34:3	41
34:12	41

Deuteronomy
3:17	41
5:17c	72
5:18c	73
6:4	228
6:4–9	248
6:5–6	61
8:3	163, 181
8:17	171
11:13–21	248
13	216
13:1–5	216
14:28–29	136
15:9	176
18:13n	71
18:22	216
19:16–20	80
19:21	78
19:21c	73
22:22	76
23:21	77
23:21–23c	73, 24, 107, 108, 110, 111, 116, 117, 118, 127
24:1	73, 112, 116, 118, 242
24:1–4	108, 243
24:4	108
24:19	136
25:4	53
28	28
29:23	42
30:15–20	208
30:19	219
32:6n	151
32:35	91
34:10–12	54

Joshua
3:16	41
12:3	41
15:2	41
15:5	41
15:62	41
18:19	41
24:15	208

Judges
9:45	42
11:30	77
13–16	217

1 Samuel
2:1–10	146
8:7n	15
12:23	208
15:22	142
16:1	16

2 Samuel
7	15
7:12–16	6, 15
7:14	15
7:14n	151
8:13	41

1 Kings
2:4	15
3–10	15
11:1–8	15
12:1–15	16
12:4	15
18:26–29	150
18:28	150
18:36–38	150

2 Kings
2:20–21	42
14:7	41

1 Chronicles
16:10	154
18:12	41
28:6	15, 151
29:11	150

2 Chronicles
13:5	42
25:11	41

Ezra
4:14	42
6:9	42
7:22	42

Esther
4:16n	140

Job
6:6	42
39:6	41

Psalms
1	27
1:6	208
2:7n	151
8:6	158
10:16n	155
33:21	154
35n	140
37:11	34

45n	155	51:4	241	2:28	7
47:2n	15	52:5	154	2:37	7
55:17	169	53	234	2:44	7, 156, 159
60	41	56:1–8	16	4	7
74:10–12n	155	58n	140	4:26	7
89:26–27n	151	58:3	142	5:23	7
93:1n	15	58:6–7	142	6:10	169
95:3n	15	60	16	6:27	7
97:1	155	63:16n	151	7	7
97:1n	15	64:8	151	7:13–14	7
98:6	155			9:4–19	146
98:6n	15	**Jeremiah**			
99:1	15, 156	3:19	151	**Hosea**	
119:105	45	17:6	41	6:6	72
		23:4–5	57	11:1	55, 57, 58, 151
Proverbs		23:5–6	16		
1	210	29:7n	90		
1:8–19	210	31:9n	151	**Amos**	
7:6–23	210	31:15	55, 57	2n	69
9:13–18	210	31:33	68	5:21–24n	69
10:25	221				
19:17	130, 136	**Ezekiel**		**Micah**	
24:29	80, 206	1	35	4:1–3	16
25:21–22	91	16:4	42, 240	4:4	35
		36:23	155	4:6–8	16
Isaiah		37:15–28	16		
2:2–4	16, 21	38:16n	155	**Zephaniah**	
7:14	55	38:23n	155	2:9	41
9:1–2	241	39:7n	155		
11:1	16	39:25–27n	155	**Zechariah**	
11:1–10	57	40–48	16	7	142
11:2–5	16	43:5	16		
11:6–9	16	43:24	41	**Malachi**	
29:13	72	47:1–12	16	1:6n	151
40–66	233	47:11	42	2:10n	151
49:1–6	47, 241			2:16	110
49:3	241	**Daniel**			
50:4–9	83	2:19	7		

New Testament

Matthew
Ref	Pages
1:1	17, 19, 62
1:16	17
1:17	17
1:18	17
1:20	10
1:22n	55
1:22–23	53, 55
2:4	18
2:5–6	53
2:15	53, 55
2:15n	55
2:17	55
2:17n	55
2:17–18	53
2:23	53
2:23n	55
3:1	101
3:2	xi, 8, 156, 227
3:3	53
3:7–10	53
3:7–12	224
3:8	xi
3:15	55
4:1–11	17, 53
4:4	32
4:14	53
4:14n	55
4:14–16n	47
4:17	xi, 3, 9, 15, 34, 156
4:17n	7
4:18–22	4
4:23	13
4:23–25	17
5	90, 119, 120, 241
5–7	x, 5, 239
5:1	5
5:1–12c	xiii
5:3	9, 164
5:3n	7
5:3–12	21, 29
5:5	34
5:9	8
5:10	5, 213
5:10–12	83, 223
5:11	30
5:11–12	30, 132
5:12	101
5:13	5, 40, 241
5:13c	xiii
5:14n	47
5:14–15c	xiii
5:16	8, 46, 137, 182, 186, 241, 244
5:16c	xiii
5:16n	152
5:17	51, 54, 246
5:17–20	51
5:17–20c	xiii
5:17–48	21
5:17–7:12	147
5:18	5, 58
5:18–19	68, 241
5:18n	8
5:19	9
5:20	6, 9, 60, 61, 62, 67, 134, 207, 242
5:21	58, 68
5:21–22c	xiii
5:21–26	73, 242
5:21–26c	72
5:21–48	59, 60, 65, 67, 119
5:22	73
5:23	24
5:23–24c	xiii
5:23–25	5
5:23–26	76
5:25–26c	xiv
5:27	58
5:27–28c	xiv
5:27–30	76, 191, 216, 242
5:27–30c	73
5:29–30	76
5:29–30c	xiv
5:29–30n	105
5:31	242
5:31–32	77, 95–96, 97, 98, 100, 105, 116, 119, 243
5:31–32c	xiv, 73
5:32	106, 243
5:33–37	77
5:33–37c	xiv, 73
5:34n	8
5:38–42	68, 78, 80, 242

Scripture Index / 275

5:38–42c   xiv, 73
5:38–42n   81
5:39   36
5:43   90
5:43–48   66, 71, 89

5:43–48c   xiv, 73
5:45   8
5:45n   152
5:46   132
5:48   x, 8, 65, 67, 70, 72, 242
5:48n   152
6   173
6:1   8, 182, 186, 194, 244
6:1n   152
6:1–4c   xiv
6:1–18   22, 129, 130, 223, 243, 245, 246
6:1–21   147
6:1–21n   130, 194
6:2   134, 137, 191
6:2n   134
6:2–4   16, 176, 184, 216
6:3   191
6:4n   152
6:5   134, 191
6:5n   134
6:5–6c   xiv

6:5–8   150, 244
6:5–15   200
6:6n   152
6:7–8c   xiv
6:7–15   147
6:8   138, 145
6:8n   152
6:9   8, 146
6:9n   152
6:9–13   146
6:9–13c   xiv
6:10   13, 22, 153
6:10n   8
6:11   162, 244
6:12   133, 244
6:13   149
6:13n   149
6:14n   152
6:14–15   166, 244
6:14–15c   xiv
6:15n   152
6:16   134, 191
6:16–18c   xiv
6:18n   152
6:19–20   130
6:19–20c   xiv
6:19–21   176
6:19–34   171, 245
6:20n   8
6:21–23   246
6:21c   xiv
6:22–23   176, 245
6:22–23c   xv
6:24   176

6:24c   xv
6:25–34   22, 176, 245
6:25–34c   xv
6:26n   8, 152
6:32n   152
6:33   12, 13, 182
6:34   164
7   197
7:1   190, 191, 192, 245
7:1–2   193
7:1–2c   xv, 197
7:1–12   189
7:1–14   22
7:3–4   195
7:3–5c   xv, 197
7:5   194
7:5n   134
7:6   151, 191, 197, 199, 246
7:6c   xv, 197
7:6–7   230
7:7–8c   xv, 197
7:8   246
7:9–11c   xv, 197
7:11   8, 151, 203
7:11n   152
7:12   189, 231, 246
7:12c   xv, 197
7:12n   54
7:13c   xv
7:13–14   207, 223

7:13–23	207	9:27	19, 32	13:16n	26
7:15	215	9:35	13	13:19	167
7:15c	xv	10:1–4	17	13:22	172
7:15–20	246	10:5–6	47	13:24	10
7:16–20c	xv	10:7	9	13:31	10
7:16–20n	72	10:14	199	13:32n	8
7:21	6, 8, 9, 22, 219	10:16–25	213	13:33	10
		10:20n	152	13:35n	55
7:21n	34, 152	10:29n	152	13:38	13, 167
7:21–23	246	10:32–33n	152	13:41	14
7:21–23c	xv	10:38	21	13:43	14
7:21–23n	60	10:38–39	213	13:43n	152
7:22	217, 219	11:1	5	13:44	10
7:23	219	11:2	8, 18	13:45	10
7:24	190, 191, 247	11:2–6	21	13:45–46	199
		11:6n	26	13:47	10
7:24–27	221	11:11	9	13:48	56
7:24–27c	xv	11:12	10	13:52	11
7:25	247	11:23n	8	13:53	5
7:27	223, 247	11:25n	8	14:3–4	116
7:28	5, 247	11:25–26	152	14:17	164
7:28–29	69, 237	11:27n	152	14:19n	8
		11:29	32	15:2	71
7:28–29c	xv	11:30	212	15:2n	5
8:11	9	12:1–14	53	15:7n	134
8:11–12	21	12:7	72	15:8	72
8:11–12n	34, 60	12:17n	55	15:13n	152
		12.:23	19	15:22	19, 32
8:12	13	12:28	6, 12, 17	15:24	47
8:17n	55	12:50n	152	15:34	164
8:20	172	13	6	16:1–3n	8
8:20n	8	13:1–23	211	16:16	17, 18
9:9–10	163	13:3–9	199	16:17n	26, 152
9:9–13	21	13:9	13	16:19	11
9:9–17	53	13:11	10	16:20	18, 21
9:11	71	13:11n	7	16:21	21
9:13	72	13:13	230	16:24	21, 101
9:15	139	13:14n	55	16:24–25	212

16:27	132	19:16	210	22:36–37	63
16:27n	152	19:21	132, 172, 213	22:37–40	62, 231, 246
16:28	14	19:23	11	22:39	142
17:1–13n	5	19:23–24	210	22:40n	54
17:15	32	19:23–24n	34	22:41–46	21
17:22–23	21	19:24	6, 12	22:42	18, 20
18:1	11	19:24n	46	22:43	20
18:3	11	19:25	210	22:45	20
18:3n	34	19:28	17, 132	23	30
18:3–4	210	19:30	21	23:2–3	61
18:4	11	20:1	12	23:9n	152
18:8–9	76, 210	20:1–16n	132	23:10	18
18:8–9c	xiv	20:15	177	23:13	12
18:10n	152	20:17–19	21	23:13–32	194
18:14n	152	20:21	14	23:13n	134
18:15–18	21	20:22–23	201, 213	23:15n	134
18:18n	8	20:23n	152	23:16–22	77
18:19n	152	20:25–28	21, 213	23:22n	8
18:21–35	133	20:30–31	19, 32	23:23	61
18:23	11	21:4n	55	23:23n	134
18:23–35	166	21:9	20	23:25n	134
18:24	133	21:12–13	75	23:27n	134
18:35n	152	21:15	20	23:28n	134
19	118, 119, 120, 243	21:25n	8	23:29n	134
19:1	5	21:28–32	227	23:32	55
19:1–9	97, 243	21:31	6, 12	23:37	196
19:1–12	105	21:31–32	21	23:37–39	32
19:3	116	21:43	6, 12	24–25n	5
19:6	117	21:43n	34	24:5	18
19:7	117, 242	22:2	12	24:14	13
19:9	98, 100, 106	22:18n	134	24:23	18
19:10–12	243	22:30	127	24:24	215, 218
19:12	11	22:30n	8	24:29n	8
19:12n	34	22:34–40	21, 90, 205	24:30n	8
19:14	11			24:35n	8
19:14n	34			24:36	152
				24:46n	26

24:51n	134	**Mark**		13:32	152
25:1	12	1:12–13	167	14:24	201
25:14–30	158, 184	1:15	9, 15, 55	14:25	14
25:31–46	21, 217, 224	1:15n	7	14:36	152
		1:27c	xv	14:49	55
		2:18–22	244		
25:34	23	3:31–35	99	**Luke**	
25:34n	33, 152	4:11	10	1:20	56
25:35	14	4:11n	7	1:27	20
25:40	136	4:21c	xiii	1:32	20
26:1	5	6:22–23	77	1:46–55	146
26:29	14	7:19	59	1:69	20
26:29n	152	7:24–30	19	2:4	20
26:36–46	150	8:38	152	2:11	20
26:39	201, 246	9:1	14	2:40	56
26:39n	152	9:43–47c	xiv	3:5	56
26:42n	152	9:49–50	40	3:10–14	107
26:44	137	9:50	39	3:14–15	88
26:52	21	9:50c	xiii	4:1–13	52
26:53n	152	10	119	4:16–21	17
26:54n	55	10:1–12	97, 105	4:17–21	52
26:56n	55			4:21	56
26:63	18	10:2	116	4:32c	xv
26:64n	8	10:4	116	6:12	137, 150
26:67	83	10:9	117	6:17	4
26:68	18	10:11c	xiv	6:20	4, 9, 30, 32
27:9n	55	10:14	11		
27:17	19	10:15	11	6:20n	7
27:22	19	10:21	132	6:20–23	30
27:29	21	10:23	11	6:20–23c	xiii
27:35	83	10:25	12	6:20–26	240
27:37	21	10:47–48	20	6:21	30
28:2n	8	11:10	20	6:24–26	30
28:16–20n	5	11:25	8, 152	6:27–28c	xiv
28:18	22, 156	12:25	100	6:32–36c	xiv
28:18n	8	12:28–34	61	6:29–30c	xiv
28:19	47, 152	12:29	228	6:31c	xv, 197
		12:35–37	20		

6:35	132	12:58–59c	xiv	21:24	56
6:37c	xv,	13:3	107	22:16	16, 56
	197	13:16	17	22:18	14
6:41–42c	xv,	13:23	211	22:30	17
	197	13:24	211	23:34	91
6:43–45c	xv	13:24c	xv	24:13–49n	54
6:46–49c	xv	13:25–27c	xv	24:30	164
7:1	56	13:28	9	24:44	56, 57
7:28	10	13:29	9		
7:36	163	14:1	163	**John**	
8:10	10	14:34–35	41	1:5	48
8:10n	7	14:34–35c	xiii	1:51	218
9:2	9	15:17–21	107	3:3	22, 210
9:27	14	16:1–8	230	3:5	210
9:31	56	16:9	179	3:29	56
10:38	163	16:11	179	5:24–29	210
11:1–4c	xiv	16:16	10, 13	6:15	21
11:2	13	16:16n	54	6:50	165
11:2–4	147	16:17c	xiii	6:60	230
11:3	162	16:18	97, 105,	7:8	56
11:9–10c	xv,		107, 119	7:42	20
	197	16:18c	xiv	8:12	47
11:9–13	201	16:19–31	187,	12:3	56
11:11–13c	xv,		224	12:38	56
	197	16:25	187	13:1–10	21
11:20	12	18:16	11	13:18	56
11:34–36c	xv	18:17	11	14:14	201
11:37	163	18:22	132	15:11	56
12	4	18:24	11	15:16	201
12:16–21	131,	18:25	12	15:25	56
	181, 224	18:38–39	20	16:6	56
12:21	131, 181	19:5	163	16:24	56
12:22–31c	xv	19:8	107	17:5	167
12:31	13	19:11	158	17:12	56
12:32	138	19:12	158	17:13	56
12:33	132	19:12–27	158	18:9	56
12:34c	xiv	19:38	20	18:32	56
12:48	183	20:41–44	20	18:36	34

19:24	56	12n	90	4:4	159
19:36	56	12:18	96	5:10	224
		12:19–21	91	5:10n	132
Acts		13	88	6:14–16	40
1:16	56	13:4	88	12:8–9	201
2	23	13:9n	62		
3:1	169			**Galatians**	
3:18	56	**1 Corinthians**		2:20	215
4:24	153	6:9	23	3:19–25	54
4:24–30	146	6:9–10n	33	3:29n	33
4:24–31	137	6:16n	118	4:6	152
8:31–35	234	7	99, 120, 122,	5:1–4	59
10	88		243	5:14n	62
10:44–48	219	7:5	93	5:18	51
13:15n	54	7:7	99	5:21n	33
17:6	25	7:9n	99	5:22	215
17:31	224	7:10	120		
19:23–26	219	7:10–16	120, 243	**Ephesians**	
		7:11	126	2:2	159
Romans		7:12–13	120	2:8–9	132, 247
1:3	20	7:12–16	121	3:20–21	203
2:24	154	7:15	120	5:5	178
3:21n	54	7:34	126	5:6	224
3:23	195	7:39	93, 121	5:8	45
4:13n	33	9:9	53	5:11	45
5:8–10	91	9:22	40	5:21–32	100
5:9	224	10	51	5:31n	118
6:14	51	11:1–16	59	5:32	93
8:1	195	12	217	6:10–12	167
8:4	59	14	217	6:16	167
8:15	152	15:24–28	158		
8:17	23, 34	15:50	23	**Philippians**	
8:17n	33	15:50n	33	2:5–8	96
8:28	203			2:9–11	22
8:35	195	**2 Corinthians**		4:6	180
8:37	167	3:6	62		
9–11n	54	3:6n	62		
10:17	228				

Colossians
1:13	22, 23, 156, 157
2:15	22, 167
2:16	59
3:5	178
3:6	75
3:13	166
4:6	42

1 Thess
1:10	224
5:17	138
5:22	40

2 Thess
2:9–10	218
3:3	167
3:10	181

1 Timothy
5:8	181
6:17–19	176
6:18–19	131

2 Timothy
2:8	20
3:16–17	51, 229

Titus
3:7n	33

Hebrews
2:14–15	22, 167
4:12	229
5:11–6:3	231
6:17n	33
9:16–17	23
13:10	24

James
1:5–8	201
1:13–15	166
1:22–25	225
2:5n	33
2:12–13	196
2:23	56
3:11–12	42
4:3	201
4:13–17	77
5:16	138, 201
5:17–18	150

1 Peter
1:4n	33
5:8	167

1 John
3:8	167

Revelation
4	161
5:5	20
5:13	22
7	211
7:3–4	211
7:9	211
13:11–15	218
21:3	36
22:5	34, 44
22:16	20

www.ingramcontent.com/pod-product-compliance
Lightning Source LLC
Chambersburg PA
CBHW032359100526
44587CB00011BA/734